# Frances Partridge

was born in Bedford Square, Bloomsbury, in 1900, one
of six children of an architect. Family friends included
Henry James, Conan Doyle, and various members of the
Strachey family. She was educated at Bedales School and
Newnham College, Cambridge, where she read English
and Moral Sciences. In 1933 she married Ralph Part-
ridge, who died in 1960. In addition to translating many
books from French and Spanish and helping her hus-
band to edit *The Greville Memoirs*, she is the author of
four other published volumes of diaries, *A Pacifist's
War*, *Everything to Lose*, *Hanging On* and *Other
People*; a portrait of her great friend Julia Strachey;
*Memories*; and a photographic album of *Friends in
Focus*.

D0933086

*Lenore Moylan*

# FRANCES PARTRIDGE

# *Good Company*

## DIARIES
### January 1967–December 1969

Flamingo
*An Imprint of* HarperCollins*Publishers*

Flamingo
An Imprint of HarperCollins*Publishers*
77–85 Fulham Palace Road,
Hammersmith, London W6 8JB

Published by Flamingo 1995
9  8  7  6  5  4  3  2  1

First published in Great Britain by
HarperCollins*Publishers* 1994

Copyright © Frances Partridge 1994

Frances Partridge asserts the moral right to
be identified as the author of this work

Author photograph © Derry Moore Photography

ISBN 0 00 654811 3

Set in Linotron Sabon
at The Spartan Press Ltd, Lymington, Hants

Printed in Great Britain by
HarperCollinsManufacturing Glasgow

All rights reserved. No part of this publication may be
reproduced, stored in a retrieval system, or transmitted,
in any form or by any means, electronic, mechanical,
photocopying, recording or otherwise, without the prior
permission of the publishers.

This book is sold subject to the condition that it shall not,
by way of trade or otherwise, be lent, re-sold, hired out or
otherwise circulated without the publisher's prior consent
in any form of binding or cover other than that in which it
is published and without a similar condition including this
condition being imposed on the subsequent purchaser.

# List of Illustrations

# *Foreword*

A human life easily translates itself into geographical terms: at times a long road seems to wind up a valley and climb a pleasant wooded hill, followed perhaps by a sudden plunge into an unexpected ravine, streams have to be crossed without bridges, tall rocks cast shadows. My readers have had to follow me through some patches of black country, but I hope that by the end of *Other People* they felt the atmosphere was lightening somewhat, while by a series of shallow steps a wider viewpoint had been reached. I have said that calm was never the main thing I wanted from life, but I began to feel settled in my London flat – it was my home, and the need to take off for foreign countries was not so urgent, although travel remained one of my greatest delights.

The title of this volume celebrates those who shared my journeys or the firelit warmth of their interiors. It also brings back to my mind a song which I was fond of as a child, when I was told that it had possibly been written – both words and music – by Henry VIII. How amazing, I thought, for a king to be so clever! The song begins:

> 'Pastime with good company
> I love, and shall until I die . . .'

I only hope I shall.

# Dramatis Personae

BRENAN, GERALD, writer and hispanologist. He had been one of Ralph's greatest friends ever since they were together in the First War, despite rows caused by his making love to Ralph's first wife Dora Carrington and to disagreements over the Second War. He was at this time living in Churriana in southern Spain. He was married to Gamel Woolsey, American poetess, and had one daughter.

CAMPBELL, ROBIN and SUSAN. Cyril Connolly had introduced us to Robin in 1948, when he was living near us at Stokke with his second wife, Mary (now DUNN). He had lost a leg and won a DSO in the war. After his divorce from Mary he married Susan Benson, writer of cookery and garden books, and himself joined the Arts Council. Robin and Susan had two sons, William and Arthur.

CARRINGTON, NOEL and CATHARINE, Dora Carrington's youngest brother and his wife (née Alexander). Ralph had been at Oxford with Noel, who became a publisher and designer, and died in 1989. They were country neighbours in reach of Ham Spray. Of their three children we saw most of Joanna.

CECIL, LORD DAVID and his family. We had known David's wife Rachel, daughter of our old friends Desmond and Molly MacCarthy, since she was a schoolgirl, and travelled with her before and after her marriage. Their children were Jonathan (actor), Hugh and Laura. The whole family were very kind to me after Ralph's death and I often stayed with them.

COCHEMÉ, JOAN, painter, especially of children's portraits, and a faithful friend for many years. She hastened to be with me when Burgo died. Her husband was Jacques Cochemé, biologist, native of

Mauritius, and a member of the Food and Agriculture Organization in Rome, where they were living in the Sixties.

DUNN, LADY MARY. Our warm friendship began in 1948 when she was living (and actively farming the land) at Stokke with her second husband Robin Campbell. After their divorce she made an unhappy match with Charlie McCabe, columnist of a San Franciscan newspaper. At the opening of the volume she was legally McCabe and dividing her time between Stokke and San Francisco. The situation is complicated by the fact that her first husband, Sir Philip Dunn ('the Tycoon') lived not far away in Wiltshire. Philip and Mary had two daughters, Serena and Nell, friends and contemporaries of Burgo's. They eventually remarried.

GARNETT, DAVID, and family. Only son of Edward and Constance Garnett, the eminent translator from Russian, David was generally known as 'Bunny'. He married my sister Ray in 1921, the year that I was taken on as assistant in his bookshop, Birrell and Garnett. He was thus my boss, brother-in-law, and a great friend for life. When his first book *Lady into Fox*, won the Hawthornden Prize he left the shop to write over twenty more. Ray died of cancer in 1940, and in 1942 Bunny married Angelica, daughter of Duncan Grant and Vanessa Bell. He had two sons by Ray (Richard and William) and four daughters by Angelica; Burgo married the second, Henrietta, in 1962; the others were Amaryllis, and the twins – Fanny and Nerissa.

GATHORNE-HARDY, JONATHAN (Jonny) and SABRINA. The popular nephew of Lady Anne Hill and Eddie Gathorne-Hardy was at the time married to Sabrina Tennant, daughter of Virginia, Marchioness of Bath and David Tennant, creator of the Gargoyle Club, and was launching a career as a writer.

GOODMAN, CELIA, one of the well-known Paget twins, who used as girls to make glamorous appearances at concerts and Glyndebourne. Her sister Mamaine married Arthur Koestler and died at only thirty-seven. Celia's husband was Arthur Goodman, who had spent a gruelling time in a Japanese prison in the war and was now working in Shell, and they had two young children.

GOWING, LAWRENCE, painter of the Euston Road Group, had married in 1952 my 'best friend' Julia Strachey. She was eighteen years his senior, a gifted but very unproductive writer, an original, eccentric and at times difficult character.

HENDERSON, SIR NICHOLAS (Nicko) and LADY (MARY). Ralph and I had been friends of Nicko's parents, and he had come to swim in our pool as a boy. After he married Mary they came often to Ham Spray. He joined the Foreign Service when he was refused by the RAF on medical grounds. They had one daughter, Alexandra.

HILL, HEYWOOD and LADY ANNE (née Gathorne-Hardy). Our friendship began in about 1938, when they were both working in the famous bookshop in Curzon Street created by Heywood, and which still bears his name. When Heywood joined the army in the war, Anne kept the shop going with the help of Nancy Mitford. In the early Sixties the Hills were living in Richmond with their two grown-up daughters, Harriet and Lucy. Anne had four brothers, of whom the second, Eddie, had long been a friend of ours and a visitor to Ham Spray.

JACKSON, JANETTA (née Woolley, now Parladé). Ralph and I met her as a very attractive girl of fourteen, in Spain at the start of the Civil War. Young enough to be our daughter, she became instead one of our closest friends, and figures prominently in all my diaries. Her marriages to Robert Kee and Derek Jackson both ended in divorce. In this diary she is married to Jaime Parladé and living in Spain. Her three daughters were Nicolette (Nicky) Loutit, Georgiana (Georgie) Kee and Rose Jackson.

JEBB, JULIAN, grandson of Hilaire Belloc, to whose small house in Sussex he sometimes invited his friends. Always interested in opera, theatre and cinema, in 1963 he was a journalist heading towards television. An excellent mimic and raconteur, and an affectionate friend.

KEE, ROBERT, Oxford friend of Nicko Henderson, who brought him to Ham Spray soon after his release from prison camp in Germany, where he spent three years after being shot down while a bomber pilot in the RAF. He very quickly became one of our greatest friends, and before long married another – Janetta. They both figure prominently in my earlier diaries, but the marriage became stormy, and by 1963 they had parted and Robert was married to Cynthia Judah. He had one daughter, Georgie, by Janetta, and a son and daughter, Alexander and Sarah, by Cynthia. He is a writer of novels and history – in particular of Irish history – and has also appeared in many television programmes.

KNOLLYS, EARDLEY, one of the three original owners of Long Crichel House, he was still living there in the Sixties, but had just decided to give up working for the National Trust in favour of his new love – painting.

MCCABE, LADY MARY see DUNN, LADY MARY

MORTIMER, RAYMOND, writer on art and literature, at one time literary editor of the *New Statesman*, then for many years top book reviewer on the *Sunday Times*. Our neighbour when Ralph and I lived in Bloomsbury, he became a close friend of us both, coming often to Ham Spray and travelling with us by car in France. He joined his three friends at Long Crichel House soon after the inauguration. Travel and reading were his greatest pleasures.

PARLADÉ, JAIME, eldest son of a prominent Andalusian family. Ralph and I met him in the Fifties in Marbella, where he owned an antique shop, which afterwards developed into a decorating and architectural business. He is now married to Janetta.

PENROSE, LIONEL and MARGARET, and their extremely clever family. Lionel was an FRS and Galton Professor of Genetics; his wife Margaret had been my friend at Bedales School, Newnham College and ever since; Oliver and Roger are distinguished mathematicians; Jonathan was British Chess Champion for ten years; Shirley is a clinical geneticist. All addicted to chess and music.

PHILLIPS, 'MAGOUCHE' (now FIELDING). American by birth, her first husband, the famous Armenian painter Arshile Gorky, gave her her unusual name. After his death she married Jack Phillips. Later she came to Europe and lived in France, Italy and London with her four daughters (Maro and Natasha Gorky, Antonia and Susannah Phillips), in all of which places she made a great many friends. I got to know her through Mary Dunn and Janetta.

PHIPPS, LADY (FRANCES), widow of the diplomat Sir Eric Phipps; she had been ambassadress at Berlin and Paris. She and I made friends late in our lives but had quickly become intimate, agreeing on such subjects as politics, war and peace, sharing many tastes in books, opera, and even for driving Minis. She was a talented amateur painter.

SACKVILLE-WEST, EDWARD (Eddy) had become fifth Baron Sackville at the age of sixty, on the death of his father in 1962. His musical talent had already appeared at Eton, and after Oxford he became a music critic, as well as novelist, biographer, and poet. One of the three original owners of Long Crichel House, he still spent half the year there even after buying Cooleville House, County Tipperary.

SHAWE-TAYLOR, DESMOND one of the three original owners of Long Crichel House. Writer on music and other subjects, in the Sixties, he was music critic for the *Sunday Times*.

STONE, REYNOLDS and his family. We first met them as country neighbours during the war, and acquaintance became friendship later when they lived at their romantic rectory at Litton Cheney, Dorset. Reynolds was a brilliant engraver on wood and stone, painter of trees and designer; Janet is a professional portrait photographer. They had four children: Edward, Humphrey, Phillida and Emma.

STRACHEY, ISOBEL, first wife of John (Lytton's nephew who had intervened in the Bussy inheritance), but long since divorced. Her only child Charlotte had been a great friend of Burgo's since childhood and was now married to Peter Jenkins. Isobel had published several novels and stories and was a dearly loved crony of mine.

STRACHEY, JAMES and ALIX (née Sargant Florence). James was Lytton's youngest brother. Both were practising psychoanalysts of long standing and James had translated the entire works of Freud in twenty-three volumes, indexed by me. Ralph and I felt towards them as though they were blood relations.

STRACHEY, JULIA *see* GOWING

TENNANT, GEORGIA, daughter of David Tennant, creator of the Gargoyle Club and Virginia, Marchioness of Bath. I first met her staying with Janetta in Alpbach, Austria in the summer of 1961, and took a great fancy to her, which built up into a firm friendship. A delightful and intelligent girl, who was at the time in a state of indecision as to what she should do with her life.

WEST, KITTY, the painter Katharine Church. She had married Anthony West, son of Rebecca West and H. G. Wells, who had left her and made a life in America. She was living in a charming little Dorset cottage to which she had added a big studio, and had also opened a gallery and craft shop in Blandford.

# Houses

CRICHEL (as Long Crichel House, near Wimborne, Dorset is affectionately known to its intimates). At the end of the Second War three bachelor friends decided to look for a country house where they could gather for weekends and holidays, and invite their friends to stay. There were two music critics, Edward (Eddy) Sackville-West and Desmond Shawe-Taylor, and Eardley Knollys, representative of the National Trust and later painter. They soon found what they wanted – a charming Georgian stone house, formerly a rectory, with three good-sized living-rooms and a plentiful number of bedrooms. Great thought and care were given to the decorations and furnishings; the garden had a well-kept croquet lawn, several statues, and a terrace sheltered from the wind by glass sides and with a floor decorated by the owners with their initials in mosaic. Two sets of what were called 'radiograms' of the highest quality, quantities of books, a series of resident staff and one or two dogs completed a ménage where conversation, music and croquet thrived. A few years later Raymond joined the original three as a resident 'Crichel boy'. In 1949 Ralph and I spent the first of many greatly enjoyed visits there. Only one of the original four, Desmond, survives to entertain at Crichel, but the house has never been without hosts to keep alive its unique atmosphere.

HILTON HALL, near Huntingdon, was acquired by my sister Ray from a legacy and is still inhabited by her elder son Richard and his wife Jane. She and Bunny fell in love with it from a photograph in a newspaper. It is indeed a very beautiful, stately but not large, Queen Anne house, and until Richard's day had been very little modernized. It still has panelled walls, flagged stone floors and a fine staircase of dark carved wood; in the Sixties it was one of the coldest houses I every slept in. All Bunny's children, by Ray and Angelica, were brought up there and loved it dearly.

STOKKE near Great Bedwyn, Wiltshire. Robin and Mary Campbell were living in this rambling, Virginia-creeper covered house when we first got to know them, along with Mary's daughters by her first marriage and Robin's two sons by his. Mary was farming the surrounding land. The large garden was somewhat unkempt, except for Robin's rockery. Indoors the atmosphere was lively and semi-bohemian: youthful feet might be heard echoing along the upstairs passages in a game of cocky-olly, while downstairs in the long L-shaped living-room their elders sat round the big stove talking and laughing with visiting writers and painters or an occasional philosopher or millionaire.

# GOOD COMPANY

# 1967

## January 1st

On the morning of New Year's Day I walked into Hyde Park. The sun was dazzling and the blood was beaten into everyone's cheeks by the cold but windless air. Every relationship was displayed there, woman and dog, young man and mum, parenthood in all its forms, contented marriage, solitude. On the whole the aspect was encouraging, making life seem a boon and people welded together by affection, and over it all the clatter of light, rippling water, oars on rowlocks, boys' falsetto laughter. A little boy pedalled by on a bicycle with brown hair glistening like a peeled chestnut; a highbrow father was trying to inveigle his little girl into an interest in mathematics ('But you see it doesn't make any difference whether they're cats or rats, they'll take just as long to get there.' Little girl: 'But how can you tell if some cats or rats won't be much slower than others?' Father looks at watch). All the pairs of men I passed had their spectacled eyes fixed on the ground, saw nothing at all of the surrounding beauty and were mumbling of super-tax and profits.

## January 14th: Alderly Grange, Gloucestershire

Arrived last night and was met by Alvilde Lees-Milne and driven through the starry night, a thumbnail moon about to sink behind the horizon. Also on my train was my fellow guest, James Pope-Hennessy,[1] whom I had spotted in the bar talking with animation to a handsome guardsman. First impression of him – too much name-dropping, and he used that offhand drawl which seems to imply that nothing really matters. After dinner I changed my views about him a good deal. He has a type of face I rather like – Russian, feline, with

[1] Writer, biographer of Queen Mary.

curious, wide, slightly prominent eyes coming round the corner of his head. There was some talk about travel to Russia, and then James Pope-Hennessy suddenly came into the open in favour of what the Russians were trying to do – put an end to class; he said it was the root of all evil and no country was more class-ridden and snobbish than England; of course what we must do was get rid of the royal family – it was 'no good to man or beast'. I was amazed and rather pleased to hear my own views supported but Jim said, 'I couldn't disagree with you more.' James is a talkative, articulate fellow and quite a lively argument went on until Jim seemed unable to say any more in defence of his views, and suddenly got up and left the room saying, 'This is so boring – let's go to bed.' Consternation was expressed by James in 'Shall I go after him? He's really cross, isn't he?' None the less we all went upstairs. 'Ought I to go by the morning train?' said Pope-Hennessy to me with a feline grin. Alvilde: 'Jim minds so terribly about all sorts of traditions being kept up.' What happens today I wonder? At breakfast Alvilde told me that Pope-Hennessy had been to see Jim to 'make it up, with absolutely no success whatever'. James Pope-Hennessy came down, pretty indignant. I left him and Alvilde alone together; she was pitching into middle-aged men who wore their hair long and greasy. (He does.) He said, 'It needn't be greasy.' She: 'It always is.' But he stayed on till yesterday evening, presumably forgiven.

## January 16th

Down to breakfast, feeling very glad to be here but that it is more comfortable without James. I took a long walk with Jim and the two whippets yesterday afternoon, and he told me more about 'Jamesy' as they call him. 'He's a *fiend*!' he said with feeling, 'he always has been,' and now 'the worm has turned.' How to sum James up? Clever, very. I've been looking at a book of his and it's well written. I was also charmed by the photo in it of his meltingly beautiful Eurasian grandmother. He's genuinely an iconoclast but out of bad motives not good, I suspect; the 'desire to cause pain', and the rather better one to 'be a rebel'. No love, I should imagine. Malicious, snobbish? irresponsible. Jim says his anti-royal feelings partly came from disappointment at not being knighted or received into royal circles because of his book about Queen Mary. I should have thought 'Jamesy' was too intelligent for that; last night he said, 'If I tell some

2

people I've danced with the Queen they almost have an orgasm.' Jim says he has broken up marriages ruthlessly, brought a handsome Malay boy back to England and cast him off, and is always sponging though he made a fortune with his *Queen Mary*. He has been much spoiled by Harold Nicolson and many old ladies, and his arrogance is the result. When he left last night the atmosphere lightened. An octogenarian Lord Methuen came to lunch today, a delightful man, speaking in the quiet voice of the deaf, ironical, charming and full of interests. He had gone to Russia with the Lees-Milnes, and had been digging hard in his garden, about which he spoke as ardently as about his three kittens. He had a noble profile like a long-nosed Roman emperor, plenty of hair, pensive blue eyes and great gentleness.

I don't really like this Cotswold country of grey stone and grey sky; it's too sad and full of superstitions and ghost stories. Jim told me Lord Methuen was in constant communication with his dead wife, and about some other couple who lived for their 'unborn child', who had miscarried years ago.

## January 23rd: London

I heard Fischer-Dieskau in *Arabella* two nights ago, and it was the most moving thing that has happened to me for weeks. I was bowled over, so were the whole audience, from the moment he advanced – tall, intense and burning-eyed, bear-like in his fur-collared coat, till the last gesture when he flung his arms towards Arabella on the balcony.

## January 24th

Janetta is due back – perhaps has already come – for a week. I don't know why she is making such a short stay. Heywood and Anne[1] have been for the last week at Montpelier Square, spreading their genial familiar warmth which Georgie and Rose[2] have certainly enjoyed. Georgie meanwhile has suddenly stepped ahead into maturity. I took her to *Rigoletto* a week ago and thoroughly enjoyed her company. I had been afraid she would be bored, but I was aware of her beside me, leaning forward attentively with Janetta's absorption and seriousness. Slightly shy with me at first, she relaxed and became a delightful evening's companion. Anne was much struck by her

[1]    Hill.
[2]    Janetta's two youngest children.

3

responsibility for Rose, and for washing-up and tidying. Also she's fast becoming a very beautiful girl – I feel sure now she'll be 'all right', and the genes will triumph.

Last night I drove Julia[1] to Quentin's[2] lecture on Bloomsbury at University College. There was a good deal of talk about various wrangles, or occasions when Bloomsbury was misjudged – by Johnny Rothenstein, Wyndham Lewis, D. H. Lawrence – mainly confirming the view, it seemed to me, of Bloomsbury's touchiness, and revealing too little of their other good qualities of reasonableness, courage, realism and high spirits. Lionel and Margaret,[3] Julia and Lawrence[4] all dined here last night. Lawrence was extremely amusing, in fact really brilliant, holding forth in a slightly tipsy, fantastic way about the artist's vision when enclosed within the globe of his extended arm (paintbrush on end), and about the 'circle subtending the movements of the painting arm'. Lionel responded and the conversation moved 'like spiders in the moon', to quote *The Voyage Out*, taking long silent steps balanced precariously above the real world, and able to dart off into unexpected corners at a startling rate.

On the way to the lecture in my Mini, Julia's conversation was one long groan about the appalling effort of having two guests to dinner the night before. 'And Lawrence never does a thing, never sees if anyone wants another glass of wine, or helps with the dishes. So all day long it's the shopping, and then off to the London Library, and then back again to more shopping, and then all this laying the table and waiting on people, and jumping up and down. No end to it till about ten o'clock. So I'm absolutely flat out today. But Lawrence likes this idea of meeting people for intellectual conversation.'

However, Margaret appreciated Lawrence (whom she'd never met before) and he her, and Julia rang up next morning to say how nice it had been.

## January 27th

The days have flowed along like a rapid river with a few corks floating in it. I often have one or two topics tucked into my cheek, like chewing-gum, and give them a bite from time to time. One of

[1]  (Strachey) Gowing.
[2]  Bell.
[3]  Penrose, Lionel, Professor of Genetics, Margaret his wife, doctor.
[4]  Gowing.

them is abortion. I asked Margaret whether the reports I had read in *The Times* the other day of the disagreeableness of the operation for doctors and nurses was accurate. 'Oh, yes – it's really horrible. With a fairly late one, three or four months, they not only kick but squeal.' A Scotch voice on the wireless described it as 'butchery'. But what's the alternative? Unwanted children? Better birth-control and per-haps temporary sterilization.

There was an irritating letter in *The Times* a week ago, signed by Kingsley Amis, Bernard Levin, Simon Raven and others, complain-ing of uncritical noisy attacks on the Americans about Vietnam, and asking, 'Whose side are we on?' They failed to see that they too are being uncritical and noisy, advocating 'America, my ally, right or wrong,' and waving their emotional flag. And how I loathe this prep. school talk of 'sides'.

At Quentin's lecture, Bill Coldstream,[1] his face alight with speculative intelligence and interest said: 'I do hate general ideas.' And the necessity to testify made me say, 'There's nothing I like better.' They are rarities of course among the corks in my stream, but when they cease to bob along at all among the twigs and old matchboxes it seems to me I shall have had enough of life. I repeated Coldstream's remark to Julia when she was here and she said scathingly, 'I don't expect he imagined you'd be so simple-hearted as to take it seriously.' This is an accusation I fairly often get from her and it calls up the vision of the literal-minded, pedestrian, unimaginative person I think she often gratingly finds me.

An old cork: how much less effort it is to think uncharitably or harbour grudges than to be sympathetic and appreciative. Particu-larly if tired, in bed at night, one's needle may slip into that distressing groove. 'Damn braces, bless relaxes' was a very profound remark.

### January 28th

I took myself to *Arabella* again alone last night. It seemed madness not to have another chance of seeing and hearing Fischer-Dieskau. Enjoyed every minute of it again. Janetta and Andrew Devonshire were there.

---

[1]  Sir William, painter and Vice-Chairman of the Arts Council.

## February 3rd

Today Janetta takes off for Spain; I saw her briefly yesterday. Her two extra days have given her the chance to carry out a triumph of generalship. What will happen when she goes I don't quite know but she told me she thought Julian[1] wanted to come to Montpelier Square, and that she would be back in another six weeks to see how they all were. Perhaps it will be quite all right. I'm just as influenced by her powers of persuasion as anyone else is, and of course feel just as much personal sadness at the loss of her incomparable company. As I left she begged me to ring up Georgie and I will. I took my *Othello* records for her to play (after her response to *Rigoletto*) and Janetta was anxious I should know that she often heard Georgie playing them. I said they were probably worn with use and she told me she had dreamed of them, and that when she looked at them 'they were pitted and scratched and grooved like the outside of the moon. Then I put them on and the most marvellous music came out.' How should this dream be interpreted?

I am full to overflowing of Turgenev at the moment – because of reading a life of Pauline Viardot, which has enthralled, moved and stimulated me. A remarkable and in some ways admirable woman, but did she deserve the lifelong devotion of this lovable genius? She obviously had a streak of austerity, or it may have been relentlessly putting Art first and uprooting her feelings for Turgenev, not letting go till they were both about fifty. And the irony of it was that both he and she seem to have assumed that she was the genius, whereas, as the book concludes, 'It was through Turgenev, who had always been prepared to sacrifice everything to her, that her name would ultimately be remembered.' What a somehow touching remark of poor Turgenev's when dying of agonizing cancer of the spine – 'Goodbye my dear ones, my whitish ones.'

But oh, Julia! She rang up in a frenzy of post-dated bitterness. She began by embarking on an attack on 'men' for not doing their share of the household chores – cooking, shopping, etc. – especially 'if the wife goes out to work all day like Katharine Whitehorn or me or Jenny'.[2] Our conversation nearly reached flash-point. 'I wish I hadn't

---

[1] Jebb, television producer.
[2] Friend of Lawrence Gowing, later his wife.

got to go down to Lambourn on Thursday. Such a bore, when I want to get on with my work.' 'Well, must you go?' 'Oh, yes! One's got to take the rough with the smooth, you know.'

So now her work has again taken first place. And *men* – personified in Lawrence – are the work-interruptors. What I foretold has in fact come to pass: now that she has got more of Lawrence's time she doesn't want it. The drawbacks of domesticity are too great, and until she has even more of the rough and less of the smooth she's unlikely to have a change of heart.

At Janetta's I saw Nicky[1] and we talked briefly about the 'drug-takers'. They had turned 'very unfriendly and scathing' towards the 'drink-takers' (such as herself and Jonny,[2] who were genial and friendly in their cups) at Henrietta's[3] recent party. Who were the chief druggists, I asked? 'The Ormsby-Gores, and one of the Rolling Stones'. Nicky agreed that their motive force or axle-pin was boredom and that there was something hopelessly negative about it.

## February 4th: Crichel[4]

A still, piercingly fresh, premature spring morning. Raymond and Desmond, with whom I came down yesterday, have gone off to their burrows. I sit at my desk, putting off my little homework task and slightly anxious because I've taken on most of the cooking. Desmond is radiant, friendly and helpful; Raymond a little plaintive (about things not being as they once had been) and – like the cor anglais, according to Eddy Sackville – 'self-pitying'.

## February 7th

That same morning arrived Pat Trevor-Roper and a youngish man called Richard Brain, who works at the Oxford Press.

There were walks in sun and spring air that was pure nectar to draw into the lungs, the whole of *Falstaff* on records, conversation, reading and some work. On Saturday night we all went to Kitty's[5] for

[1] Janetta's eldest daughter.
[2] Gathorne-Hardy, now Nicky's husband.
[3] My daughter-in-law.
[4] Raymond Mortimer, Desmond Shawe-Taylor, Eddy Sackville and Pat Trevor-Roper jointly owned Long Crichel House in Dorset.
[5] West, ex-wife of Anthony.

dinner – after which a noisy, all-shouting-at-once argument about God broke out. Brain was for Him, Pat on the fence, the rest of us against. I was struck by the curious view, held by such a very clever man as Pat, that postulating the existence of God explained anything – whereas it seems to me that it was just attaching a label to the unknown (and Desmond wholeheartedly agreed). Pat and Richard accused us – just as Koestler did once – of being 'old-fashioned'. 'No one talks about omnipotence and benevolence and the problem of evil now,' they said. As if one cared whether one's thoughts were old-fashioned or not. Thence we moved to the feelings of pregnant women that the life they carried within them was 'a good thing' and ought to be prolonged. Thence, naturally, to abortion. To a ground-bass from Kitty of '*I like* having babies' – rather as if she was still at it – there was considerable agreement, though Pat tended to take the typical doctor's view that a pregnant girl might easily not be the best judge of her own happiness. We agnostics pooh-poohed the idea that her belief in the value of Life was more than an expression of deep satisfaction at fulfilling her instincts.

One reason I cling so desperately to general ideas is that I have a horror of incoherence and pointillism invading the stream of consciousness. General ideas are strings on which the disconnected beads of sense-data can be threaded so as to make an apparently solid curtain for a door at least. Early yesterday I was overcome with lethargy – or perhaps posthumous fatigue from my cooking activities. Recovering towards evening I telephoned Julia and got her to come and share my supper. I asked about her weekend at Lambourn – she had been 'dreadfully bored. I don't like it down there any more. I don't know what to say to Lawrence. It's all unreal – and such a waste of time, when I could be getting on with my work.'

She is clearly strangling to death what is left of her relation with Lawrence; but will she be able to face renewed solitude if she does succeed in squeezing the last breath of life from it? At present she is sustained by a sort of honeymoon with the British Museum reading-room.


### February 10th

Last night with Desmond to hear *Pelléas and Mélisande* at Morley College. Though a students' performance I capitulated to it completely, as I didn't when I heard it at Glyndebourne. Slowly, this highly original, complex, monotonous material seeps into one's ears, until one's consciousness is saturated with it, and with a sensation of perfect balance and quiet satisfaction. Yet so hypnotic is it that I've never been nearer falling asleep at an opera, and Desmond did nod off briefly. The orchestra were visible (unlike Covent Garden and Sadler's Wells) and looked like a collection of insects with their strange proboscoes and mandibles sticking up in the air – particularly the bassoons.

### February 14th

I took Rosamond[1] and Julian to *Falstaff* last night; supper here afterwards. They had a curious effect on each other. Rosamond lost her usual eiderdown softness and became astringent and a little severe, an aspect of her personality I greatly prefer and shall try to touch off more often. Julian was slightly overexcited and exhibition-ist. I think they are basically incompatible. Julian told Rosamond how 'cruel' Dadie[2] had been to him at Cambridge. (Ros showed on the telephone to me later that she had resented this attack on one of her oldest friends and I agreed.) When she had fairly tartly told Julian that Dadie had felt all undergraduates were silly ('as indeed they are'), Julian took her up justifiably, and in his turn quite sharply, saying, 'If you mean what I think by that, then I must totally disagree with you.' I'm not sure whether Ros was annoyed at being thus caught out being 'silly' herself by saying that any age is silly *as such*.

### February 20th: Weekend at Snape Priory[3]

Much talk about the past, about our first meeting with Jan[4] and Janetta, Jan's character, Anne's slight feeling of surprise that Ralph and I liked her so much. It's true Jan's letters weren't very good, but then that's not a fair test of character, one might as well condemn someone for not being able to act. Lots and lots of talk of the most enjoyable sort, sometimes all three of us, sometimes Anne and I alone 'lounging' comfortably full-length on sofas and easy chairs in their

[1] Lehmann, the writer.
[2] Dr George Rylands.
[3] The Hills' house in Suffolk.
[4] Janetta's mother.

tiny square 'bicycle-shed' sitting-room: tradition came in for an attack from me and defence from Anne on the grounds that interest in the past increased historical knowledge. This didn't make one want to preserve the stocks or hanging for stealing, I said, nor should it; nor yet, by the same token, the royal family and class distinctions, etc. Delightful Punch and Judy show between Anne and Heywood; Anne abjectly apologetic after shouting Heywood down: 'Oh, I'm so terribly sorry, Heywood, I talk too much, I know I do.' Heywood's face breaks into a rueful, angelic beam: 'I've forgotten what I was going to say.' Much talk too about books.

In the Other House,[1] Eddie rose like a sleek bear unsteadily to his feet and gave a grin that has got considerably more toothless than it was. Sunk and folded into an armchair opposite was 'Mama' with her little dog clutched beside her. Heywood says she is now nearly senile at eighty-seven; I noticed little change and her old great charm. Occasionally forgetful, she breaks out often, 'Oh, I do so *hate* getting old!'

In my bedroom was a bunch of snowdrops, primroses and violets, with minuscule daffodils of heart-stopping beauty. We had a wonderful walk in blazing sun, the whole huge sky down to the flat horizon clear of clouds, and another next day with Caroline Jarvis.[2]

### February 21st: London

Hectic, breathless, why? Mary[3] came for ten minutes yesterday, arriving with my breakfast and sat for two hours talking. I had little to do but listen, but that isn't really a passive activity.

Hard on Mary's heels came Catharine Carrington. There has been quite a lot of talk about the past – with Catharine about Lytton and Carrington, with Rosamond last night about Wogan.[4] R: 'I really wish we'd never parted.' F: 'Why did you, exactly?' R: 'First it was his tremendous love affairs, particularly with Julia (I wonder how Julia squares that in her mind with her present view that marriage is sacrosanct); then it was his conversion to communism and the boring people who came to the house.'

---

1   The main part of Snape Priory was occupied by Lady Cranbrook and her son Eddie Gathorne-Hardy.
2   Later Anne's sister-in-law and Lady Cranbrook.
3   McCabe.
4   Philipps, her second husband, later Lord Milford.

## February 28th

This morning my post contained three letters about work – one from Haycraft seemingly delighted with my Charlemagne translation. I always seem to be expecting a rap from the headmaster's ruler, so that when he writes that 'I have excelled myself' I am astonished. Then Lawrence – to whom I wrote suggesting his coming for a drink, to talk about the Cézanne letters.[1] I did not add, but supposed he would guess, that I was giving him a chance to talk about his situation with Julia. Now he shows that he has taken this cue. The Cézanne project is still in the air but he thinks it 'will come off eventually'. And he says he 'would like it if I may come and see you on the way home one day, all the same. I don't suppose you want to hear my worries but it would be nice to meet.' What hope or help can I give him? Thirdly, Murray asks if I would translate a French book about Napoleon, if the project goes through.

Yesterday came a touching line from Janetta, making it clear that it is her relation with Jaime[2] (rather than the new house) that binds her to Spain and keeps her away from her children. She 'worries and thinks and loves from afar, in a disquieting way revealing itself in anxious nightmares'. One must dwell on the plus, which is her happy relation with Jaime. Julian is staying at Montpelier this week I believe, and comes to lunch today, when I shall hear something about the girls.

## March 6th

Tempo speeding up. Last week Bunny[3] and Raymond fetched up to dinner with me almost accidentally. They responded delightfully to each other; and I've never known Raymond listen so attentively to someone with a tempo so different from his own. It was worth the effort – Bunny's description of Mexico and America was seeded with unexpected and original images and phrases. (Angelica[4] too has been greatly inspired by the journey and spoke of New York with her magnificent eyes blazing from a brown face, looking as beautiful as an Inca. That was when I went for music to Islington.) I sat back and

[1] A project that never came off.
[2] Parladé.
[3] David Garnett.
[4] Angelica, his wife.

listened to the two literary gentlemen, happy for once not to obtrude my own views. Towards the end of the evening they got onto the subject of class – and agreed that the 'best came to the top', and the upper classes were cleverer and more beautiful and therefore deserved their privileges, just as if they were two Wilcoxes from *Howards End* which I'm now reading. Why have the intellectuals of today returned to the views derided by those of 1909? It is extraordinarily baffling. Forster's philosophy of love and human relationships, 'connecting' and all the rest may be a cake that is soggy in parts but it stands up very well to what has been put forth since in the sphere of Moral Philosophy. And Bertie Russell, in the Sunday papers, described the moment of almost mystical revelation when as a young man he realized the value of love and understanding and became a pacifist, which he has always remained. This side of what Bloomsbury stood for has been to some extent forgotten – and they are thought of chiefly as back-biting cynics (which some of them of course were).

This weekend with Julia to Stokke – Mary's first weekend back there after the bust-up with Charlie McCabe. Supremely perfect spring weather. I had two long walks with Julia in Savernake Forest; as we returned yesterday afternoon towards a Greek temple of grey beech trunks lit by sunlight, she amazed me by saying she couldn't possibly have walked there alone – it would have seemed too terribly sad and lonely. She wondered how Mary could bear it. Yet Stokke welcomed me and Mary with such peaceful warmth; and I believe very little, if any, sadness.

But Julia has suddenly stopped contemplating her own inner landscape and in the most marked way started to take an interest in the outside world, to read the papers and serious books, and talk about such subjects as Vietnam, which has been right outside the range of her vision for months or years. Her vitality and originality are enhanced: she seems to have shaken off a grey dressing-gown of obsessional brooding, but oddly enough the same wand that has opened her eyes to reality has also made her look older and more like the one-time 'owl in an ivy bush' instead of an ageless sleeping princess. I welcome the change and wonder if there can be a connection.

## March 14th

Last week saw the 'balloon go up' once again, and perhaps finally, for the Gowings. Lawrence suddenly rang up, came to see me and told me he had decided to get Julia to divorce him and marry Jenny. My role was easy: he only wanted me to listen. I told him of course no one could fail to imagine the strain this had all been to him. He showed more understanding of Julia's nature than she would, I think, credit him with; felt it appalling that this should happen to her of all people, with her childhood fear of desertion; deplored the purple heart habit, instituted (he said) by a foolish doctor; and said how unlucky it was that so many things she really liked – such as music – had to be ruled out because they were 'melancholy'. The bad fairy had cursed her with the inability to enjoy what was available.

Since my talk with Lawrence, he wrote to her to break the news, and I have had long telephone talks and an evening alone here with her. With the help of purple hearts she seemed to face the new crisis bravely and resentfully. Anger is a vital form of energy for getting over humiliation. She doesn't want for the present however to see Lawrence sometimes for dinner as he'd hoped. So now Julia's friends must rally round for all they're worth – the Kees,[1] the Campbells.[2] Our evening together went very well until the end when she began dismissing various friends of mine who are also fond of her and full of kindness and goodwill. Mary is really 'too silly'; Janetta 'couldn't possibly be intelligent' if she liked a certain French film Julia and I didn't care for. F: 'But surely you don't feel no one can be intelligent who doesn't agree with you?' Pause. J: 'I know *you* think I do.' Yes, alas, I do.

At Kitty West's last weekend I met John and Myfanwy Piper and liked them very much; I admired her solid, sculptured body, very intelligent face and low musical voice. The talk that evening was very much alive. At Crichel we found the Berkeleys[3] with a charming prep. school son. Everyone in the room was nice, yet the bicycle tyre of conversation went flat several times and had to be pumped up again. One afternoon Kitty and I sloshed along the muddy paths of her woods and gathered huge bunches of wild daffodils in tight buds. I read with pleasure Keith Vaughan's diary. Julia said to me: 'What a

---

[1] Robert and Cynthia.
[2] Robin and Susan.
[3] Lennox and Frieda.

13

pity we know so few people wo ever *think*.' But he certainly does: he gives a moving account of being a CO in the army on non-combatant duties; and particularly of the arrivals of German prisoners. The English expected monsters, so did the Germans. A moment of embarrassment followed by infinite relief on both sides. Oh, why couldn't this moment of truth have been made more use of?

### March 17th

Francis Bacon has a new show on in Bond Street but there isn't much 'newness' about it except his increased popularity. In the narrow gut of the gallery, turds were slowly circulating. I stepped close and hoped I was 'appreciating the quality of the paint', but it gave me no pang, thrill or lift. Nor did I get the electric shock his first shows produced. I detected a feeling of depression, and revulsion caused by the carefully and thickly laid on backgrounds in unpleasant colours, the patterned carpets, and the horrid raised boot so many of his solitary characters project at one. There they sit, mashed and mangled within the prison walls of their rooms, relieved only by a bell-rope or electric light. What is this extremely clever man trying to say? Julian last night gave an illuminating reply, which like the best criticism made me want to go and have another look. He says he is proclaiming again and again and again the dreadful loneliness of the human animal. But what worries me is the lack of *visual* element in this presentation – it seems too cerebral. The eye is not stimulated or pleased – quite the reverse – and I came away blank of feeling, either positive or negative. I feel teased by the problem he raises, and want to read his own account of what he's after – but I mistrust the high value he sets on accidents.

### March 21st

Time whirls along, gathering fearful speed. I'm torn between whipping it up (let's go to the end! it'll soon be over!) and a panic desire to brake. How long though it seems, my life, as I look back on it, and the violent onset of spring increases this sense of pace. I have sat out in the square each afternoon lately, reading in the sun. Fine tender shoots of bright green grass like a baby's hair are coming up fast through the sooty earth; there's a smell of lawn-mowings.

At Hilton[1] last weekend, however, it was cold and blowy. I walked along the flat roads looking in vain for anything in bloom and then suddenly came on a bank of sweet violets, white and purple. I drove Henrietta and Sophie[2] down with Lena, the Swedish au pair girl; Nicky also came, and Bunny and William[3] were our hosts. Impressions left: the stalwart thighs of the three girls under their miniskirts; the splendidness of Nicky's genuine and honourable character; the soft speech of collected Garnetts (Bunny speaks with barely-moving lips and his blue eyes fastened to a point on the table). Henrietta cooked magnificently, played Bach on the piano slowly and lovingly, and spoke in favour of Buddhism and marijuana. Sophie came leaping into my bed early each morning, bright-eyed and conversational. Henrietta told me she said on the last morning, 'I'm off to see Frances. Frances is a lovely person. Everyone isn't a person.' Richard's boys and a friend provided her with intoxicated and adoring afternoons.

## Easter Monday: The Slade, near Alton, Hants

Eardley[4] and I are alone here, quietly domestic and relaxed, looking after ourselves and (whenever the wild and blustery but brilliant and dramatically lovely weather allows) going out to dig in the wasteland round the house, which will one day be a garden. Eardley hacks holes in a bank and plants shrubs in them. I have taken on milder jobs like putting in pansies and herbs. I walked to the copse we see across the famous view (the shallow valley with its few fine trees and the streaming cows, a capering dog or striding man) and plunged into its green freshness and dug up some clumps of enormous primroses. Talk arises spontaneously and dies away ditto – to be buried in books.

Dreams, in my pale blue satin-striped bedroom, that Ralph was amorously obsessed by Angelica. I didn't mind that in itself, but was heart-broken that he could withdraw the warmth of his love from me. Another that I was producing an outdoor play. First the cast had to be collected together and drilled in their parts, then the audience gathered from far and wide. When they found that they had to cross

[1]  The Garnetts' house near Huntingdon.
[2]  My granddaughter.
[3]  His son and my nephew.
[4]  Knollys, whose small country house it was.

a sort of abyss they went on strike. 'All right,' I said, 'then *I give up.*' Both pretty obvious. The latter represents my sense of the effort it often is to keep my old life going. Is it worth making? Why *not* give up? But though there are threadbare moments, I believe this endless compulsive effort can become an end in itself, a solution to the problem, and I can even conceive of it gathering momentum and going on and on till I drop in my tracks.

## March 31st

The weeks to come are parcelled out into a series of visits and journeys to and fro. I am trying not to feel hectic – to take it calmly. Two foreign trips loom ahead. I'm amazed to find myself pledged to go next month with Rosamond to Sicily and looking forward to it; sitting beside her in her flat discussing plans, I peered into that over-lifesize, smooth, handsome face, like that of a vast primitive goddess, the enormous soft, deer's eyes, the pearly opalescent skin, and felt a certain wondering affection. Next week, I go for a week to Cornwall with the Hills. Where does work come into all this? I refused to take on a book for Weidenfeld this morning, for I am still in theory pledged to John Murray, with Lawrence's Cézanne hovering in the background. Of course it pleases me to have these possibilities.

I have an evening to myself – oh selfish delight! Anxiety about Julia made me ring up and ask if she were free, but I was intensely relieved to hear that she had friends coming to supper. How she is going to stand the total separation from Lawrence demanded by divorce depends very much on support of her friends. And they give it; but she runs through them rather fast. The Campbells asked her for Easter, but there was not any joy in her account of her stay. 'Are *all* parents and their children so *inharmonious*? Do they all look so *cross* all the time? . . . Of course they were entirely wrapped up in their own concerns, so they had no time or energy to spare for me . . . No conversation, no . . . Well, there was all this washing-up . . . I was thankful to have it, as it prevented my brooding . . . And then I rested twice a day, so there wasn't time for any more.' Ben Nicolson[1] has asked her for August to a large Italian house he has taken, with the Toynbees and Kees. 'I shall go, and stick it out as long as I can, but I dread it really. I simply hate Italy in August. Then there's all this

---

[1] Elder son of Harold; art historian.

16

sun-bathing and lying about in bikinis – I can't do that, and I shall feel so out of it all. And I loathe pines and sand, which I know it is all down that coast. Well, and Philip Toynbee[1] may well be an awful nuisance, so I'm not looking forward to it a *bit*, still I shall go.' I think only to me does the full flood of her critical depreciation come pouring out. What worries me most is the feeling that she does at times simply sink slowly into the bog of her own despair. It is pretty bad just now. I hardly like to go away and leave her, and noticed that she wanted to know the dates of my disappearance. I must help her somehow to get through this grim stretch.

### April 8th: Cadgwith, Cornwall, staying with the Hills

Yes, three nights of peace and equanimity, and four more to come. The magic was instantaneous. Met by Anne at Truro, who drove me twenty miles through quiet, sunken lanes crowded with preposterously huge primroses. The sight of the trees stiffly bent over to the prevailing wind, the sea lying blue and untroubled by oil, and the sound of the crying of seagulls – all this has loosened the hard, stony earth round my roots and made my flower-pot dark, warm and welcoming. Heywood's grandparents built this house in 1902 and in every detail it looks it. Thatched roof, restrained *art nouveau* (without the fantasy and curlicues), rooms lined with dark brown stained boarding to three-quarter way up and draped with pale green art silk, a glassed-in verandah – in fact a perfect holiday house, with (best of all) its position, perched on a flowery cliff and looking straight down into the little harbour of Cadgwith directly below, or two little bays rather, divided by a small rocky promontory tufted with soft grass, a row of blue boats and lobster-pots, cottages like the bricks in a toy village. Here are the whole Hill family including Harriet's[2] two children. Sheelah[3] came the day after I did. She and Heywood are revelling in the nostalgia of childhood memories combined with ancestor-worship. Heywood is *never* a bore: he longs for one to like the place – and so I do; I absolutely love it. As I do his little granddaughter Frances, a dear little English rosebud with a firm and amusing character. 'I absolutely *adore* her,' he said to me on a

[1] Writer and journalist, old flame of Julia's.
[2] The Hills' elder daughter, married to Tim Behrens.
[3] Heywood's sister, married to John Hill, the painter.

17

walk yesterday. It is reciprocated, and they make a delightful couple, sitting at a round table apart in the dining-room. What Julia calls Heywood's 'pocket Napoleon side' prevails here; quite a good thing, as someone is needed to collect stragglers and set everyone off walking or driving. Lucy[1] droops over *Anna Karenina* on the floor, goes for long and as she says 'compulsive' walks and bicycle rides, and frequents the pub. Anne told me in the car that Lucy had been worryingly unhappy, feeling her life to be pointless and herself rudderless. I would like to make more contact but don't quite know how. What will become of her? Surely her beautiful large violet-blue eyes and Undine-like, vague, willowy sweetness will captivate someone she really likes?

## April 9th

Harriet and family left yesterday morning. Their youthful vitality is a great loss. I liked Tim [Behrens] very much – such enthusiasm is a rarity. Some of it cascaded forth about Jonny's novel, which he talked of as if it were *Paradise Lost*. It was 'monstrous' that the critics hadn't appreciated it, that Julian – who so fully understood it – hadn't been allowed to review it because he was Jonny's friend. Chorus of 'I *know*,' from Anne. The way Tim took my tiny criticism of it delighted me. Amazed, he stopped in his tracks for a moment, then began furiously thinking, his words forming a popping and explosive refrain accompanying but not quite in time or correspondence with his thoughts. He did not resent what I'd said and finally gave a modest and interesting account of how certain criticisms were valuable to him as a painter. His own violent and unco-ordinated interest, appreciation, excitement and enthusiasm are very endearing. Since he evidently thinks for himself I'm not sure why he doesn't make a bit more sense of it all – chiefly perhaps because he's responding so violently and in so forward-going a way to too many things at once.

After a visit to the pub with Lucy, Anne became rollickingly funny and ribald at dinner, half-unconsciously mocking Heywood and Sheelah's talk of Cornish ancestors and various Trewithens and Tresillicks (houses owned by the family) with a chorus of 'Tregurking!' 'Trefucking!', shouts of laughter and an exquisitely comic, impish expression. Heywood didn't *quite* like it. But after

[1] The Hills' younger daughter.

dinner her scholarly side rose to the surface and she read us extracts from letters about these same ancestors, taken from family papers in the museum at Truro.

I've just had breakfast on a beautiful morning roofed by a pale blue hazy sky. Though it's Sunday three of the blue fishing-boats have come out and are floating in the bay beneath, while the gulls make a noise like an army of frantic cats.

### April 10th

All day yesterday the weather remained superb, and I was sorry in a way that we had to spend so much of it 'Tregurking' and 'Trefucking'. But not a moment of the morning's walk, northwards along the cliffs to Poltesco and back inland, was wasted. Lucy marching ahead, Heywood and Sheelah slowly stumping, I hung back and prowled at my leisure among rock-gardens of thrift, sea-campion and stonecrop high above the wrinkled sea. I enjoyed being by myself for an hour or so.

### April 11th

Drove to Kynance Cove, whose natural magnificence was set off by wind, rain and louring sky. A certain amount of thick and disgusting brown oil[1] clung to the rocks but the beautiful white sand was mostly clean and the water translucent. A helicopter was rollicking and sidling to and fro laying barrels of detergent like eggs to be received by very young excited soldiers from Ulster. The little café in the bay was full of them; smell of wet thick cloth, mackintosh and rank human flesh. As we clambered up the cliff in the teeth of a blizzard, a negro among them shouted out, 'Ah come all the way from Fiji to clean your beaches for you!'

### April 12th

To the Lizard lighthouse yesterday via Mullion with its church and junk shops. Had a drink in the bar beside the lighthouse. Though the morning was bitter cold, primroses, violets, thrift and campion sprinkled the southern slopes. Suddenly a pale sun came out and our walk home, five miles along the cliffs, was beautiful and often warm,

---

[1] From a recent disastrous oil-slick.

the sea a prettier blue than the Mediterranean, the coconut scent of the gorse filling the air. Heywood walks with a buccaneering swagger, his head held high in his touching little peaked tweed cap, his rather loose trousers and mac billowing round him like flowing Roman robes.

## *April 21st: West Halkin Street*

Dinner here last night with Bunny, Eardley, Georgia[1] and Kitty Godley.[2] Mattei[3] cried off at the last moment and after plodding round with my preparations I wondered what we should talk about. But then Georgia arrived and set everything alight at once. Her appearance was both charming and comic. From her lovely round face, beautiful long neck and torso in a flame-coloured blouse, one's eyes descended to a long cumbrous woolly skirt from which her feet peered out, incongruously arranged in charwoman's strap sandals and what looked like thick wrinkled stockings. She was gloriously amusing, starting off at once about the 'materialist civilization' of the present day, with its 'commercial standards' applied to everything, and whisking us all off into the realm of fantastic ideas woven surprisingly together. Bunny, after making a slow and slightly silent start, became completely captivated by her after dinner, and was soon making a date to go with her to a new 'microbiotic' restaurant run by Zen Buddhists, where you eat millet and drink non-alcoholic beverages. It was a pleasure to watch him, wreathed in delighted smiles responding to Georgia's emphatic gestures and statements about mysticism and drug-taking being the only possible reaction to the materialism of the present day. Looking back, I see the conversation as a mass of sparkling foam shot with illuminating searchlights and with Georgia as Venus rising from the waves.

Now here are the last few days to be got through before departure to Sicily.

## *April 22nd*

An evening with Julia, watching Lawrence on the television. I never saw anyone more at home, more of a 'natural', and Julia was amused and delighted. The evening included fascinating talk about films and

[1] Tennant.
[2] Wife of Wynne Godley; daughter of Epstein.
[3] Radev, expert picture-framer and great friend of Eardley's.

books, but ended with a tough stretch. That she was pretty desperate had been apparent all along; suddenly she was struggling in the water, asking for help. Would I think of some way she could deal with her book, make it coherent and publishable for one thing, and somehow comprehensible to a typist for another? She modestly said she felt it was too much just the 'thoughts of me, Julia Strachey, on a variety of themes – such as latency, the eeriness of the universe, scientific development and so on – and who will want to read that? After all, I'm not Proust. Can you think of any other writer who has perpetrated such a thing?' I said all I could about there being no need for a book to fall into a category. This wasn't so bad as her second problem: there were 'chests of drawers full of manuscript, so corrected and scrawled over and illegible that no typist could possibly read them'. To get an amanuensis to come to her cost £26 a week, which she couldn't afford. Unless she could see it in printed type she couldn't go on any longer organizing and correcting. I threw plank after plank of suggestions to my drowning friend; every one was rejected, sometimes for futile reasons, sometimes almost angrily. To write on a double piece of foolscap leaving room for corrections was impossible for her, she couldn't explain why, but Lawrence had understood at once. The suggestion that some typists were more gifted at reading difficult writing than others sent her scruffling through the pages to find a *really* bad bit that *no one* could read. F: 'Well, when it gets as bad as that perhaps you will have to recopy the page.' J: 'It's what I've been doing for years. I can't go on doing it.' And a tape-recorder 'made such very odd clicks'.

I had an extraordinary sense of battling with incredibly muscular, obstinate, sinuous octopus tentacles, endowed with the strength of neurosis. She didn't *want* her problems solved, yet I struggled on wearily producing new suggestions for her to beat aside. I did, foolishly, even refer to the problem as a psychological one. In any case she grew irritable with me, and yet wouldn't give up, and I longed to go home to bed, but couldn't give up trying to find a means to rescue her.

### April 25th: Palermo

Rosamond and I left London blue, blossomy and warm, and travelled smoothly to Rome, where squirts of rain were being discharged from a leaden sky, and icy gusts blew our skirts up as we walked down the gangway. Ros seemed equable, ready to giggle, and above all sane, an important quality in a fellow traveller. She told me she had never driven abroad, even in an English car; so small wonder that she wanted me to drive at first. We were anxious to get away from the unhelpful Avis official and he from us, and I asked few questions and hoped I would remember how to drive a Fiat. On the whole I did. Without too great trouble we reached the hotel I had rashly booked on the recommendation of Gerald,[1] forgetting his passion for austerity. It looked distinctly bleak and dingy, with under-blanketed beds and no hot water. Rosamond took this with great good humour, but oh dear no!, it won't do at all.

## April 26th

On the journey we had wondered which of us would be acting husband, and I realized now it was to be *me*, so I shouldered my Ros-ponsibilities this morning, leapt into the Fiat, and drove to the Jolly hotel which looks out over the sea-front. In a minute all was settled and we moved at once to warm and comfortable rooms.

## April 27th

Our new womb is a great improvement but a cold wind still rattles the palm trees. We wear everything we have, including woollen vests. Gradually Rosamond relaxes with me and her personality unfolds. In spite of having been left by at least four men (Leslie Runciman, Wogan, Goronwy Rees and Cecil Day-Lewis) she clearly nourishes in her heart a conviction of being universally beloved and desirable, and I think these defections appear to her like astonishing mistakes or just incomprehensible folly. She thinks Wogan 'would really like to be back with her' and makes no bones about wishing they had never parted. (She is innocently proud of being an Honourable, and – another curious tiny vanity – has taken a year off her age though her passport reveals it for all to see.) Julia once said she lived entirely by wish-fulfilment and I think this is true; but she's boundlessly interested in people, and likes to talk in biographical or autobiographical terms. In this, as in much else, she is the eternal feminine. Her size and her innocence together give me a somewhat odd feeling

[1] Brenan.

of having an unfair advantage over this large iridescent fish I am playing – iridescent in fact because she covers her face with some pearly opalescent substance, and this looks striking under her thick mop of white hair tinted a pinkish colour.

This morning began agonizingly, because Rosamond wanted me to drive her into the *centro* to see the various sights there. The traffic was appalling and there was absolutely nowhere to park, so on her suggestion we gave up and headed for Monreale, whose great Norman apse is lined with mosaics and features a huge and magnificent Christ. Ros was much concerned with the expression on the face of this Christ – was it 'wise', 'sad' or 'powerful but gentle'? I have the impression that she thinks of all these images as portraits – even though several hundred years in arrears – of an actual man. Back at our Jolly, I couldn't resist taking a walk while she rested, and found my way between old golden palaces crumbling into tenements and crawling with children to one which has become the National Art Gallery and contains a very extraordinary Antonello da Messina virgin. Coming home, I gazed down dark side alleys hung with washing as if with bunting, where squalid and poverty-stricken families were living, surrounded by paper and debris that swirled round their legs in the cold gusts of wind.

### April 28th

Today Rosamond decided to have a brave go at driving. I'm fascinated by her queenly acceptance of being a reigning beauty. Beamingly she advances, confident of capitulation to her charms and she certainly gets it! We both hugely enjoyed the drive to Cefalu and here again was another fine Norman cathedral built of warm golden stone and lined with mosaics and a huge all-seeing Christ. The sun came out and the sea turned a soft, bright aquamarine blue.

### April 29th: Éricé

Ros went to the hairdressers before we left Palermo. She has brought her mauve rinse with her and I think the assistant put in too much of it. Her head is now covered with bright Parma violet floss. With a pink scarf round her neck, crimson lips and a bright blue suit, the effect is striking to say the least.

Éricé is perched on a pinnacle rising a sheer two thousand feet from the plain, and Rosamond bravely drove us to the top, though she now confesses she is given horrible vertigo by heights and cannot bear to look over steep places. In thick mist or cloud we found another Jolly, and were each given a monk's cell with a big window. The wind hurled itself screaming against mine all night, and before darkness fell I looked down through the drifting clouds to occasional gleams of sunlight on the sea crawling far below. On the way up, near the top we were stopped by two men who looked to me like the police who check lorries for contraband. 'Dove vanno le signore?' they asked. When we said, 'To the Jolly Hotel,' they smiled and let us go on. I thought nothing of this, but Ros was convinced they were members of the Mafia, and has been ever since haunted by their 'evil looks and sinister smiles'. I begin to realize that her mystical views imbue events with esoteric, half-good, half-bad significance. She seems to be a sort of Manichean.

## April 30th

Ros had asked me to drive down the mountain as she would have to close her eyes not to see the precipices. Éricé was still shrouded in cold dense mist, and after a brief look at the village down we came, out of it, into glorious sunshine, with the sea sparkling and blue below us. The man at the Jolly had recommended a cross-country route; it turned out to be a slow and appalling road, at times nearly impassable, but ran through the most beautiful country, so that I'm glad we took it. Sheets of flowers now unrolled under a blue sky – either formalized in squares of dark red clover and pale blue flax, or in a wild profusion of yellow, purple and white, while convolvulus (blue and purple) sprawled everywhere. All at once I saw an extraordinary white, lily-like flower growing in a bank (I still don't know what it was). I stopped the car with a yell and came back in triumph – only to the dread awareness that we had a puncture. What now? Here we were on a small deserted road in the wildest Mafia country. Then a young farmer appeared on a motor-bicycle and we begged him to help, Rosamond actually clasping her hands in a pleading gesture. He was our saviour, changed our wheel and we set off again and by way of Selinunte finally reached Agrigento.

But my God, could this really be it? This forest of skyscrapers standing on a hill? It was indeed, and we climbed up to the town in a queue of cars, through traffic lights, hated the look of the place and didn't much like the monks' cells in the new Jolly (I see it will be Jollies, Jollies all the way, for Ros feels safer in them, with their stuffy smell of commercial travellers' cigarettes). To bed plugging my ears against the almighty racket in the road outside.

## May 1st

I've come up to bed, early as usual, after our first real talk at dinner about Rosamond's mystical beliefs. As if suddenly uncorked, out they all poured – her 'absolute certainty' of survival, the continued existence of minds 'in finer bodies', her belief in 'saints and sages' (of whom Jesus is one and her crazy old colonel with whom she wrote *A Man Seen from Afar* is another), reincarnation, the mystical experience. I can't remember exactly how it began, but I felt it was bound to some time, and was mainly concerned to affirm and maintain my own position without being aggressive. Indeed I *am* very much interested, though not exactly in the way she supposes. I asked her if she still had frequent contact with Sally? She was evasive. Not so much. She didn't need it, since she now had the certainty of survival. This part of her mind is all softness like a huge marshmallow – anything could be absorbed by it.

I have never travelled in so ladylike a fashion. Like characters in an E. M. Forster novel, we seem to be gliding through Sicily in an invisible barouche, gloved and veiled, provided with a primus to make cups of tea at any moment. We haven't once sat in a café. I suggested it this morning, but met with reluctance; I think she felt it looked 'grubby' or 'squalid'. Her appearance often creates a sensation and I'm sure this delights her. The guide in the cathedral here asked if it was the English fashion to wear hair of such a colour. In Palermo a woman also asked politely about it. She sometimes half-complains, half-boasts of being pursued by men, that the waiter puts his head into her room and wishes her goodnight, for instance. 'It's so maddening and silly.' This morning among the temples of Agrigento two quite young and handsome Sicilians offered to accompany us to Pirandello's house, and while we were watching a pretty little bride being photographed clasped in her husband's arms against the sunburned pillars of the Temple of Concord, the photographer asked if he might take our photos too 'as a memento'. What in the world does it mean? Was it just the possibilities of a striking colour photo offered by mauve hair, orange dress and blue cardigan? I'm faintly embarrassed by such incidents but not much, and this evening I feel rather hilarious, perhaps because the supernatural has popped out like a Jack-in-the-box. I would like it to go back and remain there, however.

Agrigento is completely spoiled by its hideous encircling fringe of skyscrapers, and its inhabitants deserve their reputation for surliness. But the valley of the temples is beautiful, well-ordered yet lavishly overrun with flowers, and the day has been divine.

### May 2nd: Piazza Armerina

The barouche rolls on. The queenly figure bends her head like a swan and smiles sweetly from under her sunshade; the little companion looks beadily and inquisitively about her. A brilliantly fine morning and May Day crowds welling up and oozing slowly everywhere led to something of a *dies non*. Driving east along the coast we found them coagulating and streaming along the road. Gerald had told us to 'spend half an hour at Palma', where the ancestors of the Leopard[1] came from. We drew up and walked up a flight of broad steps sprouting with grass and weeds to a handsome baroque church, but a crowd of little boys so nagged, hustled and pestered us, and I was so disgusted when one spat into the car at me at close range, that we soon left.

### May 28th: Syracuse

The Roman villa at Piazza Armerina was a splendid sight. Set in a luscious green valley full of singing birds and the sound of water, it is very well arranged, so that one can walk round an unobtrusive plastic roof and gaze down from a height on these extraordinary mosaic floors, where elephants and other African animals are to be seen being embarked on a ship, where cupids catch enormous innocent Edward Lear fish, and female athletes wear bikinis.

I did most of the driving to Syracuse today. We had tried to reserve rooms by telephone at the Grand Hotel, the only one in the old town, but when we got there we found that by some 'mystical'(?) error we had actually been booked at the Jolly instead. It stands on a large

---

[1]   The Prince of Lampedusa, author of the book of that name.

main road halfway between the classical sites and the old town. While Ros rested I went to the post office on the port, where I found a letter from Alix – and when I saw how short it was I instinctively knew what news it contained: the unimaginable fact that James had died of a heart attack. Why had the possibility never occurred to me? Why did he seem immortal? Simply I suppose because it was useless and painful to contemplate his death.

Ros had a letter from her 'boyfriend', the old precognitive, Jesus-conscious colonel. He warned her of the evil influence of the Mafia who 'definitely practise black magic' and this has reinforced her impression of the sinister viciousness of the faces of the two men on the hill at Érice. When we were talking and joking about the number of earthquakes and eruptions of Etna that Sicily is subject to, she said, 'I think he would have told me if we were in danger. When I went to Egypt he told me I should be in need of special protection.' Well, I'm treated to a good deal of bunkum daily!

### May 4th

Last night I had another dose of spiritualism, mysticism and reincarnation, and I am getting a bit bothered by the suspicion that Ros has hopes of me; for my isolation with her here, natural curiosity and even politeness make me not only refrain from saying, 'Shut up; you're talking utter rubbish!' but actually draw her out. Each evening we repair to one or other of our rooms and drink whisky from tooth-glasses before dinner. I did seduce her to sit briefly in a café for a cappuccino yesterday. In the afternoon we visited the catacombs and the quarries where the Athenian prisoners once worked. Bus-loads of schoolboys and girls followed us screaming like starlings wherever we went, carrying their vitality and noise right into the strange depths of the cavern called the Ear of Dionysus. They were convulsed by the sight of Ros's hair, and several girls came up and asked what nationality she was, and (with broad grins) whether English people always had 'pink hair'.

To return to last night's conversation. Whatever she may have felt about my convertability, I had momentary qualms as to whether I might have unsettled *her* beliefs, though this I don't think is possible and God knows I want it still less. She told me that I obviously loved life more than anyone she knew. Why then, did I want it to come to an end? For that very reason, I said. I could neither envisage nor desire a 'finer' or more attenuated form of it; it should have an Aristotelean beginning, middle and end, and this shape (developing from birth to sexual maturity and declining towards the grave) was, to me, as necessary to life as to works of art, perhaps in fact necessary to art because an essential element of life. I said much more that was trite and embarrassing now to remember. She said Sally's death would have finished her off utterly without the revelation she had then experienced; but that I (in a tone of infinitesimal disapproval) 'had got over Burgo's death'. I've always known she didn't put a husband's death on a par with that of a child, but she invariably speaks of Sally's death as unique among all bereavements. Does she think she was the reincarnation of some goddess or the Virgin Mary? She has shown polite concern for Alix, but that's all it is. And what does she think about her old colonel? Is he a reincarnation of one of the apostles or even J.C. himself? He claims to have known Him in a previous life. He sounds a real psychotic. I asked if he believed he could know the future as well as the past. Ros: 'Oh, yes. I've had several proofs of this.' I told her about my frequent 'false premonitions', and said I didn't think I would want to know the future even if I could. I'm aghast at the woolliness of her thinking, and to find how easily she soaks up any comforting rubbish about vibrations and higher spheres and finer forms.

She told me as a great confidence how when she was in Egypt she noticed that an Egyptian guide who was showing her round a museum suddenly began to tremble and shake as he stood beside her, until at last he said: 'Forgive me, but I've known you before. This is terribly agitating. I can't go on being your guide. Perhaps you were formerly some Egyptian queen.' I told her I thought her long eyes going round the corner of her face did give her rather an Egyptian appearance, and she at once agreed. But how much of this episode and the guide's remarks have been fished up from her unconscious? I must try and keep her to more mundane subjects.

N.B. I mustn't forget to chalk up in Rosamond's favour a fit of really abandoned, uncontrollable, infectious giggles over the expression and manner with which one of the waiters described the various available ices to us.

On the whole the people of Syracuse are very friendly and lively and quite different from those of the said-to-be Mafia-ridden Agrigento. We have seen a number of astonishingly handsome Sicilian men, black-haired but sometimes with bright blue eyes and classical features, strong and well-built and dandyishly dressed. In comparison their women are quiet little hen-sparrows, clad often in black, and we have seen few female beauties.

## May 5th

Heading towards the end of our holiday, I feel a growing anxiety to get our trusty little white eggshell of a car safely to Catania. We had decided to devote yesterday to Noto, and as we were missing out the other baroque towns (Ragusa, Modica, etc.) it was perhaps a relief to find it very slightly disappointing. But we saw and admired the cathedral and several other golden baroque churches. Their strikingly *lay* appearance, more like town halls or ballrooms than churches, offended Rosamond. Then to eat tough rubber tubes of macaroni in a small restaurant whither we were directed by a policeman. While we were there in came a couple of South Africans. Ros instantly fell for the bronzed, blue-eyed, virile-looking husband, who spoke good Italian and obviously knew Sicily well. She'd met him before, seen his photograph, known him in a previous existence perhaps, thought he might have been a general in the last war (too young by far) and found him 'extremely attractive'. This *déjà vu* impression has taken her by surprise several times; she had it about a man in the Syracuse Museum. It is part and parcel of the esoteric quality she likes to attach to ordinary circumstances.

Back to Syracuse; later in the afternoon we set out for the Fonte Ciane, an enchantingly peaceful and rustic place reached through a leafy country lane. A deep pool of pure and translucent water is fed by a stream winding between extraordinary mop-headed papyrus plants, coloured green, or yellow with dryness, and tricked out with occasional touches of scarlet. It had of course its classical myth attached, but its great charm came from its contemplative, serene and strangely clear atmosphere at the other end of the gamut of possible sensations from the noise of lambrettas or eager haste of Jolly waiters. It is Ascension Day and therefore a holiday, so one or two family parties had driven there in cars. We had seen others earlier at the port setting out to sea in bright blue boats with eyes painted on them, dressed in fancy hats and streamers and ribbon bows; and passed cheerful parties driving along the road in carts pulled by gaily bedizened horses or donkeys.

There were huge crowds at the Jolly last night. Armies of grey-haired ladies regimented by cynical couriers, and our South African couple from Noto. I think I shall feel fonder of Ros after this holiday, however cruelly I may have dissected her here. She's a good, sweet character. What I find hard to understand is how some parts of her brain can function critically, and even stigmatize Juliet Duff as a 'goose', while others have been invaded and submerged by a concentrated solution of her own goosishness. Considering her femininity and helplessness, her fear of squalor and of heights, she's brave. I feel a masculine desire to protect her and do things for her, and then fear I may have been absurd or bossy. I started with the determination to be acquiescent and adaptable. I hope my natural egotism has not become too rampant.

## May 6th: Catania

Last night for the first time I began to feel wound-up and exhausted, after a day when I had done all the driving as Rosamond has strained her wrist. In bed I read about the earthquakes, and eruptions of Etna, the lava's slow crawl down the mountain, repeatedly destroying Catania. What a queasy uncertain part of the earth's crust we are on, I was thinking, when suddenly my reading light went out. Going to the window, I saw that the whole town was in darkness, and I was seized by the impotence of being unable to strike a light. Suppose it *was* an earthquake, suppose the Jolly hotel began to crumble, what a horror to be able to see nothing! I stared at the cheerful lights of passing cars and thought how spirits and even sanity absolutely depend on light, and wondered how medieval prisoners ever kept going in pitch darkness. But after half an hour it magically returned and I read and slept.

## May 7th

Episodes from Rosamond's past come out in the course of conversation and I am gradually joining them together. The impression I got of her being an unconfident blushing girl when she was at Girton and I at Newnham was only partly correct. She must already have been a spoiled beauty and her father's darling. Some innocent but unhappy love-affair was the basis for *Dusty Answer*; then came marriage with Leslie Runciman, about which she says little or nothing. Wogan and

Day-Lewis were the great passions of her life; Goronwy Rees, another Welsher, was also passed over in silence (not *once* mentioned) though I remember how she confided in Ralph and me at the time of his defection that it had been an appalling and 'incomprehensible' blow to her, she felt 'he still loved her though he didn't seem to realize it.' Her family and Wogan's both tried to stop their marriage, and she was sent to America to forget him. Then she spoke of Tommy.[1] Wogan adored him, and she had fallen completely under the spell of his charm; he often stayed with them at Ipsden. Once, while she was dancing with Tommy at a party, she 'told him how much she loved him'. 'Oh, you do, do you?' he said, looking coldly at her. 'Well, you'd better not, because I'm doing all I can to break up your marriage.' Cecil Day-Lewis's desertion was a complete surprise and shock and she still cannot get over it, or recognize it as genuine. It's a measure of her innocent vanity that she still thinks of it as 'wrong and mistaken'.

Yesterday was sunny and blue. I came in from a short walk before lunch to find Ros in full contact with the attractive South African and his wife. Far from being a general in the last war, he is a scholarly doctor, who spends a lot of time studying archives and antiquities, and travelling. His adoring wife tells one with every word and glance what a marvellous man she has married.

Rosamond has a deep horror of heights and had to steel herself to climb to the theatre at Taormina which has only a very slightly plunging view. She told me she was worried about this – it seemed to be getting worse. As we started home, another unfortunate experience: following a sign saying 'To the autostrada' we wound up a twisting road behind the town, only half-noticed that a passing car shouted 'Attention!' and came round a corner, Ros driving, to find ourselves at the edge of an unprotected cliff. She jammed on the brakes (the handbrake is very feeble) and got hastily out. I went round the corner to investigate and found that the road more or less petered out between a new building and the cliff. We retraced our course, me driving, and she said, 'I couldn't have done it. I should have passed out.'

Yes, I not only feel I know her better but am fonder of her. Almost all barriers have been crossed, our different attitudes to the unknown have been plotted and left as they are. Among other things we talked

---

[1]  Stephen Tomlin, first husband of Julia Strachey; sculptor.

of today was the unfortunate meeting between Hester Chapman and Elizabeth Bowen[1] at Crichel. Elizabeth was so appalled, and no wonder, by Hester's attitude of prurient interest in and exposure to the world of her stepdaughter's sex-life that she suddenly burst out violently, 'Shut your bloody trap.' Hester returned to London and told Rosamond about it in floods of tears. I can't quite make out the relationship between Ros and Hester; some rivalry certainly comes into it. She told me Hester had been indignant because she flirted with the guide of their Egyptian tour, allowed him to hold her hand, and call her 'darling'. Hester thought she was 'making a fool of herself' as she doubtless was, but what did it matter? She also snorted with indignation whenever mysticism or the supernatural was mentioned.

## May 10th: West Halkin Street

I have been back here for two days. I think of Alix, who is said to be desperately low, and wonder what counsel and advice I can give – alas, there is nothing but brute courage. I have rung her up and am going to see her on Friday.

## May 14th: Stokke

I came here last night after spending the day with Alix at Lords Wood. I arrived here soon after twelve and we talked without stopping until after five. It seems to me astonishing now that I could have wondered if she would want to talk of James's death and her feelings. (Perhaps because I think I'm right in saying that when I went to see them after Burgo's death they never mentioned his name *once*, and I marvelled at such ignorance of human emotion and its workings on the part of professional psychologists.) There was no question this time – Alix started at once with simplicity, directness and moments of breaking down, on the story of James's last days. We talked of other things also of course – politics, Sicily, Julia – but far the most about James, the past and how she was to deal with the future. Now and then she struck with a sharp metallic clang on some painful truth recognized by me years since, as when she said with almost a sob: 'I'm so terrified of forgetting him.' I tried to reassure

---

[1] Writers.

32

her, 'You *won't*,' but of course in a sense she will – only so very, very slowly, and by losing first the unbearable sharpness. It's in a way a drawback that I know so much about the state of bereavement. She didn't ask, 'How soon does it get better?' or I would probably have answered with unpalatable truthfulness, 'It gets worse for at least a year.' As I knew she would be, she was absolutely realistic, dignified and courageous in spite of total grief and loss. My awareness of it was agony. I drove through the matchless beauty of green woods and fields from Henley to Streatley and Newbury, aware that I was sitting bound up and tense in my seat, spent the evening talking to Mary, and then (after getting into bed early) the delayed effect of my pain for Alix zoomed out of the darkness like a huge crow and clutched me with its claws and beat its great black wings at me. I couldn't sleep but lay tormented and doubting. Had I done all I could for her? Was she all right? Two things moved me greatly and in a particular way: when I was leaving, the voice of genuine feeling in which she said, 'Goodbye, dearest Frances, I'm fearfully glad to have seen you,' and the fact that when I asked if there had been no one she could summon to her side, she said, 'Well, I had thought perhaps you might come.' It took me a long time to take this in. All the time I was with her I was reacting and counteracting so furiously to her sorrow and mine that there was no time for weighing or sifting. Hence my tortured thoughts last night. Should I not have firmly announced that I was coming down to stay till her brother Philip comes back from America in a fortnight? Or would this be an invasion of her privacy and the desire to 'collapse' at times? Would it be taking too much on myself? Her remarks had surprised me because I'd never thought of her as setting me high among her friends, but rather that she and James were two of the people I most loved and admired and was delighted and amused by, and whom I thought of as a mythical, indissoluble pair. And as I'm cursed with hypersensitivity to other people's feelings, which sets my heart racing as it raced last night, I doubt whether I'm fitted to support and sustain someone in the extremity of grief.

### May 15th

I have written to Alix, suggesting coming again next week for a night on my way to the Carringtons and perhaps another on the way back. I thought a lot about how I should word it, making it easy for her to say no or yes, or allow me to go for one night or more. Discussing this with Mary led to a talk about sense of guilt. She claimed not to know what it was – if you've done your best then there's nothing to be gained by self-castigation. But even so un-neurotic and kind a prson as Mary must surely have factual doubts sometimes where the material in question is the subtly vulnerable and complex stuff of human feelings. How can anyone be sure they have done the best they could? Yet Edward Glover[1] would perhaps have agreed. For I seem to remember he thinks both sense of guilt and anxiety are neurotic, whereas to me there are many cases when it would be irrational not to feel them.

One thing Alix and I talked about was aggression. If James had been there I don't feel she would have dared put forth the very interesting suggestion that Freud was mistaken in taking the death instinct as basic and aggression as a form of it turned outwards. And that, on the contrary, aggressive instincts have an obvious part to play in biological terms of self-preservation, and it is more correct to say that the death instinct and suicidal impulses are a turning inwards of the primary instinct of aggression.

I have loved being alone with Mary. All yesterday the birds kept up their mellifluous, surprisingly loud, sweet and complex music. They still do today, though it is as wet and dismal as yesterday was sunny and cheerful. A morning such as this makes one remember how lonely one can be in the country, how the mercury in one's thermometer can sink like a plummet. During green, sweet, musical, scented yesterday, everything we did was a pleasure. Mary and I spent an hour or so planting out begonias, asters and marigolds in a well-dug flower-bed and watering them in.

We have just been to have a drink with Serena[2] at Ham and then to lunch with Teresa Waugh, wife of Auberon – an interesting girl, sharp in both good and bad senses, an efficient mother to three dear little children.

### May 16th

I'm oppressed not by what Julia calls the eeriness of the universe, but by its tragic grimness; by the swoops made by death and the horrible necessity of wondering where it will strike next; by fear of my own;

[1] Freudian psychoanalyst.
[2] Rothschild, daughter of Mary and Philip Dunn and wife of Jacob.

by U Thant declaring that we are seeing the preparation of a third world war; by reading that one in every ten people is now doomed to be killed or seriously injured in a motor accident; by the prevalance of futility, drug-taking and boredom; by finding myself so quickly able to subside into the morass when I believe that I have found stability; by effervescence and restlessness and noise. And, constantly, by the absence of Janetta.

5 p.m. What would Rosamond make of the above? I have just been rung up by Rosemary Peto to tell me that she lent a very old car of hers to Serge[1] and Katharine Fedden[2] to drive to Morocco in, that they have had an appalling smash near Vittoria and that Serge was very seriously, possibly fatally injured, and Katharine herself terribly bruised and shocked. Nicky and Renée Fedden have flown out there, Janetta has been wired and is coming to meet them. Robert has proved as usual a stalwart support in time of need. God help us, what a world!

## May 18th

This horrifying crash still looms at the back of my mind. Further details have come through from telephone calls from Janetta and Renée. The car was being driven by the third member of the party, a young art student without a driving licence. It is therefore a police matter and is likely to remain so until Serge recovers or dies. He's still unconscious and there seems no certainty which will happen. Janetta is staying with Nicky at a Vittoria hotel, and there are great complications about money. The accident took place at 6 a.m. and both Serge and Katharine were asleep; perhaps the driver was also.

Julian came to dinner and an evening of steady, absorbing and now forgotten talk.

## May 20th: Lords Wood

I drove down here yesterday, and am spending one night with Alix on each side of a weekend at the Carringtons'. Although I had the greatest difficulty in sleeping last night, the actual topics we spoke of

---

[1] Brodskis, husband of Janetta's eldest daughter Nicky.
[2] Daugher of Robin and Renée.

for so many hours yesterday were not actually so harrowing as before. James's name of course came up a great deal, and I noticed the pathetic change from the 'James likes' or 'James always does this' of last time to 'James used to' this time. Alix has taken on a superhuman task in contriving to be here alone since he died; I believe she has seen very few people. I'm full of admiration for her, and as I looked at her distinguished profile in the lamplight last night I thought she was still really beautiful. She says the 'evenings are rather fearful'; she does what she touchingly thinks of as 'taking to the bottle' – that is to say she drinks one not very large glass of South African sherry! She was anxious to 'break the habit' of being unable to look at television because of the sadness of the empty chair in the darkness. It was my task last night to fill that empty chair. She can't bear to listen to music. She confesses to 'panic fears' in the night, yet doesn't like to wake up the Johnstons above. I think after the first shock, she is just able to envisage the bleak future, and she confesses that from her point of view the atom bomb going off (which seems highly likely at the moment) would be a relief. I think her powers of adjustment are pretty good – and her brother Philip, I'm glad to hear, arrives on Wednesday, the day after I go back to London.

## *May 27th: Hilton*

Drove Bunny down here yesterday through greenery pale and viridian but always strikingly luminous under towering storm clouds, with heavy showers beating up and departing. Angelica and Amaryllis[1] arrived soon after us, William was here, the fiery Nerissa[2] arrived for dinner. I have the room with the smudged grey walls on the top floor and am happy there, in spite of the sheets on my bed being dirty and crumpled, dead flowers in a vase, and the bathroom next door an inconceivable chaos of stained and battered objects, forests of dirty tumblers, old bottle tops and decayed toothbrushes. The personality of the house is still unique and original. I spread my work over a rickety table in my room – feeling the necessity for a private bolthole, away from Angelica's endless violin-playing and William on the oboe, probably later to be joined by Fanny on the horn. Much talk to Bunny on the way down; later some to Amaryllis.

[1]   The eldest of the four Garnett girls.
[2]   One of the Garnett twins, the other being Fanny.

36

Being an actress has set its indelible mark on her, so that I feel she can never be anything else. I do hope she will be a success. Her large soft eyes, low voice and cloud of soft hair make her look vulnerable, and the compulsive need for dollops of indulgence (cigarettes – the act of lighting gives a necessary hoist to the ego – drinks) is not a symptom of happiness. Nerissa and Henrietta also need these things, but clutch at them fiercely and positively. I'm fascinated by these girls and their ethos and habits. Their hands are covered with rings old and new, one on each finger. Last night Nerissa asked me to play chess, her present enthusiasm, and beat me soundly. Then talk to Bunny about why the young hurl themselves into this dangerous, expensive and self-destructive habit of smoking. Richard and William never did, apparently. I suppose smoking is a sign of weakness of character – a need to shore oneself up by the signs of maturity and ritual movements, a crutch, a walking-stick. Natural therefore to adolescents, but a rational person ought to be able to shake it off afterwards. Talk also about fear of heights and other phobias. I'm amazed how many people own to them; they describe them variously as 'feeling I'm going to pass out, or throw myself over, horrible dread' – but not giddiness.

## May 30th

My days are packed much too tight. I deplore this congestion and the fact that conversations, scenes, faces flash by without my being able to take stock of them. Argument was pretty lively at Hilton, ranging from subjects like the difference between sarcasm and irony, to violence, and the 'new philosophy of the young' which seems to be tinged with Zen Buddhism, and voiced by the Beatles. A new record by the Beatles was played; I see little talent, or originality, no power to excite in them, and of course said so. 'Yes,' the cry went up, 'that's true, but then they don't aim at that. What they give off is a sort of serene acceptance. You feel *happy* when you listen to them.' Hitching this on to a later conversation with Georgia (who arrived later with Henrietta and Sophie), it seems to me this current philosophy of youth is above all passive. Acceptance is good, so far as it goes, but I cling to my belief in activity being better than passivity. The younger generation seem like opium-smokers, lying about soaking up sensations, pouring cigarettes, drink, cinema, television and marijuana in at the portals of their senses until near-satiation is reached. Yet Georgia said, 'Surely youth is the time you're supposed to feel excited.' Her face wore its puzzled look. An eerie impression of a lot of people endlessly sucking on hookahs comes to my mind.

Sophie ran about excitedly from person to person till at last she became overstimulated and fretful. Angelica and Bunny toiled for our benefit and I fear tired themselves out. Nerissa helped valiantly, Henrietta looked rather wan, Amaryllis went off to visit Leonard at Rodwell, Fanny came with her lover, a professional conductor. Their love was more exhibitionist than any I ever saw; they were constantly entwined in its tense throes, exchanging loud kisses. She has grown up with a bang, like Alice after eating the mushroom. There was music one evening, and she stood in the doorway playing softly (and then suddenly very loud) on her horn, looking like a Piero della Francesca angel.

By Sunday afternoon I wanted to come home, and did, bringing Nerissa. Ever since I have been typing and toiling, in a stupefying fashion.

## June 1st

Yesterday came a letter from Janetta, who starts driving home next Monday. She says of her week at Vittoria, 'It was *appalling*. I still feel in a state of total shock from it all and obsessed by the horror of it. It was the most brutal destructive thing in the world to be near someone so hurt, in such agony. Beside the appalling anxiety, it was all fearfully difficult, a non-stop series of things to be done. And then Serge's amazing Mum . . . This camp of anxious women developed in the only hotel in Vittoria, with whisky and scrambled eggs in the bedrooms. I kept trying to make people sleep, I certainly used to cry in the street with exhaustion. I was *terribly* worried about Nicky and fearfully moved by her. She became very quiet, childlike and utterly dependent.'

In bed last night in the small hours I began reading Lorenz on aggression – fascinating. He describes how some animal species 'run themselves into a blind alley', for instance male peacocks almost overbalance, stags' antlers are useless except for fighting other stags, and suggests that western man is doing the same thing – running into a blind alley of high blood-pressure, senseless speed, lung cancer, as a result of competition 'within the species'.

## June 3rd: Lawford Hall

Beauty, faint uneasiness and also sadness. Phyllis,[1] Leslie Hartley, Jimmy Smith and I are off to Aldeburgh Festival this afternoon. Leslie has got portentously fat, and what with his hypochondria and his care for his shapeless carcass (taking his temperature every day and having a check-up every week) I'm slightly put off by him, amiable old geezer though he is – an old baby, that has never passed through maturity. Jimmy Smith, not met before, I like; he is alert, interested and intelligent. Inclined to drop names, he says, 'What?' in a P. G. Wodehouse way after every remark.

## June 4th

At the Dolphin Hotel, Thorpeness – a village of 'refined', select, mock-Tudor seaside dwellings, two imitation Tudor gateways in red brick and a bogus Norman church (Leslie Hartley thought it genuine, the old ass) lined up in front of a long shingle beach stretching all the way to Aldeburgh. Our party has settled into four little rooms side by side and found a workable, mutual wavelength fairly easily. But there is some spring that has to be wound up to maintain it. Last night we went to see the two new operas, Walton's *Bear* and Lennox Berkeley's *Castaway*. Packed in to the uncomfortable seats of the Jubilee Hall, we found Anne and Heywood and Alvilde Lees-Milne beside us, Celia [Goodman] behind, and when we drifted out in the entr'acte innumerable familiar faces – Desmond, Pat Trevor-Roper, Frieda Berkeley, John Julius Norwich. There was a charm in floating about in the still, twilit, pearly space between the hall and the shingle bank, a disembodied feeling of being wafted rather than supported on legs. A certain rivalry, as I had foreseen, between the two operas. Greatly hoping that Lennox Berkeley's would be good, I thought it only moderately so, while Walton's was an uproarious success.

## June 6th

On Sunday we lunched with Lord and Lady Gladwyn, a cold spread with delicious wine after drinks – of which I took too many – in the garden. At lunch I was pleasantly situated between Desmond and

[1] Nichols, widow of Sir Philip.

Jock Cranbrook.[1] On then to hear some choirboys in sailor suits from Vienna singing in Blythburgh church. On the whole I remain stony to these disembodied voices, their famous 'purity' seeming a purely negative quality – amounting to a lack, in fact, of various things like maturity, emotion, expressiveness. I was pleased therefore, as well as amused, to hear Desmond say with feeling (and only partial truth): 'I *loathe* boys!' Another splendid concert in the new hall at the Maltings, Snape, whose acoustics are magnificently warm, rich and alive without being in the faintest degree fuzzy. And yesterday I left the others behind in what was obviously burgeoning into a hot summer's day, and returned home to be greeted in London by headlines two inches high: IT'S WAR. The Middle Eastern crisis between the Arab States and Israel has developed, as how should it not when both sides were longing to fight each other. So here we are. My own feelings are leaden, but a dreadfully soulless lead, throwing off no reflections. How quickly they could blaze up, of course, I know. On the wireless last night various brave young voices declared their intention of setting off at once to fight or work for what they believed right, though their vagueness as to why they thought it right or even what it was was quite amazing. In the streets everyone was buying papers, and words like 'call-up', 'they're horrible people anyway' floated round, while a sympathetic girl gave an exaggerated shudder – 'Brrrr!' – after glancing at her paper. So here, I suppose, we go, at the very least into total dishonesty, corruption and mass hysteria. Frances Phipps[2] has sent me a heart-broken wail. Such a situation almost literally 'breaks her heart'.

Janetta comes back today. I look forward immensely to seeing her, but to nothing much else.

### June 10th

Janetta's talents for organizing have as usual begun to make sense of her difficult problems. Arriving full of strength from Spain, sun, love and hard work, it is in a way sad to see her courageous barque nearly sunk by the weight thrown onto it. She sits up to Spanish late hours and gets up with English earliness, brooding over her problems. She

[1] Anne Hill's eldest brother.
[2] Left-wing widow of Sir Eric Phipps, diplomat.

has already planned to let Montpelier Square, find a flat or independent lodging for Georgie and carry Rose off to Tramores, where a tutor will be found for her for the next two terms. Altogether she has the reins of her life pretty firmly in hand.

The Middle Eastern crisis has presented an extraordinarily swift-moving series of events, and much 'side-taking'. Mary: 'I thought of going out there, not sure in what capacity.' F: 'Oh, which side would you join?' M: '*Really*, Frances!' Tim Behrens has gone out to join the Israelis. It is this excitement and real love of fighting that is so horrifying. I'm sure he, Tim, believes he's moved by high-minded feelings. After four days of sensational success by the Israelis and admirable moderation on the part of the Great Powers the war seemed to be over and Nasser last night resigned. But the Israelis and Syrians are flushed with battle, and won't stop fighting, like two frenzied dogs who ought to have pepper shaken over them.

### June 21st

A day of steady work and no human visage, not even Mrs Ringe's (her husband being ill).

### June 22nd

This morning, still no Mrs Ringe, and David and Rachel Cecil expected to lunch. I pulled myself violently together, tackled the mountainous pile of dishes from the last four days, watered plants, sorted laundry, went out and shopped, dusted a bit, cooked – and feel better. Also because two friends in distress, Alix and Julia, have asked for my company. Tomorrow is Julia's divorce from Lawrence; she will come to dinner after it. On Friday I drive down to lunch with Alix.

David and Rachel illumined my flat with their delightful presence. They refused wine, but I noticed that their company had been more intoxicating than the small aperitifs we all swallowed. Now the last crystals of antipathy to life have been drained away by my continued sensations as I sit in Belgrave Square: warm sun, sound of tennis balls and children's voices, sight of their flying limbs and the trimmed lawn. A little boy of about two keeps asking me to watch him jump off the edge of the grass.

## June 27th

And again I'm in the square gardens and the same small boy is showing off his jumps to me. Violent tropical showers and interims of burning sun have brought all the ugly floribunda roses out into bloom. The imminence of Janetta's departure for heaven knows how long (for she has let Montpelier – the last link – and Georgie is to move into Nicky's flat) casts a cloud as black as the huge one that is about to open its mouth and swallow the sun. I have seen a lot of her – last night we went to *Frau ohne Schatten* together, subjecting ourselves to the immense, sometimes shattering noise of a huge orchestra, even the two stage boxes being stuffed with extra, more vigorous noise – harps, trumpets, cymbals. At one moment all hell broke loose. Some stalwart men advanced in military fashion to the front of the box nearest us and sang with deafening strength, while brass trombones brayed and in the opposite box men beat frenziedly on what looked like tin trays.

## June 28th

An urgent need to pick this book up and stand it opposite me; to hold a conversation with it, since I have no other vis-à-vis. If only it would answer! How impossible it is to manage without a 'best friend', if one cannot have a 'best beloved'. Janetta's disappearance has, I suppose, emphasized the fact that though I have many friends, none is 'best' in that he or she can be summoned to my aid when, as now, I suddenly feel myself uncertain and foundering, after years (literally) of apparently 'getting along'. Last night after my orchestra I went round to Montpelier Square, and found a curious scene. In the back room was a rather subdued party – Robin and Susan Campbell, Sonia Orwell, and Julian dressed in brightest pink and seeming rather overexcited and probably drunk. I had no private talk with Janetta, and am not sure if she really wants me to go to Spain in the autumn. All I have to go on is that when I said the Hendersons[1] had asked me to Mijas, she said she 'would be furious if I didn't come to her too'. To be honest I feel a curious antipathy to that whole coast and its life – not, of course, to lovely Tramores, and if I do go there I would like to bury myself up there among the mountains and hardly approach the horrible coast. Then I must take some work.

[1] Nicko and Mary.

Oh, I don't know, I don't know. I'm floating on a mounting tide, a very unaccustomed wave of uncertainty mixed with a feeling of not belonging anywhere. I'm distressed at my own prickly inability to fit into the lives of other people. Julia has asked me to go to Lambourn, and I've said I will next Monday, but shall I be able to stick it out? I think she would like me to go for more than a week, and in theory perhaps I could, but I so dread my own irritability, though I never stop trying to gulp it down.

Tonight Julian comes to dinner, something I look forward to very much. At his best he is almost the truest sounding-board and metronome I know. I have an idea why he vanished completely into another room when I was there last night. Perhaps I shall discover whether I was right.

### June 29th

Yes, partly, and also as he candidly avowed, he was in a state of upset and sorrow about the occasion for our being gathered together: Janetta's departure, with her three nymphs, all looking particularly nymphlike, attractive, graceful and in a state of excitement about taking wing – Rose to Greece, Nicky to Paris, Georgie with Janetta to Spain. This was the reason why Julian had dressed in such brilliant pink clothes and wore a hectic pink expression. He honestly admitted what I see I was not up to admitting – being painfully saddened by Janetta's departure. His pink clothes were a touching attempt to hide the deep sadness which later exploded into tears in her bedroom. She is so important to us, we all miss her so, and worry rather broodily over her. Julian confessed to irrational anxiety-feelings centred on August.

### July 2nd

On the eve of departure to Lambourn on yet another Julia-rescue operation, I wonder if I was mad to undertake it. She arrived to have supper with me tonight in such an almost visible and certainly audible *spangle* of rage, and began to discharge it so rapidly and furiously at me, that the fat was in a moment nearly in the fire. When she arrived I had on the wireless playing some folksy music. I turned it off at once, but in two minutes she had found fault with everything I said – thought the music nice because I didn't, then said the human voice was always unbearable, and when (trying to find grounds for agreement) I said I particularly disliked counter-tenors and choirboys, she at once excepted these from her disapproval. But then, she said she didn't 'like human beings, as I did'. Thank heavens I had the wit to stop her before it got worse. 'Julia, you're upset – what has happened?' In the nicest possible way she at once agreed and apologized and explained. But the tension of our evening together has left me palpitating and restless. Well, I'll do my best, think before I speak, bite back disagreement – but I don't look forward to it at all. Not at all.

## July 5th: Lambourn

Two nights here have passed in perfect amity. Julia has been charming, friendly, and the best of company. She is even somewhat euphoric, and was saying this morning that it was so nice here that she might consider keeping the house on. 'And give up Percy Street?' I asked. 'Oh, no, just as a weekend cottage.' All of a sudden she doesn't worry about money, and yesterday explained to me that she had decided against trying to cut a chunk from her present novel to send to the *New Yorker*, because it would spoil the plans for the novel itself and 'she was not going to put money before work. She never had,' which is strictly true. I sleep in the tiny coffin-shaped room overlooking the garden. Its low window looks straight out into the green branches of a tree. After breakfast I settle at a table in my favourite room – the morning-room (not liked by Julia) and struggle with a tough bit of Arts Council translation sent me by Robin. We take a walk in the afternoon, more work and then I help Julia sort her books and she helps me – very effectively – with my translation.

Industrious, routine life.

## July 7th

Day after day of summer, delicious to be in the country in them, but I brood over my poor unwatered London window-boxes. Robin's bit of translation is a real teaser; Julia has been extremely helpful with it. Yesterday however, she got on her high literary horse and thought I wasn't respecting the author's style enough. A dangerous corner. 'I don't mind what you're saying,' she said, 'but you mustn't mind if I shout at you.' In her view certain adjustments altered the flavour or sense, in mine they turned the syntax from a French to an English one. She wanted a sentence to begin: 'Microbes, held to be animals, are more like forces.' I disliked the concatenation of 'Microbes held'. But this, she said, was a turn of words used by all the best writers, from Sterne to Herzog, and any intrusive words between 'microbes' and 'held' would distort the author's intention!

## July 9th

Julia is amazing and fascinating – the qualities of her mind delight me. There is actually in it a potentiality for philosophical speculation, though imagination takes over so quickly and whirls it up and away that one doesn't always recognize it. She told me how absolutely thrilled she had been when as a child Oliver[1] explained to her something about sameness – how a thing could be the same as another thing, yet not identical. This was in the course of a long ding-dong argument about the desire to have children. There was a moment in the middle when we both fell silent for a few minutes, and then began again amicably and finished so. Julia even declared herself convinced to some extent by what I said, and for my part, I think I now understand the reason for her opening contention, which was 'that the desire to have children in the abstract (i.e. not *with* a certain person you are in love with) is unhealthy and hallucinatory'.

I brought up, of course, the primary instincts, the desire of small children to play with dolls, other longings for things not yet experienced but about which you have evidence from books and other people – such as sex and Italy. Julia declared she had never had a general longing for sex, always been in love without a pause ever since a child, always wanted to have a child by the man she loved, but never in the abstract. She could not conceive of 'longing to go to Italy' if you'd never been there, it was a 'hallucination'. You couldn't tell what '*a child*' would be like, it might be different from your imagined picture, therefore it was unhealthy to long for it. Sexual desires, she strangely suggested, were merely evoked step by step by male caresses. I brought up Freud and his theory of the instincts in vain, I described the process of a child longing for '*a pony*' and the images that coursed through its mind. What affected her was my

[1] Strachey, her father.

45

referring to the physical organism of females, producing each month a possible child, and its inevitable effect on the mind. What interested me was the sudden realization that it was the gambling element in desiring '*a*' child she hated, the risk, the lack of planning. Just as she can't bear to leave anything to chance, hates adventure, improvisation – when travelling in particular, but virtually always – and feels it uncivilized. So that even to desire so recklessly unknown a relationship as parenthood was to her uncivilized.

## July 11th: At Kitty West's

Kitty and I had a drink at Crichel – Raymond, Pat, Desmond, Richard Brain, and Munro Wheeler[1] (a perfectly delightful, well-polished walking-stick-handle in the shape of a monkey, intelligent, highly polite, with an American's interest in famous people). I liked him very much and was pleased when on our leaving he took a beautiful white rose from a vase and presented it to me.

Yesterday was one of those rare, utterly flawless, still, hot, summer days that come at most once a year, and we ate and lay out of doors, creeping from sun to shadow, embraced by the smell of the garden flowers, attentively watched and hopped around by a sparrow.

## July 25th

Like a powerful red express train the heat wave drives its way steadily along its track. The stations are crowded with crimson-faced travellers, great or small, white and black, turning up their tortured faces towards the announcement board, then dragging their suitcases and paper bags and fretful children towards the grille where they stand sweating for hours like prisoners in a concentration camp. Around the Slade, where I spent last weekend, the trees have bulked out their dark green, full, summer silhouettes and the cornfields begin to turn yellow. The sun was almost too hot, yet how delicious was the air and free from flies. Eardley and Mattei were radiant with happiness, feathering their nest – and it has begun to bloom and flower, even though I'm surprised at their apparent vagueness about colour combinations. We were all happy I think, cooking, weeding,

[1] Very important figure in the American art world.

digging, translating. Yet there were moments when Eardley chilled me with his relentlessness about Crichel. So anxious is he to take away from them everything that is legally his that the Slade overflows with sofas and more and more pictures. 'And I'm going down to *swipe the lot*,' he ended up saying. He also asked how I thought Crichel was getting along, and said he 'thought it was running to seed terribly'. I'm afraid he wants it to fail, and I don't quite know why, now that he's quit of it. Ungenerous, surely?

## *July 27th: West Halkin Street*

Dinner last night here, with Julia, Julian and Robert[1] – three of my favourite companions, yet in a way I would have preferred being with any one of them alone. However, it seemed vital to support Julia through the remaining evenings before she leaves for Italy, and so the party evolved.

Julian arrived first, wearing the pink jacket that now seems to me rather like a hurricane cone. As a comforter and distracter of Julia he was perfect, and she was enthusiastic about him after-wards, but he brought a small tornado into my flat with its four inhabitants. Yet he was extremely amusing, and entertained us with brilliant imitations of Cyril Connolly and television life.

Robert started several of the general themes I so love. One of them arose from watching a would-be suicide trying to throw himself into the Haymarket for several hours on end yesterday afternoon. Robert's own inclination had been to turn away and escape as fast as possible. He dreaded seeing the man jump. But most people behaved quite differently. A youthful crowd was making a gala of it, thrumming guitars and watching with detached interest. Not ghoulishly, Robert thought, though a girl in his office said she 'longed to be there, it would be so exciting and interesting'. Perhaps their indifference was much healthier than his fear? Robert wondered. I said it didn't sound like indifference, which never keeps anyone waiting about anywhere for hours. Thence we got on to the difference between pity and sympathy – sympathy is surely far more desirable than pity – and to the fear of death and how it affected one's beliefs, with Malcolm Muggeridge as an example.

[1] Kee.

## July 30th: Crichel

Lovely to be alone here with Julian and Desmond. I wish I did not feel so horribly tense, though, and I do not sleep. Ugh. I hate my physical, or rather nervous constitution, but I am saddled with it, it hangs on my back like a heavy knapsack which can't be put down. I must just make the best of it, haul it along. Julian has been his gentlest and most sympathetic, no fizz at all. Desmond, on the other hand, though all Irish charm and solicitude for our happiness, is a bit inclined to blow up, and his hair which forms an unusually long, thick fringe round his head at the moment gives him a wild appearance. Last night he put on that feeble Beatles record after dinner (three guests present of whom more in a moment) and shouted quite angrily at Julian because he went on talking, as though he was being distracted from some major work of art. Julian either didn't hear or decided to ignore him.

The weather having soured to damp greyness, we have got into an effortless gear of work, record-sorting and playing, short walks for Moses, talk, jokes. I now sit in what used to be Eardley's and is now Pat's room, translating at a good solid table looking out at the level grey-green landscape. It is extraordinary after these weeks of brilliant colour – as if the plug had been pulled out of a basin of dye.

Last night's guests were Dickie Buckle,[1] Ed Gilbert[2] and a tall, well-built and almost ludicrously handsome guardsman whom Dickie fancies. He was a nice friendly fellow, carrying off the situation well and telling amusingly a hair-raising story about being dragged round Hyde Park Corner by his horse. Apparently guardsmen are killed like this occasionally because their stirrups are so arranged as not to come loose from the saddle. Nothing must be changed, not even this. One died at the trooping of the colour last year 'but it was hushed up'. I did not feel strange among these five homosexuals. Not a bit, I'm thoroughly used to it, and I liked the guardsman.

I enjoyed talking to Ed and looking into his ocelot's face. A feeling of sympathy sprang up between us. We talked of the burning, everlasting topic of the drug-taking, flower-loving, Zen-Buddhist young. I don't know how much he is 'of' them, but not entirely as he

1  Writer and authority on ballet.
2  Architect and designer.

tucks into whisky which they deplore. He mentioned someone who 'was very much "turned on"'. F: 'What does that mean, exactly?' 'Taking drugs and wearing flowers and bells and loving each other and calling each other beautiful.' According to Ed, bells are the badge of drugs. We only talked a little but I took to heart all he said; he was in favour of their non-violence, but they aren't 'doers', he said. Of course not if they 'think it important for some people to do nothing beautifully'. They do seem to have got hold of the wrong end of the stick, yet I suppose that sticks have no right end, or rather that their rightness is relative to the civilization they are in, or, in other words, lies in the eye of the observer.

Last night I dined with the Campbells at Charles's restaurant off the Fulham Road. Afterwards there was a tinkling at the door and Susan said, 'Oh, here come the bells.' It was Henrietta with two friends, wearing a bell on a string round her neck like a farm animal. She looked lovely and came up and kissed me warmly.

### August 2nd: West Halkin Street

The silence of August has settled on London, except for voices speaking French, Spanish, German; the telephone is mute, the post non-existent.

Henrietta rang me up yesterday. I'm going to see them on Friday, and am very glad she wants me to go. But the only thing I seem to have much heart for is reading about the Hittites – nothing could seem more remote from the present.

### August 4th

Worry, when it takes over and fills the available space in consciousness, is like a sound starting small and faint and gradually swelling, and when you think it can get no louder, doing just that – swelling, blaring like an air-raid siren spelling danger, yet not having the saving grace of sirens – that they eventually descend again from their summits. Worry merely goes on shouting in one's ears until total exhaustion or restlessness takes its place; and it is always waiting in the wings to return.

Bunny came to dinner last night. He says he lies awake worrying; he is worried about Angelica, who has had what seems to be a small cancer removed from her breast. Yet in spite of all he gives a rather unearthly impression of being immune, detached. I do wish that the passing years would bring me such detachment and immunity. Instead I find myself increasingly involved and vulnerable, sometimes absurdly so. For instance, I have been re-reading Turgenev, beginning with my favourites, *Smoke* and *Torrents of Spring*, but when Ganin (in *Torrents of Spring*) deserts his sweet Gemma for the predatory vamp, I could not bear to read it. Quite literally I leapt ahead to the tragic conclusion and after swallowing it at a gulp (which seemed somehow easier than slowly advancing into doom) I went back over the ground again more slowly. It was a relief to talk to Robert yesterday – there is almost no one with whom I feel more in agreement about nearly everything. He at once put his finger on the flaw in the drug-takers' philosophy: its scorn for the reality principle. If one is to live in this world one must want to understand it as it is, be fully conscious and appreciate it with both mind and emotions as it is. To do otherwise is to be with Rosamond in her spirit world.

## August 7th

Now that Julia has gone away, taking with her the need to maintain that life is worth living, it seems to me plain that it is not. Julian has just lunched here; tomorrow he too departs, and I suppose I shall clatter off to Spain as planned the week after next. I'm reminded of travelling hand over hand along the boom of the gym with legs dangling. I've a feeling of having said everything before, done everything before, thought everything before. The only thing I take an interest in is Turgenev, and it is with pure joy that on re-reading his books one by one I find them just as good as I'd remembered them and for the same reasons.

## August 12th: Snape

I'm doing a little East Anglian tour, instead of resigning myself to spending the weekend alone in now depopulated London. On Thursday I drove Margaret Penrose, her 'cello and my violin to Thorington where I spent two very happy nights. We talked about drug addiction much of the way down. She is wildly against it, almost intemperately so, yet when her housekeeper Bessy irritates her, she rushes to the cupboard for a swig of whisky. Why then be *so* down on marijuana? When picking bunches of brilliant dahlias in the garden there was a loud crack of thunder overhead and she ran indoors, shouting to me to come in, and quite anxious because I stopped to gather up my flowers. They are both timid – is this perhaps a common trait of very intelligent people? Lionel took a more cautious line about drugs – it was not proved how much harm they do, and certainly you would have to take massive doses of LSD to affect the genes of future children. I didn't get much new information from them, and not the ghost of a suggestion how anyone could be cured. But I did adore their company and delighted in the relaxed, ramshackle life, casual meals, odd swigs of whisky, Haydn trio-playing, stimulating conversations, sitting down together to correct the grammar of anti-war articles by illiterate psychoanalysts for some pacifist magazine. There is never a moment when one wonders what to say or do next.

This morning I drove to Snape and lunched with Anne and Heywood. From my bedroom window I see the poor hunched figure of Lady Cranbrook creeping round her tousled garden, her white wig of hair now yellowing with age, like a copy of *The Times* left out of doors, and after her creeps her little dachshund, faithful and nearly as decrepit as she is.

### August 13th

It is utterly peaceful and nice being here. I work a little, sleep well, and feel calm. The sudden change in the landscape these last days has been astonishing, the trees scorched at the edges, the cold hand of autumn clutches and holds one's own as one goes walking in the fields.

### August 14th

Sitting up in bed waiting for breakfast to come; watch stopped, I do not know the time. Outside, a grey windy day, and rain spatters the panes. I have been plotting a cross-country journey home, based on Heywood's advice.

This house inevitably becomes sadder, as it watches the slow dehumanization of a delightful old lady – yet her charm still gives a watery gleam from time to time. So does her intelligence. But the repetitions, over and over, within a few moments, of the same remarks in exactly the same tone force one to become a hospital nurse. She is only twenty-one years older than me, don't forget it. She gets nothing but touching kindness and consideration. Yesterday a walk turned into a drive for her sake, with many little stops to get out and look for something, like a rare and enormously tall and exciting plant, found by the river (*Sonchus palustris*). Everything has faded for her, even the flowers she once knew so much about. She gazed wonderingly at a yellow water-lily laid on her lap by Heywood, and asked me what a pink campion was. Anne is fiercely protective, and said to me how impossible it would be to think of sending her mother to a home. I reflected, but didn't say, that unless she dies soon it will also be impossible to keep her here. The awful, insoluble quandary of old age.

### August 15th: London

Yesterday I set off in streaming rain and drove slowly and gently and by rustic routes to the very outskirts of London where I spent a hectic three-quarters of an hour trying to get to Golders Green and return Margaret's 'cello.

Back home about four – a pile of letters. From the fact that there were *three* from Gerald, and that his usually neat writing betrayed strong and painful emotion, I think I guessed what they were about. Gamel[1] is gravely ill, in fact, dying. Gerald writes in an ecstasy of despair – by which I do not mean he is getting vicarious pleasure, but hurling himself head first into his emotion without reserve. His letters were written in a quavering hand and blotted with tears. Xavier's[2] arrival had led to his discovering that Gamel had not had hepatitis at all but a heart attack; also that one of her arms was swollen and she had a lump between her neck and shoulder (Janetta wrote that it was plainly visible), which a specialist at once diagnosed as inoperable cancer. That neither her doctor nor Gerald had noticed it is pathetic and terrible. Xavier thinks she might live six months or a year, or more. 'It is really I who have the cancer,' Gerald writes, 'because the knowledge of her having it eats into me and I cannot get rid of it for a moment. I feel as if I were living in a nightmare. I can't contemplate life without her – the awful loneliness, the longing, the

[1] Gerald's wife.
[2] Gerald's son-in-law, a French doctor.

guilt . . I can't sleep . . . I can't think of anything else. I just feel this throb, throb, throb of sadness and pity.'

He is desperately anxious to keep the news from Gamel, and believes she thinks the radium treatment she is having is for 'a ganglion'. But she is much too intelligent and well-informed *not* to realize, and I feel almost sure she has known for a long while and not wanted to face it or make Gerald unhappy. The last of his letters says they are arriving in England the day after tomorrow, whether for treatment or consultation I don't know, and returning on September 2nd. I was enjoined to tell no one.

## August 17th

Precarious calm and sanity has foundered, I don't quite know why. Yesterday I worked peacefully (though bored to tears with my current book) and saw no one until I dined with Jonny and Sabrina[1] in the evening. Jonny was very helpful about the Brenans' arrival and suggests our driving to the airport to meet them. His house is in a state of almost exemplary squalor, dirt and untidiness – the walls newly covered with wallpaper whose colour scheme was 'designed by' Sabrina, the carpet more stains than not, and well seeded with tiny shoes, dolls' cots, prams. Suna Portman, who was there, suggested 'livening up' this lavender-blue-grey and white wallpaper with 'some cheerful emerald green curtains'.

## August 18th

It's strange – more than that, deeply disconcerting – to think of someone with love and sympathy and then come up against the not altogether attractive side of their personality. So it was with Gerald last night, and of course it's often happened before, and of course the endearing, original side will reappear when I see him again, and the mechanical taking-for-granted, almost *boring* Gerald who taps away *sotto voce* like a tinny typewriter will disappear like one of the figures in a cuckoo clock.

Jonny came in his car in good time to fetch me and eat a hasty snack; added to his sensitive charm is a new kindness and responsibility. We arrived at the airport and soon discovered that there was

---

[1]   His wife at this time.

three-quarters of an hour's delay on the Malaga flight. Out on to what is absurdly called the 'Waving Deck'. A huge Pollock-theatre moon goggled at us through dramatic streaky clouds, and below (like some neat child's game) the aeroplanes lined up, little buses trundled round, gangways were moved – all brilliantly decorated with lights of all colours and giving a reassuring, jolly, busy, even efficient impression. We gazed into the dark sky where an occasional red, lurid, winking eye showed that an aeroplane was approaching. Then it would light up suddenly with three white stars, and float towards earth quite silently, apparently very gently and softly, so that one expected it to land without a sound. But a terrifying transformation took place on touching down; the quiet settling swan all at once became a ferocious dragon and an earth-shattering, bestial roar filled the sky as its lights turned red and savage. Afterwards, neatness and efficiency again.

Suddenly I saw Jonny waving – he had found the Brenans, and beside them stood a tall clergyman. 'Oh, don't you know Charles Sinnickson?' It now became clear that he too had driven to meet them and was also prepared to have them to stay. Jonny said afterwards he felt 'jealous' of Charles Sinnickson, and it was a bit damping to find that we were quite superfluous. 'Charles' obviously wanted to have them, and they would probably be better cared for there and quickly accepted his hostship. Meanwhile it was somehow decided that we should drive them to his Chelsea vicarage in Jonny's car. Curled up like a foetus in the back, no room for my legs, I listened to the dry tap-tap of Gerald's compulsive talk about Torremolinos and all its denizens, including Hetty, who was 'Queen of the Hippies' in San Francisco; it all seemed arid and soulless. Gamel looked really rather well and spoke cheerfully; perhaps she *doesn't* after all know what's the matter with her.

### August 20th

Last night the Brenans came. Yes, of course a different side of Gerald appeared, and a far more lively and inventive one. The fact that he is overwrought appeared in his violent attack on Bertie Russell – why do this if he is anxious to make Gamel happy, why, why, why? She took it calmly, and I must say looked serene, rather plumper and handsomer than usual. I began to wonder if Gerald had got it all wrong about her mortally stricken state. Almost anything is possible.

He made his usual attack on Ralph for practically being a half-wit. 'Of course I was a dolt – like Ralph,' he said, and not for the first time I told him to 'speak for himself'. It pleased him to say that 'all the rest of Bloomsbury thought Ralph stupid.' Well, more fool they. But what use is it to get angry? There is a strong streak of the Judas in Gerald and of course he always was and always will be jealous of Ralph. So he is prepared to label himself a 'dolt' also, if by so doing, Ralph can be called one. No two human beings could have been more different than Gerald and Ralph, and I think Ralph (being a realist, while Gerald is almost totally uninterested in reality, but a creative artist) understood Gerald much better than Gerald understood Ralph.

## August 24th: At Nicko and Mary Henderson's rented villa, Mijas, Spain

The change is so easily effected and all my surroundings are so violently familiar that only last night when sleep was almost entirely unattainable did I realize what a shock of adaptation there always is. Fingers of consciousness kept going out into the night, and I couldn't stop being exquisitely aware of what I couldn't see – the land sloping down from this villa across humped hills towards Fuengirola, the nearer folds of hillside and their houses, the olives, the road winding off to Torremolinos, the mountain summit seen year after year from varying distances and always with a futile craving to be on it. All these imagined sights were the more vividly imprinted because this basin-like fold of the hills acts as a sounding-board and echoes every noise clearly and faithfully (dogs barking, cocks crowing, a stray motorbike, babies squalling), with acoustics as good as Snape Maltinghouse. Last night as we sat eating on our balcony, voices came very clearly from the restaurant in a pretty little old house opposite.

Mary very kindly met me at Malaga airport in the full heat of 3 p.m. and whisked me up into the hills. Almost like last year, there is a heavy, crushing heat hanging over everything – the sky partly veiled – and I should think there will any minute be an enormous storm. The sound of crickets all the time is deafening. The dry aromatic smell and the dusty brown landscape are old friends, and as we drove at once off the hideous main road we left the horrors behind.

Nicko is away, returning tomorrow. Staying here with Alexandra[1] are Rosamond's granddaughter, Anna Philipps, and an old-fashioned-looking, solid, blonde cousin of Alexandra's. Anna is attractive, bespectacled, dark, with a sensitive interesting face. They all seem very young for their age, and squeal and coo and make a fuss over the dogs.

Very delicious bathe in the little pool here. Later a walk into Mijas village – though almost every shop sells Mexican hats and brand new plates it is still a pretty village, and as we walked further we reached streets where the shops sold fruit and *alpargatas*.

Today the two girl visitors go.

I've eaten my breakfast – the heat is *tremendous*, the sky deep blue over the mountains, hazy over the sea. I'm wondering a very little how I shall pass my time – reading, I suppose, and writing letters. In the evening a visit from Janetta, Julian and Rose. We all sat on the balcony – the soft evening light had by now slipped away over the monticules between us and Fuengirola, over the sea, over the far horizon. Down below us Rose and Alexandra swam like slim, elegant crayfish in the pool, and were joined by Julian. All three visitors combined very sweetly to give me a sense of being welcome and its being worthwhile to have come out to see them. My room at La Fonda[2] awaits me – I begin to get a notion of what it is like there. Janetta looks smooth and happy.

## August 26th

The ferocious heat changes moment by moment to a sky overcast with long tresses of pale grey seaweed and hot wind. Nicko due back from Madrid; the whole house – wife, daughter, three servants and above all the dogs – were visibly awaiting their lord and master. The large elegant dalmatian stared out anxiously at the landscape, started at every sound, and last night in the moonlight suddenly left the house and dashed across the valley looking for Nicko. Now and then he flops down with an impatient sigh, flinging out one leg sideways like a ballerina dancing *Le Cygne*. Mary told me the vet said of him, '*Estos perros son siempre muy comediantes.*'[3]

[1]    The Hendersons' only child, now Countess of Drogheda.
[2]    Hotel beautifully decorated and run by Jaime, with Janetta as chef.
[3]    'These dogs are always acting.'

## August 31st: Marbella

Yesterday I moved to La Fonda, and now at nearly ten, I am sitting up in the Greta Garbo suite waiting for my breakfast. My rooms are *extraordinarily* pretty – they couldn't possibly have been done up with greater taste. I have a large bedroom and sitting-room looking onto a jasmine-covered terrace and a huge old Victorian bed draped in lace. Its chief drawback is that it is directly above the bar, where chatter, tinned music and long, inane conversation goes on until two o'clock. Janetta had chosen me a quiet one on the top floor, but the occupant flew into a rage and threw my suitcase downstairs.

Janetta, Rose and I drove to Tramores. It simply is a masterpiece, looking as if it had always been there, and surrounded by matchless freshness and greenery and the circle of the lovely mountains. Even the fact that an absurd collection of film people were trying to shoot a scene under the Moorish castle couldn't rattle it. It stood firm and didn't yield a particle of its personality. Below the house, down to the huge swimming-pool of very warm water, everything that has been planted has sprung up and flourished. There are *huge* thorn-apple bushes, dangling their great cream-coloured flowers, morning glories, marvel of Peru, stocks, zinnias and a thousand other plants, while below the pool came fields of sweetcorn, laden fig trees, greengage and walnut trees. This then, is my first impression of Tramores – total subjection and admiration – not a single word of criticism. It is as if I had been confronted with a work of art and I bow down, most humbly and gratefully. I must get up, so will write no more now.

(Later) A man from the *Sunday Times* has come to interview Mark Culme-Seymour[1] and Janetta about Donald Maclean. Hearing I had been at Nicko's he pricked up his ears. He too was on his list. Items of gossip momentarily aroused interest among the few sluggish occupants at the Fonda – 'Melinda Maclean has gone off with Philby.' 'No! Really?' 'And have you heard the very latest from Churriana? Bayard Osborne[2] has gone off with a mother of three.'

This morning I asked for my breakfast on my terrace, and am now lying on the lace cover of the big garden bed, protected from the faint morning sun by the roof of jasmine. It keeps dropping large, white, scented aeroplane propellers on me and they blow across the tiled

[1] Janetta's half-brother.
[2] American painter.

floor in light drifts; I enjoy the isolation and peace, and have a mind to spend today very quietly and much alone, writing letters and not being at anyone's beck and call. Also I think it is Janetta's last day with Jaime before he goes on holiday and I very much don't want her to feel responsible for me. I have seen her a lot each day, and she has been sweetly solicitous for my comfort. But we have not had a lot of deep-going conversation. When she gets up to Tramores – we went again yesterday – she is a bewitched princess, and moves slowly round looking lovingly at each fruit tree or datura, considering the placing of a tile or the colour of a door. Her tempo becomes slower, and she must need this relaxation after several hours working in the Fonda kitchen each night.

## September 4th

Jaime gone, Georgie gone, and soon I shall be gone too. I took a taxi to the Beach House yesterday, equipped with papers and book and a determination to do nothing contentedly all day, and in this I succeeded. No thinking goes on on this coast; conversation is fragmented and the most *suivi* I had was with darling little Rose at dinner. There is something almost frightening in her rare sensitivity, the highly-tempered, delicate but strong material of which her character is made. I feel often as if a valuable, fragile and irreplaceable vase was within range of my fumbling hasty movements. I asked her if she could imagine living at Tramores and her face suddenly shone as if a candle had been lit inside it. It's clear she is in love with the place, almost as Janetta is, and she was pleased when I praised it wholeheartedly.

## September 10th

Back to West Halkin Street and the Brenan crisis. A last visit from Gerald, and this time he didn't attack me. I was relieved when Julian said today that he had noticed how aggressive Gerald always was to me, though he believed he was as fond of me as of anyone, because I had begun to ask myself if I somehow provoked him. But on yesterday's visit he was all kindness and dulcet sweetness. Gamel has had two goes of her treatment. I can't help thinking she knows, and perhaps would rather 'play it' Gerald's way. This I felt when I said goodbye to her. 'I may never see her again' was the thought that echoed inside the tin can of my head. My brain is full of 'hundreds and thousands' and I cannot make much of the prospects lying ahead.

## September 12th

My visit to Alix was only painful in that it is distressing to be aware of such unhappiness and loneliness. She is extremely brave and always an interesting companion, not self-pitying at all. The question of the general index to Freud[1] was rather easy – I think I convinced her that she herself was the right person to deal with it.

Private life becomes more and more like life in wartime, under constant pressure from circumstances, I thought, as I sat in a block in my Mini on the way back from Marlow, and looked round at the motor-bicyclists in full armour or motorists in their tanks (like me) advancing into battle.

## September 13th

Dinner with Raymond and Paul Hyslop in Islington last night. Raymond looked exhausted and shut away, his brushed, little-boy appearance was touching. 'Two old bachelors' though. Paul says he has retired, not exactly voluntarily but because he has no work to do, and is glad of it because it made him so anxious, and 'put him all of a tremble'. He intends to learn to cook, and already works hard in the garden. Their ladylike housekeeper has gone, and a tiny deformed Italian manservant skipped round with our dinner. It was his first effort with company, and there was much agitation. 'He must be told to be quieter,' Raymond boomed softly. I don't know why, but I was rather saddened by these two with their mutual irritations and affections. Paul does marvellously neat *petit point* to his own designs. They both seemed to have stepped further into isolation and silence, and Raymond showed that very significant symptom of total lack of interest in what I had been doing, so that I hesitated to speak of Tramores or the Fonda and when I did it obviously fell on deaf ears.

[1] I had indexed the 22 volumes of James's English translation.

## September 14th

Yesterday morning Julia rang me from Sonia's house, where she had taken refuge, and asked if she could come 'and rest on my bed that afternoon'. I gathered that things were not perfectly smooth between her and Sonia, who was just off to Paris. Julia arrived at two sharp and lay on my bed with the curtains drawn, neither reading nor sleeping for a good three hours. This, she says, just gives her strength to face the evening; she rests, but 'has never in her life fallen asleep'. I remember she used to do it in Rome. I am amazed by such a disrespect for the valuable waking hours. Before disappearing she amusingly described how impossible Sonia had been — bossy, hectoring, downright rude, finally saying that she 'was quite exhausted, and part of the reason was having to have Julia to stay'. Julia: 'Do take some sleeping-pills, won't you, and get a good night's rest.' S: 'Sleeping-pills? Do you want me to kill myself?' With teeth set: '*Do you*?' She then bustled Julia off to bed, where she was going anyhow, and came back saying: 'Now into bed with you. I'm Nannie and I'm going to see you undress.' Julia has taken a great fancy to the young librarian who has been helping Sonia with the collected works of Orwell and she thinks Sonia is jealous. It's quite possible. Her other fixed belief is that Robert is a homosexual. In spite of acknowledging his great kindness to her in Italy, she criticized him because in company 'he never once addressed a single remark to her, but always either to Ben Nicolson or Philip Toynbee.'

## September 19th

I have been toiling steadily at revising Napoleon,[1] and am anxious to burrow through to the end. Meanwhile I have seen dozens of friends, and read the first volume of Holroyd's life of Lytton, which Raymond kindly lent me in proof. What will the world say of it? I wonder. It is a monument of hard work and conscientiousness, yet I don't think it will fail to rouse shrieks about who these arrogant Bloomsberries thought they were, and why they were so beastly about each other. Nearly a dangerous corner with Julia about the book the other night. I don't quite know what emotion was the source.

[1]  I translated four books on him by the French consul on St Helena.

## September 21st

A disconcerting letter from Gerald. Half is written by a disconsolate husband ('We sit round watching her slowly die'), yet the emphasis has subtly shifted and he is now anxious *not* to prolong her suffering. 'It's like the case for capital punishment, twenty years' imprisonment is infinitely more cruel . . . When Gamel ceases to enjoy life I shall hope for a quick end . . . She has been a little despondent . . . [The cobalt treatment] *might* prolong her life by a few months but of what use will that be if it is to make her feel depressed?' Then with almost shocking suddenness he reverts to his new girlfriend Lynda. He has asked her 'to come and live with him when the time comes' . . . and she has 'gladly accepted'. Then – really, really! – 'the very fact of my loving Gamel as I do makes me require someone on whom I can turn my affection when she is no longer here. *I feel Heaven has sent Lynda!*' (My italics)

## September 22nd

When Michael Holroyd comes to spend the evening with me I describe the same graph each time. A surprised feeling of sympathy and easy communication to begin with: then (as he gradually becomes more at his ease) I begin to wonder: *is* he too confident of his literary judgements and criticisms? How much can one plot a human shape by what it likes? He loves Chekhov (good start) and also Turgenev, whom he read when quite young. But doesn't like Henry James or Proust – and his newest enthusiasm is for Sylvia Townsend Warner.

I talked about the account he has given of Carrington's suicide, and how I had not had the faintest recollection of Bryan Moyne's gun being borrowed by Carrington; moreover felt completely sure that Ralph, Carrington, Bunny and I had *not* driven back from Biddesden with the gun in the car. Possibly she asked Bryan on this occasion and went to fetch it later. All this because he wrote as if this had happened under Ralph's nose. I had talked to Bunny, Gerald and Julia about it, and all from various sources confirmed my view. But last night Holroyd told me that it was from *Gerald* that the story had in fact come! F: 'But didn't you realize how uninterested Gerald is in the truth?' M: 'Perhaps, but I admire him so enormously as a writer?' What makes someone into a 'great friend'? This I feel Gerald to be, and yet, and yet, on two of my last four meetings with him he attacked me violently. I am aware that he has done all he can to depreciate Ralph in print, and may well do more.

## September 25th

Grey damp Sunday in London yesterday but full and busy, and the evening – with Julia and Julian – informal, stimulating and enjoyable.

Julia arrived about an hour before Julian, and with an air of great exhaustion and despair told me she could not any longer bear leading such 'an unsuitable sort of life'. I think it's a good long time since she's done any writing; all the more important does it bulk in her eyes. If she 'sees people' she is too preoccupied to do any writing the day before and too tired the day after. Ergo, she says, people must be cut out of her life. Yet it is her loneliness that forces her to get drunk and waste the whole evening looking at tosh on the television and take more and more blue pills, if she has an evening unfilled.

Talk about poetry. Julian put in an interesting plea – for second-class but modern poetry. Julia and I, neither of us real poetry-lovers, boggled a bit. Surely poetry was literature in its purest, most concentrated form (Julia had a good simile: 'like making gravy – the process of reducing') and therefore 'nothing but the best' etc? But Julian, who is a poetry-lover, saw it as just another form of expressing ideas that had value because they were – contemporary, I can't avoid the beastly word.

I very much enjoyed a visit to poor Dadie[1] in the morning, sitting up in bed at Moorfields after two eye operations, in black spectacles. His vitality and charm bowled me over, and we talked hard for an hour, mainly about people and books, and then drank champagne and ate caviare. The combination of these ingredients – conversation and delicacies – sent me away very cheerful.

## September 26th

I took Sophie out from school and brought her back here last Thursday. She is such a darling little girl, so full of rare qualities, sweetness, sense and fun, that I find it unbearable to contemplate any

[1]  Dr George Rylands.

possible unhappiness for her. This is, and always was (perhaps disastrously for Burgo) my besetting failing, leading to self-torment and guilt, but perhaps not to the beloved creature's happiness. Sophie has grown up enormously through her holiday with Quentin and his family and her mind has leapt ahead, stimulated no doubt by his older children. There is nothing she seems unable to take in – except perhaps death, of which she is frightened. When someone was mentioned (not Burgo) who was dead, she gave a noisy shudder and said, '*I* shan't get dead, shall I?' And I loved the way she sat at the piano, not vaguely banging, but picking out notes in a really musical way with curled fingers like hammers, singing as well, often trying to and succeeding in singing the note she was striking, or if she failed, saying 'No, that's not right.' Always perfectly in tune, and often to fanciful, imaginary words.

## *October 1st: Crichel*

The long window of my room – once Eddy's, and I feel easier in it now that the crucifix and praying-stool have gone – goes right down to the floor, and my eyes slant down across the bright blue-green carpet to the soft yellow-green croquet lawn where several birds stalk sombrely about. I have woken fairly early to think about human life – the latter stage of it – and why we cling to it, and whether if it were easy and simple to lay it aside hundreds of us would instantly (with hardly a pause or a farewell) do so. Mrs Winters, the cook, is in Salisbury hospital pretty desperately ill with leukemia. When Raymond and I arrived on Friday she came forward with the curious but dignified outspokenness of the uneducated and said the doctor had told her 'she might go at any minute.' I felt a *sort* of envy, as one might when waiting one's turn to perform in a concert, if other people are called in front of one. No more waiting. And there's poor old Gamel – her time nearly up. Yet I know if that simple exit was handed me on a plate, some tiny bolus to be swallowed, I should not swallow it. When I walked along the road with Moses yesterday under tearing clouds in a warm Irish wind and sun, I had a positive feeling of well-being, a physical glow.

## October 2nd

This morning the sky is a washed blue as bright as the cloak of morning glories that drapes the house. It has been *awfully* nice here this weekend, with relaxed and spontaneous conversation even at breakfast (best of times for it): yesterday it was the concept of 'mystique' which has crept (with the word itself) among us. What exactly did it mean? Was it entirely derogatory? Most of us thought it means a nexus of irrational beliefs and emotions all centred round one notion or activity. All of us save Pat thought it an unpalatable idea – he has a hankering after 'spiritual' values. This morning we ate our baked eggs to the difference between prose and poetry, concentration versus allusiveness, and whether it was possible for genius in the arts to be appreciated by those thirty years older than the artist.

I hear Moses snorting hopefully and I shall now take him a little walk.

## October 6th: West Halkin Street

The aftermath of Crichel was a terrible railway journey, when our engine apparently caught fire and immobilized us for two solid hours in the middle of a field ten minutes out of Salisbury. There were Desmond, Pat, Raymond and I stewing together in the juice of restlessness produced by being inside something that should move and doesn't, matters being made worse by Desmond having a fairly bad cold and exploding into sneezes and flourishing a huge silk handkerchief like a flag in this confined space. (Raymond fled to another compartment.)

Returning from errands today, not for the first time I met a young man whose dark burning eyes brought me an agonizing memory of Burgo. I feel unarmed against stray impressions and unequal to pursuing such thoughts very far.

Reviews of Holroyd on Lytton come out – Malcolm Muggeridge took the book as a text to jeer and jump and stamp (like a red-faced little boy with his face contorted with rage) on all homosexuals, as if they were derisory as such. He pitches into Bloomsbury as a dead dog, and can't of course bear its attitude to religion or sex, and in fact grows more frenziedly puritanical weekly. Perhaps a little mad? Leonard has written a good but rather crushing review of the book –I couldn't help being delighted by it, partly because it was so completely in character.

Another train of thought started off by an article in *The Listener* – how the physical facts of birth, growth and death form a pattern on which works of art are based. We need to appreciate them as ending because we know we must end ourselves. Perhaps those novels that trail away into a fog of 'everything goes on as it always did' are trying to deny the fact of death. Even the sound of a clock suggests that writers are shaped by their minds – it is really 'tick-tick-tick', but we hear it as 'tick-*tock* tick-*tock*'. I am always prejudiced in favour of attributing patterns of experience to the mind rather than the universe.

The whirlpool of other people's troubles sometimes nearly submerges me, and I can only keep my head above water by quelling my own sense of guilt – which is always ready to stalk out of the corner and stand over me like a menacing spectre saying: are you quite sure you've done all you could for them? Of course I never do. My own life dwindles to a skeleton leaf and in a way I'm thankful for that. When I realize the difficulties of living with other people I am more reconciled to loneliness.

I think – perhaps wrongly – that I'm not very vain personally speaking. Yet something that submerges me with gloom is the sight of my ruined and ancient face in the glass. I look at it no more than is barely necessary, but I feel ashamed of inflicting it on my friends. I wonder how the scarred or deformed surmount this hurdle. I wish one were allowed to wear a mask yet oddly enough this confrontation of naked faces is as essential to human relationships as naked bodies to physical love.

## October 18th

No one writes to me, I was just thinking, and then suddenly a huge fat envelope from Gerald came through my letter-box – thirty-eight pages, covered in small, close writing. Fascinating, of course, yet sometimes terrifyingly inhuman: here (jumbled together) were Gamel's character, her relation to him, the torturing conflict between wanting her to die quickly (so that he shan't miss the chance of his Lynda[1]) and genuine pity, his views on all Lytton's books, Freud,

[1]  Price, his new friend.

Wittgenstein, death, life, love, determinism. The only subject he cannot see clearly at all is himself, as is much and comically in evidence. He is the innocent, unworldly 'poet'; so far as I know he has never convicted himself of the slightest malice even. I laughed aloud when I read that *Gamel* was responsible for his peering at girls over cliffs, 'there is nothing of the voyeur in me'(!!) He has been peering over cliffs ever since I knew him and long before Gamel ever came to England. He also says, 'Of course I couldn't tell anyone about Gamel's drinking', implying that he nobly suffered in silence, while the truth is that I've never met anyone he *didn't* tell. But his letter is extraordinary, enthralling; it's strange but true that I count myself as fortunate in having *such* a friend. The letter took me quite an hour to read and I was shaking with agitation, indignation and amusement when I finished reading it.

### October 23rd

Arriving in London on a warm, scented and golden autumn day – euphoria. Why? I travelled up from Crichel with Pat (he drove me at a steady ninety miles an hour, but much too well to alarm me, into Salisbury), thence by train. Here is someone I liked and was drawn to and interested by at first meeting, but a sort of wooden barrier erected itself from the feeling that he despised women (hearing so, in fact, from Julian). Well, perhaps he does; but now I feel he has become a friend. He has quick sympathy and the power to grasp other people's thoughts. On the platform he told me about his father, a doctor over eighty years old, who had taken a mistress the other day, though sincerely grieving for his recently-dead wife.

### October 27th

Last night I dined with Maud and Boris and the rather over-smooth John Malet. Got on well with Maud; Boris was all suavity and broad Russian smiles until he suddenly looked black and angry as he denounced Art and all museums – 'the Prado, Louvre and National Gallery should be blown up at once' he said with a thunderous expression. Then he sat beside me on the sofa and I looked into that huge face with a feeling of deep tenderness, noticing with concern that his upper lip was a pale turquoise blue colour. I do not think he is well, though at first blush he seems so.

Janetta is due back next week, and I'm longing to see her. I suppose I should feel gratified that I have already received four invitations for Christmas and am asked away the next five weekends. I *do*. I *am* grateful to my dear and kind friends, and my feeling of affection for them is by long chalks the most enjoyable sensation I am now capable of. After Georgie had left me the other evening I felt a wave of love for her wash over me like a warm sea.

## October 31st

It is I'm afraid true that Julia has 'gone right back' and is again seething with concentrated hate. Not a good word last night for anyone or anything; many vitriolic ones. Sonia was 'impossible, and she never wanted to see her again', Julian had offended her deeply by calling another 'living woman novelist' the *only* one who could see into the male heart. She fell on Rosamond's new book on her experiences of the next world with sparkling eyes, and was with difficulty dissuaded from working herself into a frenzy by reading it. To my suggestions about food that did not need cooking or very little she put up a blank wall. (She had implored me on the telephone the other day to give my mind to this problem.) She 'simply couldn't be bothered even to peel an apple when she was alone'. Why does one struggle to solve her problems? It is useless. For the tenth time I resolve not to. I fear her, quite literally, in this mood. How she forgets anything not concerning herself! Telling her about my enormous dossiers from Gerald I said there was a lot about Gamel of course. 'Why about *Gamel*?' 'Well, you know she's dying.' J: 'No, I didn't know' (looking, I must say, shocked). I reminded her of a conversation we'd had on the subject, and I think she was shaken a little. She had described a visit to ninety-five-year-old Pippa[1] in her old folks' home. The sight of the poor old oblivious creature revelling over the glories of the subject of Holroyd's book infuriated Julia and she confronted her with Lytton's homosexuality and (quite gratuitously) told her he had had an affair with Duncan. 'With *Duncan*?' said Pippa. 'Well, you know he was very beautiful?' '*Beautiful?* I know he looked very much a Grant.' Julia said she forced Pippa to admit that she had known about Lytton's tendencies, that she remembered an Eton boy going to his bedroom, and that she was

[1] Lytton's sister.

67

shocked by it. Not a sign that she felt any remorse for badgering this poor old lady on the brink of the tomb, and forcing her to face what James tried his best to shield her from.

At Stokke last weekend: hard work on my new translation by the Cuban writer Alejo Carpentier; not much outdoor life and rather too many social occasions. The world looks to me to be full of tusslers – a Dantesque inferno of figures wrestling with their private devils or in the toils of huge serpents. No rest or peace anywhere – an endless fight against loneliness, cancer and the pains of love. It's all very well to say like Gerald that you 'love life'. So in a way do I but it seems at times a senseless, an irrational passion.

### November 1st

I spin home through the London streets after my orchestra evenings calmer and more resigned to the universe than on any other day of the week. How I love them, yet why should they be so peculiarly soothing and relaxing that I get into bed feeling as though I had been gently massaged by invisible hands? I got Margaret to come there, hoping to seduce her to take part in this delightful therapy. I think I may. She wanted to go to the pub afterwards, so we went; unlike Julia she didn't groan about her troubles but merely said things at home were 'dreary and unpleasant'. This is written all over her face, which has temporarily lost its intelligent sparkle, and anyone who didn't know would think of her as one of the innumerable housewives rolling down Oxford Street with heads full of shopping lists. I find her company salutory after the sour taste left by Julia's last visit, the simple difference being that Margaret enjoys loving people and Julia enjoys hating them. The vital importance of loving, quite apart from being loved, has been much on my mind. If someone has the secret, as Mary has (unconsciously and naturally) they are 'all right', in Janetta's sense.

Ah, Janetta – she has been 'expected' at Montpelier for three days, arousing an increasing and rather painful tension.

### November 6th

Back from my Cambridge weekend, I rang up Julia to hear how hers had gone at Philip Toynbee's. 'Oh, *beastly*. I *hate* them; they're barbarians, not my sort at all. Then it cost me four pounds – quite a lot. Philip attacked me all through the weekend for being an intellectual snob, and then Sally's terribly stupid really.' I asked if the house was cold. 'Oh no, much too hot. We sat in this narrow strip of a room, fearfully overheated, and then Philip has a passion for these terrible dogs, so the room was half full of a ghastly great *dog* with bloodshot eyes seeming to be spouting blood; it was so tall it reached the ceiling, and had a squashed-in nose.' For entertainment they had gone to the ballet, to a neighbour's to see an amusing film taken on their Italian holiday, and been treated by Ben Nicolson to a dinner at the Hole-in-the-Wall, a first-rate Bath restaurant. 'But I really hate these grand restaurant meals – unless of course they're really good French ones – I'd much rather eat quietly at home.' So her mood of depreciation still has all its stops out and everything under Laperouse standards must be ruled out.

More harrowing cries of grief from Gerald (two letters yesterday – he has inevitably quarrelled with Honor[1] but made it up again). 'The situation here is becoming absolutely unbearable . . . an awful feeling of strain and exhaustion has come over me . . . If Gamel should linger on like this till the spring I shall not be able to endure it. I shall have a stroke or a coronary. Not that I mind. Anything to escape from this situation . . . Rosario yesterday said to me, "I love the Señora like my mother but if she has to die I pray to God, if there be a God, that she should die soon for she is killing you."'

And a touching letter from Alix. 'I cannot disguise the fact that I am quite sick with misery – with the dreadfulness of James being dead and that I shall never see, or hear or touch him again.'


### November 9th

Bunny came last night to talk about his present situation.[2] I have never known him nicer, more realistic, without pride, complaining that he didn't enjoy feeling self-pity but was in no way indulging it. All that I like most in his character came to the fore. He talked of Angelica without any bitterness but with great sadness. He himself was after all twenty-four years older. 'When I married her I didn't expect she would stay with me so long.' Then he made some very accurate comments on Angelica's character. He said he had stronger

[1] Tracy, writer, and devoted friend of Gamel's.
[2] Angelica wanted to leave him.

paternal feelings than she had maternal ones. I asked if she went in for self-analysis? 'Not usually. But a year ago she tried hard to analyse herself, and after a long time she reached the conclusion that it was *my* fault she wanted to leave me. I told her I didn't hold myself responsible in the least, and that quite shook her and she said I was probably right and we'd better try again.' I asked why he thought she really had wanted to leave him? 'The need to express herself; she's full of talents and has never given enough time to them, or else gone off on some side issue like mosaics.'

### November 16th

Bunny, Julian, Julia, Janetta to dinner. Bunny a little sadder than the last time I saw him. When Julia repeated her condemnation of the Toynbees as being second-rate, I asked her whom she considered first-rate and the only people she suggested – rather quickly – were 'Lawrence and Tommy' – her own two husbands! I then proposed Alix and Duncan, whom she accepted, and Janetta, whom she did not. But of course such all-round rating of human beings is monstrous. Bunny, Janetta and I discussed this after Julia and Julian had gone. Bunny said he was glad Julia recognized Tommy as first-rate; I said he didn't pass on moral grounds, although he did on intellectual; we all deplored the rating system and realized that Julia's depreciation of people as second-rate was a form of Strachey arrogance. But *we* also agreed that a little arrogance, like a little aggression, was attractive.

An absurd detail: some time after dinner Janetta got up and started prowling round the room. Julia, irritated beyond endurance, got up sharply and said: 'Well, I shall walk about too; like Janetta I like fidgeting.' No one paid any attention to her and after a few minutes circling round her chair as if playing musical chairs she sat down in it again. I commented on this incident to Janetta later, wondering if she had noticed it. Yes she had, but regarded her own restlessness as impossible to resist. Julia's trouble is that she is a born school-mistress and wants to improve us all; she cannot, cannot, cannot accept people as they are.

## November 20th

Jogging along in one of the new uncomfortable cattletruck trains from Oxford to London. The world is submerged in an unflattering greenish mist. A plump little man opposite has been scenting the air and afflicting my ears with the bull's-eyes he noisily chews. His fat hand steals into his pocket for another the moment one is finished. David and Rachel's little villa was crowded with comings and goings, and they – poor dears – somewhat exhausted by it all but bearing up bravely, by dint of going to sleep on their beds in the afternoons managed to keep up the ceaseless talk until after midnight.

Conversation about the forthcoming diary of Cynthia Asquith, which is to be published with an editor's comment suggesting that she might have been the daughter of A. J. Balfour, not Lord Wemyss, her theoretical father, or perhaps even that all but one of Lady Wemyss's children were bastards. David remarked airily that Gabriel Herbert's mother was *known* to be a bastard. No one seemed to mind this, but there was considerable agitation about its being published to the world, and about aunts and other relatives possibly minding, and some criticism of Leslie Hartley, who was contributing a preface, for letting it pass. It was reasonable I suppose to complain of things that weren't true or could never be proved being set forth for scandal-mongering reviewers to pounce on, but as I had been plunged all weekend into Holroyd's Vol. II (which completely 'goes into everything'), I felt the contrast between these two modes of life – the aristocrats wanting to wear flattering veils while on the whole the Bloomsberries were prepared to stand up for their way of life. Reading the account of 1924–32 at Ham Spray and my own part in it left me curiously blank. I think on the whole Holroyd has been accurate – but my *word*, there's much too much of it.

Jonathan and his wife Vivien[1] brought an intense, obsessional waft of back-stage atmosphere. David and I went to see Jonathan perform in a play by Ustinov, which goes to London next week. David gets into such states of agonized empathy on his children's behalf that I felt it important to be amused and was unaware if it was good or bad.

[1] Jonathan Cecil and his wife were both actors.

## November 22nd

Gerald's two latest letters are so shocking in their chilly egotism that I feel almost physically sick. Self-pity and self-praise, combined with calculation: 'I have had some resentful feelings towards Gamel on account of her refusal to send for any of the money her nephew was offering her from her account,' he writes. 'I do feel strongly she ought to make some contribution to the expenses of her illness . . . Last night I had a frightful night . . . I had horrible thoughts, chiefly about Honor's attempts to eat her up and remove her from me, and woke up giddy and ill.' He goes on to say that the village doctor says her swollen leg is an embolism, and she might die at any moment. Then he describes another appalling squabble between himself and Honor over poor Gamel's moribund body – in the next room it is true but she probably heard. It ended by Honor saying she would leave next day. 'I think that when tomorrow comes she will have decided to stay . . . but you see what I have to put up with.'

Next day the sorely-tried Honor, who is sleeping in the next room to Gamel and virtually acting as nurse, had decided to go on as if nothing had happened, and was, even Gerald admits, being 'absolutely nice. We are not going to quarrel again.' And he ends with an astonishing pat on his own back: 'I think I have really behaved throughout with tact and sensibility, for there is a strong practical side to my character, not often revealed. After all I am descended from endless Colonels and Generals'! Is he going mad? I almost ask myself.

His second letter reports greater calm but more financial preoccupation. He goes on to say he is going to the cemetery 'to make terms with the undertakers. For the last foreigner's funeral out here they charged £200.' The clergyman's fee is also mentioned and he now says he has finally persuaded poor Gamel to write for the money her nephew has for her. He returns next to how he will live when Gamel is dead. 'I suppose that what with Gamel's drinking, her two illnesses, her visits to London, Honor's three very long visits of at least three months each, she has cost me apart from her ordinary living expenses around £3,000 in the past three years . . . I think I have also found through Manolo, Maria's future husband, a cheaper way of arranging for a funeral.' What *is* to be made of all this? Is it unjust of me to feel utterly revolted by it?

## November 23rd

My horror over Gerald's last two letters kept me in a fever all yesterday, and went on even after I had tried to discharge it in a fairly strongly-worded letter. I told him his letter had 'greatly upset me' though I didn't say how, and then went on that I felt a violent need to say one or two things. First, *Money*: Here I told him what I was trying, with Janetta's help, to do; and suggested that the bills could be met later or by selling some object and I begged him not to worry Gamel in any way about money. His cruel insensitiveness about this appals me. My second point was that he must get in a nurse at once; the moment has come. It is too awful for Gamel to be in the hands of two jealous squabbling people. Of course I didn't put it like that, but I did write less sympathetically to him than I ever have before. Janetta completely shares my blood-curdled horror. Julian was disposed to be more sympathetic and understanding towards Gerald, and to interpret his behaviour classically as showing a sense of guilt. But *does* it? I'm not aware that Gerald has ever shown any signs of such a thing in his dealings towards anyone, and of course I think of Ralph and Carrington and the events of the past. What sense is there in saying someone is 'suffering from a suppressed sense of guilt' if they show no trace of it except violent egotism and unawareness of others?

## November 27th

There was the pleasure last weekend at Hilton of seeing Bunny cheerfully providing delicious roast pheasants (plucked and cooked by himself) for three of his girls and Sophie and William and me. And the counterbalancing feeling of shock when I heard the three girls and William planning to go north to their cottage in Swaledale and leave him quite alone for Christmas. And Sophie is to be sent off for a whole fortnight, to stay with one of Lucian Freud's mistresses called Bernardine and her two little girls.[1] Postponed a day or two because she wasn't well, she seems to be going today, and Henrietta says one of the little girls is her best friend and that Sophie wants very much to go. I expect she will have great fun with the other children – and it seems that the Swaledale plan may be off, so perhaps Bunny will have company for Hilton. So I can set aside my fanciful plan of taking

[1] Esther and Bella.

rooms at Brighton for Julia, Sophie, Bunny and me! None the less I go on moving around these chess-pieces endlessly in my head, particularly when I wake in the night and their movements are informed with the weak-mindedness of my post-flu mood. I long to drag myself into a more profitable orbit. But if I glance further away – to Spain, say – there is Gamel dying and Gerald probably angry with me for my interfering letter; or there is Janetta who writes to no one.

### December 18th

I move thoughtlessly rather than unhappily from one thing to another. Now, sitting in a warm little stopping train from Salisbury, I am aware of the *relief* at heading towards my own *querencia*, even though it is Crichel I leave behind.

### December 21st

Arrived in London to find three letters from Gerald and a very good one from Janetta describing the Brenans. She had found Gamel 'better and worse' than expected – better because lucid and serene, worse because terribly swollen, even her face crooked and distorted. 'Gerald is nearly off his head. He's frenzied. He never stops gabbling, talking, quivering, exhausted, ferocious, on and on and on, contradicting himself, never calm, awful things being said amongst practical ones. Uninterruptable, totally unreasonable . . . Then he and Honor really *loathe* each other. I do truly feel they might either of them murder the other. Gamel must sit with her lop-sided calm while this savage war hurtles along the icy corridor and through half-closed doors . . . Honor's affection for Gamel was very touching, and at least she *has* some and I really don't think Gerald has any now.' She goes on to describe 'the arrival of Xavier and Miranda[1] trying to persuade Gerald to get a nurse and accept money (all your things in fact). Gerald raved.'

These last two days I have been working like a black. (Napoleonana suddenly arrived from Murray and put out my working schedule.)

---

[1] Gerald's son-in-law and daughter.

Tomorrow I take my Mini and drive down to the Slade for five peaceful days.

## December 23rd: The Slade

Yesterday morning I drove quietly down through silent mist, and here I am away from everything. Julia came to dinner the night before I left, looking fantastically young and pretty, dressed for a cocktail party which she had failed for some reason to get to; she was interesting but peppery. At last having 'done her budget' – a fatal move – she had decided that 'after the essential expenses she had only seven pounds a week for everything, so couldn't possibly afford whisky. She had therefore tried something called 'Dry Fly sherry' and not found it to her taste. There was about twenty minutes' fulmination against 'the cosmos'. My shameless canvassing had got her a second kind Christmas invitation, to go to Golders Green with the Penroses. But the other evening she was furious because Margaret had 'rung up to ask when I wanted to come' in a practical rather than a welcoming way.

Last night a long, interesting stimulating conversation with Eardley, ranging over such subjects as artistic creation, how a work of art develops and all the problems arising from the Grünewald altarpiece. We both I'm sure enjoyed it. Mattei arrived lateish from London, in all his usual black and white distinction.

## December 24th: Christmas Eve

Sweet and blessed peace is what one gently inhales here like the incomparable air. Yesterday was a day of method. I translated all morning at the table in 'Mattei's little French sitting-room', warm, silent, a few logs speaking quietly from the hearth, and (outside) the rural scene lit by mild sun. Lunch of cold things – salad, the ham I brought, cheese and fruit. After lunch I walked for a while up the lanes by myself, while the others toiled planting fruit trees. How I did *not* envy them, and how intense was my pleasure as I looked up at the fast but quietly moving clouds (moonstony, pigeon's breast-feathers, pearly pinks and blues); or into the hedges where there were such surprising signs of life – ferns fully decorated with orange spores, catkins and buds; and collected a bunch of these springlike twigs and ferns as well as ghostly skeleton grasses and umbels, to add to the pale pink chrysanthemums in the drawing-room. My lane was new to me and provided sudden dips and climbs and sideways glances along field-paths and hedgerows bloomed over with Old Man's Beard. I had to return, but hardly wanted to. The immense sun, almost as pale as the moon, had nearly vanished behind the hill.

A little more work; gramophone records, reading and bed. My room is very snug with a comfortable bed; I like the fact that no one goes into it, and it is all my own.

## December 26th

Raining and blustering with a soft and distant roar most of yesterday; we didn't go out at all. Turkey for lunch, work, reading Van Gogh's letters, at first unattracted by their constricted, religious, adolescent quality and the feeling of his charmlessness. Then comes the extraordinary explosion into articulacy and feeling as well as writing – page after page of it, when other careers are abandoned and he takes to painting. And again when he falls in love. Before one's very eyes a genius bursts into flower from what was a nondescript, cramped bud.

Meanwhile Eardley and Mattei play Canasta as they do every night, revealing their characters and the nature of their relationship. Squared up face to face across a table set in front of the fire, it is a flirtatious battle, in which Eardley becomes more masculine and Mattei rather feminine.

## December 28th

I rang up the Penroses, unable to resist asking how Christmas went off with Julia.

Margaret: 'It was *marvellous*. Frightfully nice. We enjoyed it enormously and I really think Julia did too. I hope so, anyway.'

This morning I rang Julia: 'A bloody awful Christmas. Oh, they were very kind of course, all of them, but I simply felt like a stray cat.'

Why does the stray cat feel no gratitude for being taken in, I wonder, as a stray cat of many years' standing. I didn't hear much more about the horror of staying at the Penroses'. Lionel and Shirley had passed with honours; Margaret failed. Julia three times said she was 'inharmonious' whatever that meant, her food was appalling and her housekeeping ditto. She added: 'Some of it was quite funny really, but I should feel *disloyal* telling you over the telephone.'

## December 30th

I am to see the new year in at the Tycoonery.[1] Mary met me this morning at Bedwyn station and took me back to Stokke for coffee and a talk, in which the Tycoon began to figure as an ogre looking about for someone to kill or flay alive. Like everyone else in the house he has had or is having 'flu. I drove off with Mary in a *Who's afraid of the Big Bad Wolf?* spirit. Answer – they *all* are – Mary, Serena and Jacob Rothschild and the servants. Not perhaps the children. He greeted me with a friendly kiss, and had – so Mary said – refused to let my visit be put off. But a rolling bulging eye kept lighting on some cause for anger ('*Who* left the lid off the ice-jar?'). Lunch was apparently all right, and Mary said they 'hadn't had such a jolly one for days'. She and I strolled through the cold winter afternoon and beside the French-looking canal to see Frances Phipps. Talked to her in her warm little drawing-room, whose life and untidiness, and reality above all, contrasted so notably with that great gloomy, unreal and not very comfortable Tycoonery. Children's toys lay about, papers, books, sewing. Before we left Henrietta and William[2] came in with a troop of pale gentle children, with thimble-shaped heads, tiny faces and soft slow voices. One carefully carried a sugar mouse. Walked home in the dusk. Like an actor in some improvised performance, I was prepared to take my cue from Mary, and that cue was 'a cup of tea in your room and rest till about seven'.

Unfortunately my room was icy cold – the radiator only tepid, no electric fire, a few sticks in the grate but no coal, logs or matches. The hollowness of millionaire life was emphasized by this, and by the fact that there was no heating at all in the big bathroom, and the cold tap in my basin gave no water of either persuasion. I got under my eiderdown and read however, and thought about the rich and their insufferable arrogance. Philip let off some Roman candles against the 'little man', the 'privileged poor', the Welfare State, etc. I took up none of them; having decided this beforehand I found it perfectly easy – it is only when the wool has suddenly left one's head that all is

[1] 'The Tycoon' was Mary's first (and last) husband, Sir Philip Dunn, and so Stowell Park was 'the Tycoonery'.
[2] Son and daughter-in-law (née Lamb) of Frances Phipps.

lost. Anyway such arguments are too futile – it's not worth talking to him about politics or any moral issues. How riches rot the cockles of the heart, though!

Philip felt too ill to come down to dinner, so we had quite a jolly evening with Serena and Jacob, a young banker called Sam Baring and Annabel Lindsay (née Yorke). All the young are bright-witted. Serena has just had a third baby girl, tiny and charming; and looks pale and thin. I like Jacob.

# 1968

## *January 1st: Stowell (the Tycoonery), for the New Year*

Sunday lunch with the Barings and Annabel Lindsay at Shalbourne. A large Victorian gathering with delicious food and wine. Quite a lot of talk to the Tycoon in the morning. He has read a lot, with interest and care; he tells me he rehearses the book he is reading if he wakes in the night. He's not a clever man nor a stupid one, but he's fierce to anyone who gets in his light. Even this has exceptions – he is an adoring grandfather and loving father. I think I got on with him rather well, by dint of talking a lot about books and letting his outrageous expressions of opinion fly by, like cricket balls you don't attempt to field.

I had tea alone with him – everyone else 'resting'. Heavens, what a lot of *resting* the rich do, and why? Then I took myself off aloft for a rest of a different sort. The nearest to an argument was about the traffic problem. 'Why not more railway carriages?' I said. 'It would decrease the deficit.' P: '*I* don't want to pay for the railways.' F: 'Well then the roads will become impossibly crowded.' P: 'Let "them" all go on the roads and kill themselves; then there'll be fewer of "them".' F: 'They may kill *you*, you know.' He laughed. He 'only does it to annoy' and the great thing is not to make him think it 'teases'. But I do wonder when he talks about 'them' never doing any work, what work he thinks *he's* done for the past thirty years.

Now I'm speeding back to London in a warm buffet car, frosted with human breath, through which I see the country covered in thin snow. I feel as if I were abroad, especially as three women are talking French. At dinner last night the Tycoon was positively jolly. I talked a lot to Jacob. Everyone spoils and humours the Tycoon like mad, whether because he's a millionaire or just an ill-tempered man I don't know, but I have to admit there's something likeable about him.

## January 3rd: London

Last night Robert and Henrietta came to dinner. What a pleasure to look at them both, listen and talk to them, to feel warmly to them, to forget myself or even what was being said in the interest of the conversation, which was very equally supported as on a tripod by all three.

I thought of this again, after coming back from visiting Sonia this evening. How sour she is, her face twisted between false amiability and true jealousy, and envy. The telephone rang several times and the person the other end was deluged with her insincere warmth. '*Darling* Bee' was one. Sonia remarked as she put down the receiver that she had never liked Bee and she was the worst mother she knew. She was more guarded over talking about Janetta than usual, but 'hated' Jaime, thought him totally superficial; and knocked off Nicky and Serge and several others in a word or two. When I said something nice about Julian she said, 'I don't really know him.' In short, she tore everyone limb from limb with relish (Julia had 'been quite demented when she last saw her'), until the smell of human blood and crunch of bones filled the air. No chance to sidetrack her onto books or ideas. As always, she seemed just to want unlimited cruel gossip. I tried to get away several times, but she detained me with a greedy expression.

No, it's no use. I can't do with her. I had been drawn by sympathy for the fact that she has just had all her 'insides' out. I sent her some flowers and was touched by her reply – it was insincere.


## January 10th

A blizzard of snow has fallen and is fast turning to slush; it had set so hard I couldn't get my Mini out – its wheels spun and didn't grip, for a bright moon and clear sky had brought on intense frost. London looks extraordinary – like Moscow. Cars all lidded with snow, people picking their way over iced whiteness, dressed as Eskimos, laughing and excited. Nothing has been swept or cleared but there's a dangerously shiny black path in the middle of the larger roads. I took a taxi to orchestra and a bus back. Only one other second violin at first (one other later). I much prefer sitting near the front and came away purring because our conductor said to me at the end, 'Thank you very much for coming along, you did fine.' Ridiculous, childish pleasure! We had Jean Pougnet as the soloist for our practice. He was amiable and uncomplaining but slightly bored.

### January 13th

There has been trouble at the Kees – fairly bad. Robert came to lunch yesterday. My fear that he wouldn't talk, that I should see that shut – more than shut, locked – expression was not fulfilled. But my heart was wrung by the pallor and anxious sadness of the face waiting outside my door; though it melted quickly in conversation, it is of course the understratum. Certainly our conversation did no harm; I don't know that it could have done much good. I did get him to talk quite freely though, curbing my own natural volubility. Nor did he reject my suggestion of a London working room, with weekends of family life – but I doubt if he could face a more definite breach. I said my dread was that he'd let things just slide till they got as bad again, and he seemed to accept this possibility. We talked on such subjects as why he had to ill-treat his wives and be angelic to other people, without really clearing them up. He knows it's true, refers it back to early childhood. Some talk, too, about mind and brain, and of a suggestion he had heard or read (not new, surely?) that there is only one entity, not two – that all mental processes can be put in terms of brain, and that what we call 'mind' occurs only when the brain reaches a certain degree of complexity. Computers will achieve it in time. Yes, I can take that – easier perhaps than their having feelings (in what terms can the affective side of life be expressed on this new view?): a computer is to give a concert of its own work at the Festival Hall. Would it feel stage fright, its proprietor (owner, husband, what the hell must one call it?) was asked. 'Oh yes, very probably.'

To go back to Robert: he obviously wants to try and make a go of the marriage, but does Cynthia? Or rather, can she face going on trying? When I think back to her quiet voice saying she must leave, and that perhaps she should just have done it without saying so, I feel doubtful. It was because of this that I tried very tentatively to see how much the marriage meant to him. He said that 'he was very fond of her,' that she was 'a good companion', that he 'admired her'; but it's clear he knows that their minds work on very different planes.

## Saturday morning

I watch huge snowflakes descending, with my usual claustrophobia. I am supposed to go to Brighton this evening for the concert tomorrow, but wonder if it will come off at all. And the snow and a sense of unutterable loneliness shuts me in.

6.0 p.m. On the Brighton Belle, not at all what its name calls to mind. No sign of the bar carriage in which I had promised myself a large drink. Just the old cattle-truck in which we jolt fairly uneasily along. I'm quite glad to get out of London. My Mini has let me down again, the starter went dead, and I arrived at the afternoon rehearsal too disgruntled to enjoy it to the full, though I worked hard.

## January 18th

The Kee crisis has left me in a hyperaesthesic state. I wonder continually how they are 'getting on', but have not dared ring up. Also Julia; and then there are Gerald's letters describing Gamel's approach to death with increasing vividness, obviously moved by it to his maximum degree of sensibility. He has great power to convey what he feels, and I feel it with him – particularly that sense of the loneliness of dying. In trying to avoid Gamel's feeling too much alone as she goes into the dreadful arena, he spends hours and hours holding her poor hand or stroking her forehead. I am deeply touched by this, and I believe in some way he has come nearer to fully loving her, now that she is dying, than ever before. And this is something to do with his being in no way a realist, but appreciating things acutely through his imagination.

Yesterday I saw no one bar Mrs Murphy, and quite looked forward to it. But when evening came and I sat down to read for the second time an essay by Lionel on Consciousness lent me by Margaret, and when I tried to marshal my wits and read it critically, thinking what the implications were, and whether he made out his case – or indeed what it was – I began to quiver all over with the effort and agitation, and after I got into bed lay awake for hours of sparkling but futile consciousness, almost hating this stuff I generally rate so high in my scale of values, or wishing I could at least temporarily be quit of it. I'm interested in the difference between the scientific and the philosophical approach. Lionel writes entirely as a scientist; he sets before one strange patterns of facts (that can only be mutely accepted), and then leaps forward to throw out a number of 'hunches' – for instance, can people 'share' the 'same state of consciousness'? He worryingly, and rather unphilosophically however, doesn't say whether by 'same' he means 'identical' or 'similar'. Of course great discoveries are made by hunches and Lionel *is* the man to have them, but unless they are supported by some evidence – just a little – they strike almost as hollowly as Rosamond's about the spirit kingdom.

I have rung Cynthia; they are going on much as before, except that Robert seems calmer. I have also rung Julia, who has been looking after a girl living in her flat who has 'flu. It has taken her out of herself.

Julia was condescending about Lionel's Consciousness paper – to *me*, not him, needless to say. 'When one's reading these scientific papers week by week, one begins to realize that all scientists work by hunches. *You* won't like that. Mystical, eh? I don't suppose you liked his saying inanimate matter possessed consciousness.' F: 'But he didn't say that.' Julia: 'Well, he thinks so anyway; he told me so. And I was pleased that my hunch was the same as his.'

Later Margaret rang up, asking my opinion of this paper, and said, 'I can't think why Julia imagines he supposes inorganic matter to have consciousness. He doesn't believe any such thing.' It delighted me when Margaret said at the end of our conversation, 'You've cheered me up, no end,' and I realize (and wished that I'd been the first to say it) that *she* had cheered *me* up.

## January 19th

Bunny to dinner last night, and lots of what Desmond called 'good talk', among other things about communication. He said, what I have always believed, that losing the loved one through death is in a way easier to bear than their simply taking themselves off. (He has after all experienced both.) There is inevitable resentment and bitterness against the once loving person whose other life has bereft you. Bunny said he felt he didn't know what to do with his desire to communicate – to make a present to Angelica of everything he did. This is immensely understandable, and I so very well remember that awful sense of amputation.

What happens when in the long run one does adjust? A sort of parleying with oneself is set up and goes on almost continuously.

You could call it thinking, but sometimes it doesn't deserve the name. When I wake in the night words are nearly always running through my head. Real thinking is harder work alone than when one has a shadow-boxing partner, as I did always with Ralph. Last night too with Bunny I noticed how much easier it was to think when there was his wall to bounce my tennis ball against. Thinking all by oneself is a fearful effort.

Oh, God – another twenty pages of feverish rambling from Gerald – poor Gamel is not dead yet and the doctor won't give her morphia 'as it would certainly kill her'. The barbarity of the religious!

## January 23rd

Gamel died last Thursday, thank God. I had reached a point of wondering if I should telephone Janetta to ask her to get a doctor from Malaga or Gibraltar to overpower the local monster and give morphia. Yesterday I found a short, calm, *relieved* note from Gerald.

Pressure of work and the lives of friends has risen. Sadness too is rising all around like a green tide, and I'm haunted by poor Julia's voice saying brokenly last night: 'I'm *wild* with desperation.' Her writing problem has now resolved itself to the equation: 'The *only* thing I can write will be written with my heart's blood, and will be about myself and Lawrence. Nothing else can I write, but am I to do it?' It gives her a new way, I imagine, of finding a reason not to write.

Lunched with Magouche.[1] She isn't happy either – she feels her life has no purpose without someone to focus her warmth on.

## January 26th

I came home from the first night of *Aida* to find a letter from Janetta, crossing mine. She described – what I had been aware of – Gerald's gentleness and calm during the last terrible weeks of Gamel's life. Also the briskness with which he was dealing with what was left of her – burning bedding, stacking and giving away clothes. A very good thing, and I remember doing it myself, but it brings home how very dead the dead are. Memory is all there is of immortality. I think his mainspring may recoil quickly and we may soon hear of Lynda again.

[1] Phillips, later Fielding.

Dined with Margaret and Lionel last night. Lionel doesn't look very well, but he talked as usual enthrallingly and our three-cornered colloquy was lively, interesting and sometimes funny.

### February 2nd

Two nights ago Julia, Eardley and I dined with the Kees to look at Julian's television programme. Julia came straight from a visit to Dr Henry Dicks,[1] and I could hardly forbear to snort when she told me that he had suggested her getting help or criticism of her work from some literary figure like Dr Leavis or Bonamy Dobrée. To my astonishment she quite took to the idea. Is it because she would have to pay him? Yesterday I found her sitting at a table in the London Library, a much crossed-out sheet of paper in front of her. Her face was turned to the cruel white light of the sky and I had my reading glasses on, so that I suddenly saw the thick coating of make-up and the wide black lines drawn round her eyes and the Dan Leno brows. They are all part of the tragic decor.

Georgie and her French boyfriend came to dinner at the Kees. Georgie looked lovely in a demure little black velvet frock with miles of splendid black silk leg, but she was rather shy and speechless. However, they are a beautiful pair; Jean-Pierre is quite remarkably handsome and also intelligent. Only just eighteen, he is faced with the horrors of military service. He likes to read philosophy and literature. When I asked him about French writers his reply was old-fashioned – Gide, Proust. 'And there is an English writer whom I adore,' he said with suddenly starry eyes – '*Shakespeare*!' He reads him in French and I urged him to try the Sonnets in English.

### February 5th

I've returned from a visit to Anne and Heywood, with (in the background) Eddie and the poor old lady, who has taken a big stride towards the tomb. Her life seemed to me unbearably sad to contemplate, and anyone who loves her must surely long for it to end; but Anne said firmly that she was positive she enjoyed many things and didn't want to die. I wondered if this was that old brute guilt in Anne trying to cancel out her natural longing for her mother

[1] Psychiatrist.

to die. Last night, with a full gale blowing, lashing rain and pitch darkness, I was appalled to see a mop of white hair waving outside the window of Anne and Heywood's 'bicycle-shed'. Heywood, gently and tenderly as ever, helped her in, and she sat down panting in a chair, and began to talk confusedly about the nurse who is fetched from the village to spend every night with her. Lady Cranbrook can never remember why or when she comes, resents and complains of her coming, but would be frightened without her. This evening, hours before it was time for her to be fetched, she must have suddenly begun to fuss about Heywood having to drive and get her. She evidently suggested that Eddie should go instead of Heywood. 'He refused. He said he was sixty-six,' she said with a sudden flash of amusement in her dead blue eyes. 'Was he cross?' said Heywood. 'Not cross. *Firm*,' she said, still smiling. Then she burst into tears. Why should she have this nurse? She didn't want her in the least, and she was quite unnecessary. 'No, you know you really *love* having her, Mamma,' said Anne in a brisk but comforting voice. 'She's just like a sort of *lady's maid* – she does all sorts of things like filling your hot-water bottle in the middle of the night.' When she had gone, Anne and Heywood dismissed the tears as unimportant. It was always happening. But I felt that what she was crying about was her hateful plight – not just a brush with Eddie – and that she does not want to go on living, even though she may be frightened to die.

The *Sunday Times* has a wide spread from Holroyd's next volume – my Carrington portrait of Lytton is very large across the top, with Carrington and Gertler on either side. Next week I suppose it may be Ralph or Gerald. Heywood has read the book and feels it quite astonishingly outspoken and that I, and other living people involved, 'must' – or should? – 'mind'. Roy Harrod also feels, so I hear, that I shall be very upset. But then he is a conventional man who thinks that homosexuality and illicit love should be hinted at but not described. I am at a loss to analyse my own feelings, past and present, and certainly to prognosticate the future.

### February 10th

A dinner party two nights ago, and not having had one for ages I took an enormous amount of trouble. Delicate cucumber soup, *boeuf créole* (with rum, black olives and pimentoes) and even a *crème brulée* which I have never made before. Duncan had been the focus of the party, and he was ill with a cold and couldn't come, but Boris made as good a substitute as anyone could, looking like a monumental Buddha in his elegantly cut, wide suit. Georgia at once noticed the 'yards and yards of stuff' that had gone into the trousers. Someone else noticed the special chic of his square-toed shoes. No one could fail to be struck by his splendid presence.

Bunny was bowled over by Magouche, and I was rather surprised by her on-coming response, which made Bunny's face radiant with pleasure.

Now next day I feel rather flat. Am going to peg on and finish my task. Then wing off to Spain.

### February 13th

I asked Julia to dinner, to eat the remains of my dinner party. Was she perhaps annoyed at not being asked to it? She arrived in a rather dictatorial mood; asked for – or ordered – a pot of tea at 6.15 – '*Strong, please*,' and then settled down to go on reading one of Gerald's letters written when Gamel was dying. I could tell from her comments that she had been planning to pull him to pieces as she came along the street, and I don't like these blood-sports. She soon began saying that he seemed to her 'frog-like', 'inhuman' and 'boring'. Didn't I agree? Then came the sinister remark, 'I can detect it in his voice and face.' Ever since this traumatic phrase was applied in her stinker to me, I cannot help feeling it is really aimed at me when I hear it. However, nothing could have gone more smoothly than the whole evening. She got on to the 'stray cat' theme, and I said the world was full of stray cats and we were all stray cats, and listed a few others. They were all disqualified in one way or another. She hugs her misery to her and desires no competition. My claim to be a stray cat was waved aside – 'Oh no, you've got your boyfriend Eardley.'

Since then – two nights at Cambridge, with Tom and Nadine,[1] taking in two cultural events. One was a performance – chiefly by undergraduates of both sexes – of *Iphigenia in Tauris*, the other a lecture at Newnham by Denis Page on the Minoan bull. This was amusing and interesting, thoroughly trouncing Sir Arthur Evans; and it was a strange sensation to find myself in the Newnham Hall for the first time since I came down. In two rows around me were no

---

[1]   My brother and sister-in-law.

less than three of my contemporaries. I was amazed also to brush across a female dwarf looking rather younger than me, and recognize Enid Welsford who tutored me in Shakespeare when I was eighteen, and seemed quite old then!

Sunday brought another dollop of Holroyd – really very vulgarized by the Sunday paper. 'Trouble at the Mill House,' and a huge portrait of Ralph and Carrington. It shocked me, and the next lot may do so even more. I mentioned it on the telephone to Julia. She brushed it aside – she won't hear of any criticism of Holroyd, yet she has only by her own admission 'pecked about' in his first volume.

Duncan came to see me yesterday. How magnetically delightful he is! He says Angelica writes ecstatically that she is wildly in love with George Bergen[1] though she admits he is difficult.

As I grind to the end of *Doctor and Patient*,[2] I think more and more about Spain, but I still hear nothing from Janetta. I think I shall go, however.


## February 17th

Saturday morning in London. I am already ducking in anticipation of the next instalment of Holroyd tomorrow in which I suppose I shall probably figure, and already my friends have been commiserating with me, one and all (except Julia) appalled by the vulgarity of newspaper popularization, but it is rather feeble only to object to this treatment by the papers when one is the victim oneself. Everyone (except Eardley) to whom I have talked about Holroyd's book thinks it 'very badly written'. Julian had a very good phrase: he is a 'literary buccaneer', and in this case has cashed in on the Bloomsbury belief that the truth must be told. I'm going to see Alix today – I wonder what her attitude will be.


## February 22nd

Calm, oh calm, where have you gone? I have been making frenzied, useless efforts to regain it, and I believe (until I am in Spain) it may be out of the question. So that although Janetta wants to put me off I shall, I think, go and throw myself on Gerald's mercies on March 7th. Unless he too rejects me, which he hasn't exactly done.

---

1 American painter, had been a lover of Duncan many years before.
2 A book I was translating from Spanish.

What is the source of my horrid agitation? The end of my translation and the explosion of Holroyd's book and violent anti-Bloomsbury feelings, as well as finding that I *do* mind the appalling vulgarization of my own and Ralph's and dear friends' lives in the Sunday papers. Roy was right then to some extent. I don't mind the book, but I suppose none of us would have produced the information we did had we known it was to be distorted by the Sunday papers into the likeness of a *News of the World* account of the lives of film stars.

Last Sunday there was a picture of sweet Ham Spray's face (a photo taken by me, as it happened) with a screaming headline about the 'Abode of Love'. I was overcome by a wave of indignation, but what on earth is the use?

Everyone else I have spoken to about it thinks the Sunday extracts appalling. I was delighted by a postcard from Desmond saying; 'Would my prosaic and unfanciful old friend (my hat!) consider coming with me to the *Queen of Spades*?' These adjectives were Holroyd's estimation of Lytton's view of me.

Meanwhile some of the reviewers acclaim the book *as* a book and others like Muggeridge and Grigson take it merely as a text for an anti-Bloomsbury and anti-Lytton screech. Muggeridge, going particularly far, says that Holroyd's Carrington is a 'marvellous *comic* portrait', that she was a 'nymphomaniac weirdy' and 'the poor lady took her own life.' Squelch! – it is all rather disgusting and I wish now the book had never been written. I'm glad James did not live to read these frenzied hymns of hate. I am now starting to read Volume II carefully and with as much detachment as possible, and I do find it absorbing.

I must remember some very nice things to counterbalance these murky agitations: going to *Mastersingers* with Julian, on the very night of Heinemann's party for Holroyd. Six hours of rich all-enveloping experience, and the music having such powers of penetration that it is with me still, all the time circulating in my head. Poor Julian was quite exhausted by many nights of too little sleep, but he sat attentive and wide-eyed beside me like a touching child. He is the perfect companion for such things.

Again and again and more and more and more do I feel that loving people is the one great pleasure in life. Sophie, darling little girl, provided more of that pleasure when I took her to lunch at the Kees' at Kew. Paralysed by shyness at first, she suddenly unfroze and when the children of Caroline Citkovitz[1] joined us, all six had a wonderful time running in the park. It was a great joy to see Sophie running with scarlet cheeks, clambering on trees, turning somersaults. I had to run too, she wanted me to turn somersaults. 'I'm much too weak,' I said. 'You're *not*!' She asked me if I had a grandmother. As I drove her home she fell fast asleep, and I looked at her ravishing little profile beside me, knowing I should remember this moment.

### February 26th

The last instalment of Holroyd has appeared in the Sunday papers, and, perhaps because of the genuinely moving nature of the material, it was not vulgarized. I'm glad it's all over, however. I wonder what Ralph would have felt about it. I'm unable to guess when I meet people I don't know well which camp they will be in. I've finished Volume II and think it on the whole extremely good and (to me at least) enthralling. Nor do I charge my agitation over the last weeks to Michael Holroyd, but to the vulgarity of the papers. How good Lytton was as a writer I now propose to reassess for myself, and leave the critical chapters till after doing that.

I stayed with Kitty last weekend: iced beauty, pale blue skies, blue tits doing acrobatics just outside the window, only one brisk solitary walk, a lot of talk and reading. Frank Tait and Billy Henderson,[2] who came to dinner one day, questioned me closely about Carrington. So did the Sterns[3] with whom we lunched yesterday. I try hard to get her right, but even allowing for all intrusive emotions it's not easy. Also I'm bewildered by the nature of the antipathy aroused in Muggeridge and Grigson. I don't see how any reader of the book can be unmoved by such touching and constant devotion.

Now I heave a rather deep sigh and feel a sort of catharsis about the whole thing. I'm sure I shall continue to be questioned, as a survivor from the sunken ship, but I think or hope the feverish agitation and uncertainty of the last weeks will now die down. Amen.

### February 29th

Am I perfectly mad to persist in my plan of going to Spain next week, in face of such slight encouragement? Gerald writes short, sad,

---

[1] Née Blackwood.
[2] Doctor and painter.
[3] James, writer, and Tanya.

distracted letters, showing plainly that he is desperately keyed-up at the thought of Lynda's arrival, but not revealing whether it would be a relief or the reverse not to be quite alone with her. Nor if he can face having me for a week until Janetta returns from Morocco, which seems to be her plan. Both he and Janetta write of a fortnight's incessant rain, the road to Tramores being cut off. When Gerald's last letter came I nearly cancelled my whole trip, he seemed to show so little enthusiasm for my visit and the ghosts of his lack of welcome in the past rose up suddenly to haunt me. I wonder, too, if his aggressive mood of last September may be revived, and though I feel I can stand it at the moment, and want to try to help and comfort him I may well fail to do either.

The rain in Spain is mocked by our perfectly dry but iron-bound weather here in London and yet I long to get away; I long to get out of it; but no doubt it is myself I want to get out of.

Last night's dinner at Magouche's with Cyril and Deirdre,[1] Bunny. Cyril was positively twinkling with benignity, and I have a feeling that for some reason I'm in his good books. A lot of the talk was entertaining and lively, some about Bloomsbury and Lytton. One or two sharp disagreements, as between Bunny and me over whether Lytton would have supported the last war. Of course he wouldn't.

## March 1st

I don't think I invent the desire mere acquaintances show to grill me about the past and my feelings about being 'in the book', whereas my friends all go on speaking with horror of the *Sunday Times* extracts, and many assume that the book is the same. I defend it as best I can, and particularly on the score that it is the first book about Bloomsbury that is not a *suppressio veri*, like Roy Harrod's on Maynard for instance, as pointed out by Goronwy Rees in *Encounter*. A few days ago I took the typescript of my translation to Jock Murray, who was I felt too gentlemanly to mention the subject. Not so Colin Haycraft, who fixed me with a glittering, unwinking eye and turned on the heat just as I was about to leave. What did I feel about it? Wasn't it awful? He would hate to be put in a book. I said, as I generally do, that I didn't mind the book but had hated the *Sunday Times* articles. And found resentment against this swarthy staring man rising within me. I must avoid persecution

[1] Connolly.

mania at all costs, but I do rather want to get out of this country.

Last night a very pleasant evening with Lionel and Margaret and the Hills – first at Rossini's *Queen Elizabeth* then out to dinner. They obviously liked each other, which makes half a host's happiness.

### March 5th

Weekend at the Carringtons', and *endless* discussion of 'the book'. No, my agitation over the whole subject has not died down, and I am really somewhat dreading the re-turning of the soil that will be started off by Gerald. Julia this morning suddenly spoke with warmth and kindness of Ralph, saying how fond she and Lawrence had both been of him and that she had looked up Holroyd's description of him and found it 'totally inadequate'. I was moved to sudden speechlessness. This image is of course Gerald's creation and had it not been for interpolations of mine it would have been further still from the truth.

I went to London to find a further letter from Janetta still mentioning no dates, but saying they would be 'going to Morocco almost at once', and I pictured myself marooned with a hostile Gerald, waiting, waiting for Godot. A slow bruise emerged as a result – but Janetta has applied Ellerman's embrocation by a touching cablegram today saying she is putting off Morocco and will collect me on the eleventh. *Infinite* relief, but I do feel guilty lest she has put off Morocco for me, though I telegraphed her not to. She ends: 'Secretly fear Gerald's house rather cold.'

The best comment on Holroyd's Lytton is Frances Phipps': 'Oh, that *book*! When I die I'm going to have SHUT UP put on my tombstone.'

### March 7th

I'm just off. Yesterday was a frantic day, made more so by an icy northeaster and gusts of violent wind. I drove to Canonbury to lunch with Raymond, whom I found brown as a berry and not looking a day over forty-five. He was totally unamused by the story of Frances Phipps' tombstone. Perhaps he wasn't listening.

Airborne at last. Flying almost bores me now; I never even bothered to look out, but munched my way through re-heated meat and tinned peaches. I had expected sweet warm air to enfold me at

Malaga airport, but it was as cold and grey as London. At Gerald's I found Rosario and the little girl Mari. Soon Gerald appeared, looking years younger. How totally unexpected! Lynda had arrived the day before but gone to ground with a bilious attack. Gerald: 'She's a *very* nice girl, very intelligent, quite different from what I remembered. I wouldn't have recognized her. I've done very well for myself. I think she'll be happy here. She wanted to be quiet and read, but she's very attractive and if she wants to have her boyfriends to stay she can. I shan't mind. We sat up till two or three last night talking.' F: 'What does Rosario make of it?' G: 'Well I don't know, but she said to me, "Don Geraldo, you must get yourself a girl." I've been terribly lonely, especially in the evenings. I can't live alone. I never think of Gamel. I don't think of her *at all*. Sometimes I dream of her, but I don't think of her.'

The house is extremely cold and smells of tom-cat. I am evidently to sleep in Gamel's room, in the bed where those ghastly scenes Gerald's letters described took place, and where she died. Do I mind? I don't think so, but I feel a lack of sensitivity in putting me there. Also I've had to ask for another blanket.

After tea in the *mirador* Gerald and I strolled up the familiar hillside path while he talked with unseeing eyes, mainly about Holroyd. He half-identifies himself with him, feels *he* has written the book or at least contributed most of the material, is delighted with his own portrait in it. He is making Holroyd his literary executor, and has asked him to stay. (I wonder if Julian and Jonny know they have been ousted.) He was very friendly and warm to me, without prickles or raised hackles. Lynda appeared before dinner, wrapped in a warm, blue dressing-gown. She has a wide, pale, oval face with truthful brown eyes and a friendly catlike smile, a soft voice. I liked her.

I have told Gerald I don't want to be entertained, and will fend for myself. Of Gamel he said, 'We were very remote these last years; perhaps I was to blame, but we had hardly anything to say to each other. I have no desire whatever to talk about her illness. Most of what I felt for her was intense pity.' It's extraordinary, come to think of it, that so voluble a man should ever have been short of things to say. He never is with anyone else. His lack of desire to talk of Gamel and her death is unique in my experience of bereaved people – but a huge relief.

It *poured* with rain, drumming on the garden lilies, this evening.

## March 8th

A night of shallow sleep, seeming very long and strange. Each time I woke I thought, 'I'm lying on Gamel's deathbed.' This made me want to open the window and it was terribly cold. 'It's the coldest day we've had,' said Gerald calling me. But the sun is shining and I'm sitting in it now against the far garden wall on a small hard iron chair. There's a border of freesias in front of me, clumps of violets beside me. I shall hope to spend every morning here till the sun goes off. Gerald told me Lynda would 'be reading in the *mirador*'. Actually she was talking hard to him in his bed-sitting-room as I went out. I don't think he'll waste much time before he starts making up to her after his fashion. He says he has been feeling ill, and the *practicante* comes every day to inject him, but he looks very well, and I now think much of the scattiness of his recent letters was due to anxiety about Lynda. I think he is really quite pleased for me to be here, but there is nothing I can do for him, none of those services most of my friends seemed to think I could provide. He is *perfectly all right*. What an extraordinary being!

As Gerald truly says, his mentality is 'forward-looking' not retrospective. So he is totally uninterested in anyone but himself – and Lynda. As we sat, rather chilly, eating our lunch at the glass table in the patio, Bill Davies[1] silently appeared. I got a warm hug from him and we are invited to dinner tomorrow.

## March 9th

Oh yes, Gerald is an astonishing character. It is all to the good, no doubt, that he does not miss or think of Gamel at all; yet surely this means total lack of love for her, in the ordinary sense of the word, all these years they've lived together? He makes an impression of being happy as a sandboy now. I went to my room to lie down after lunch but it was much too cold. He came in and asked me eagerly, 'Do you like Lynda?' I said truthfully that I did, very much. '*Isn't* she a nice girl? *Aren't* I lucky? *Lucky Brenan!*' She appears to me sweet-natured, serious, a reader, reserved, attractive rather than actually pretty, thoughtful, but does not give herself completely away. Gerald is in an excitable state, shows off a good deal ('I never show off'), and is beginning to reveal that he feels like a boy again by running when

1 An American neighbour.

other people would walk, even hopping and jumping, and saying *what* a pity it is he never learned to dance almost as if he still might. I can't really imagine what there is in this situation for Lynda, and wonder whether her poetry means much to her and how good it is.

In the late afternoon Gerald took us both on an enormous three-hour walk on the hillside (in itself a show-off), nearly to Torremolinos and back, among olives and carobs, orchids and iris. Lynda was amazed and exhausted by this performance.

Much Holroyd-Lytton talk. I refused to agree that Lytton's *Landmarks* was taken in chunks from textbooks or a pot-boiler, or that he had read none of the originals. Again I was struck by Gerald's seeming to feel that Holroyd's was *his* book. 'I wonder why he speaks of Valentine Dobrée as being deformed,' I said vaguely, 'I don't remember that she was.' He looked slightly cornered. 'Oh yes, I told him that. I think one of her legs was longer than the other, or something. I'm not sure what.' F: 'And then was she ever in an asylum?' G: 'Oh, that was what *you* told me, I think.' (!!) I traced the source of this – a long letter – destroyed by me unfortunately as too prosy – from Bonamy to Ralph saying that he (Ralph) was upsetting his wife or words to that effect, but I don't think anything about asylums or even nervous breakdowns was mentioned. There has been little talk about Honor except that she slept under eight blankets and with this I now sympathize deeply. I go to bed in my underclothes under three blankets and with a hot-water bottle and wake in the night, frozen.

### March 10th

I've begun reading Gerald's autobiography and find it of course fascinating, though he stands over me talking and talking as I read, so that it is hard to concentrate. He's like the fountain in the patio, gushing night and day without pause. Yesterday I took the autobiography out into the last pale rays of the sun to read in peace. When I came back the torrent was still pouring over Lynda.

Our evening at the Cònsular was pretty dull. Bill's throat and ears are closing up altogether so that he can neither hear nor properly articulate: 'Whassat you say, Frances?' Annie was a little complaining and said, 'Bill's getting so terribly fussy.' There was much talk of poverty and economy, and the dinner wasn't good. But after the dank and draughty chill of Gerald's house it was glorious to roast oneself into a stupor in front of an olivewood fire. Lynda's social manner was modest but perfectly assured. Other guests were a French Moroccan with an American wife. He talked to me about Holroyd's book. 'Did you ever go to Ham Spray House?' F: 'Yes, I lived there for nearly thirty years.' I heard Gerald talking about the importance of not washing, and his appearance strikingly illustrated this theme.

But he disarms all criticism by anticipating the words just forming in one's head – such as that he can't bear listening to other people talking, and knows he always interrupts, and likes to talk entirely about himself. How will Lynda manage him? Gerald says she tells him nothing so wonderful has happened to her before coming to live with him.

This morning the cold was worse than ever. The starry sky under which we walked to the Cònsular gave way to rain and icy wind, grey sky and fresh snow on the mountains. I ran through the patio, where the huge leaves were being drummed on with a melancholy sound by the rain, and into the little dark bathroom, to revolve frantically for a few moments under the shower turned as near scalding as possible. No matter how hot the water or how long I stay under it, I am freezing when I come out and blot myself with a curiously unabsorbent towel. Impossible to spend the whole day crouched over the butagaz heater in the *mirador* so I put on coat, fur cap (thank heaven I brought it) and walked alone up the steeper slope of the mountain.

At nights the long hollow corridors of this house echo with the sound of Gerald clearing his throat. By day he champs ceaselessly on his false teeth. No laughing matter, look at it any way you like, and an indication that though Gamel has only recently died, he has been fundamentally a solitary for many years.


## March 12th: Tramores

I'm quite knocked out by the astonishing change in ambience. I was right to trust Janetta – she even came earlier yesterday than I expected. I was therefore only at Churriana for four nights. Janetta is more sensible of the gloom, discomfort and cold of that house even than I am, and attributes a deep sadness to it. But to me it also trails an aura of seigneurial grandeur and romantic beauty.

Yesterday morning, Lynda asked me to walk into the village with her and we were just setting out when we ran slap into Janetta. Did Lynda want to ask my advice as an old friend of the strange septuagenarian she has settled in with? I shall never know. Gerald has repeatedly said to me, 'Of course there will be no love-making. I shall just make a companion of her and grow fond of her,' in his obsessional muffled monotone; but he has already started exploding into scabrous remarks and reminiscences (boastful on the whole) about his youth, and bringing out naked photographs of girls he once went to bed with. I feel touched by Lynda, who seems to be sensitive and reserved, and might react against his prurient voyeur characteristics.

Janetta drove me, talking all the way, along the familiar coast road to Jaime's house in Marbella. Sitting in his little patio under a blue sky, I felt I had crossed into a new continent. I had self-inoculated myself against the inevitable delays and didn't therefore mind them in the least. We finally set off to Benahavis where we waited for Jaime in his Land Rover. Weeks of rain and flood have nearly destroyed the road beyond and we shook and bounced up it and through the swollen river to Tramores. Met by Serge[1] and pregnant married Nicky, beaming with happiness. Janetta bought her some blue and white wool and she at once started knitting a tiny vest, calling constantly for help and advice. Serge was rather silent as we sat round the fire last night. Janetta and Jaime both feel that he is 'against the world', and to some extent out to get from people what he feels the world has denied him. He and Nicky have lingered on and on here, and their departure has been several times postponed. How they will live when they get to London no one can imagine, as he has no money and no work. I grope for the key to his character, and it interests me. I asked Janetta what Georgie thought of him. 'She's very impressed by him.' Janetta and Jaime seem extremely close and happy, and Jaime said he adored Tramores and could hardly bear to tear himself away. Janetta is absorbed in the things growing in her garden, almost to the exclusion of everything else. Each bud is lovingly inspected every day. The house is a marvel of taste and beauty, and basic furniture has sprouted as it were from its walls. The silence and peace are wonderful. There is as yet no electricity; that is the only real deprivation, for our tiled bathrooms are useless, and beaked jugs of hot water arrive every day. But I love the soft light of candles and lamps, and a log fire burns in my room.

[1] Brodskis.

Woke this morning fairly early, and was brought breakfast by a little girl in black called Luisa, whose *tia* also works here. The sky is clear of all cloud and I am sheltering from the slight north wind under the cracked dome of the ruined Moorish castle. I feel I've spent hours scribbling in this book and done little else. Stray-cattishness has made reading rather difficult, but I propose this very moment to start a huge fat life of Voltaire in French, lent me by Raymond.

Janetta and Serge have driven off to Marbella. Nicky paints in a little shed. Voltaire and I share the lower terrace with a peach tree coming into bloom, a small orange tree (dropping its fruit) and neat box-edged beds of lettuces, anemones, arum lilies and carnations.

## March 13th

Voltaire was fortunately absorbing, for Janetta returned very late, bringing a carpenter with her, and we lunched about four. Dinner nearer eleven than ten. After lunch I started to walk up the bed of the stream behind the house; but as I advanced into the huge circle of wooded mountains they rose up menacingly as if to swallow me, so that I was suddenly submerged in a nightmare feeling of loneliness. There was also an almost complete absence of flowers into which to project my libido. I turned home sadly and helped Janetta weed her terrace, which I enjoyed. How much does she think about the future? Hardly at all I believe. She has a letter from Derek[1] saying he has married a French widow and that it 'might be better for financial reasons that she and Rose[2] shouldn't return to England for a year'. I asked if she had thought of doing so, and if so, when. J: 'I don't think I *need* go back, do you?' She warned me to keep off Vietnam with Serge as he felt so violently about it. But he came back from Marbella, drank more whisky than usual, and started the subject himself. I can't resist an argument, but I was on my guard. I think he was surprised to find my sympathies totally anti-American (I'm told this is the litmus-paper he tests everyone with. I thought he had taken a dislike to me, but since this talk he has been very friendly.) He said he thought we should give military support to the Vietcong. I declared my pacifism – and pessimism. I asked Nicky if she was still a pacifist; she looked thoughtful and torn. Serge launched an attack on

[1] Jackson, Janetta's ex-husband; professor of physics.
[2] Daughter of Derek and Janetta.

pacifism as being unrealistic, saying one ought to compromise. I said my deepest belief was in correspondence without compromise between beliefs and actions (including speech).

## March 15th

Janetta's new car has already collapsed. The resulting total isolation is alarming. One is now used to depending on modern inventions and communications, telephone, post, newspapers. The element of our isolation that I like – the peace, quiet, restfulness, beauty – is mixed with a tinge of escapism which only seems justifiable as a change from my 'real' life. I can be happy here for these two and a half weeks, composing my day with reading, writing letters and rather frustrating walks. But no longer, I believe.

Rose arrived today from school for the weekend.

## March 16th

I have been surprised by Janetta's complete absorption in her life here, and lack of any thread of desire leading back to London, Georgie, Julian, Magouche, all that is happening there. When Nicky and Serge have left, and after Rose goes to live with Derek, what will take place on these cleared decks? I'm not at all sure how much she plots the future, nor how. But her pride in this magic creation of Tramores, and love for it, is of course completely understandable. I question myself: what do I feel for Tramores? If I were Janetta, should I love it as I loved Ham Spray? Yes for its beauty and atmosphere and the fact that it is a growing organism, but with its appalling road and the village quite a trudge away, and without light, hot water or telephone, I feel we are putting back the clock to the eighteenth century.

Janetta off to Marbella. I talked a lot to Serge, interested by him and puzzled. He's certainly intelligent. Talked about Russia, his family (his father was born a Russian), books and Spain. He said he was 'disappointed in the Spaniards', they're too suburban, and have far less nobility and poetic sense than the Moroccans.

This morning I woke about eight, opened my shutters and lay looking out at the serene morning; only part of the mountains were as yet lit by the sun, but it gradually crept up and picked out the branches of the fig tree outside my door. I lay happily reading

Voltaire for about an hour and then went to the kitchen and asked for breakfast. Luisa came back later to say, 'Señora, no hay pan.' I said I'd have a boiled egg. By ten o'clock Nicky, Rose and Serge were all champing and prowling. Serge at last set off in the now mended Citroën to the village. At eleven I saw him returning, and at the same time Janetta came out of her room holding some tiny biscuits and smiling her most cajoling smile: 'I brought these *for you*. How *stupid* of Luisa not to see them!'

## *March 23rd: Seville*

Drove here yesterday with Janetta – a lovely road and crystal-bright morning. Arrived in good time at the airport, took a long deep breath and we were at Lisbon, taxi-ing up to the castle where in a marvellous position overlooking the Tagus, was the flat of Jaime's friend Duarte, in which Jaime was still asleep. After coffee, brought with a lot of 'oosh-ooshing' by a stout red-faced maid, we went out into the drizzling, then pouring wet, town. To a plant shop where Janetta and Jaime chose and bought plants for Tramores with care and love.

Back for a long and glorious sleep on the sofa in Duarte's sitting-room and then to the opera, where by great good luck we struck the first night of Donizetti's *Maria de Rohan*, not performed for a hundred years. We sat at the very top and looked down through a letter-box slit at the stage far below, all faces reduced to pink blobs.

## *March 24th*

Woke to find the Tagus muffled in thick white mist. We kept waiting for over an hour the chauffeur of an English queer and Lisbon tycoon, Dicky Wyatt, who was to drive us to his country house in an idyllic homosexual setting, with blue and green parakeets flying loose in the trees, wild orchids in the grass, *soigné* lunch on the verandah. Wyatt was very put out by our tardiness, as he had meant to take us to see a beautiful house nearby before lunch, and had instead to sacrifice his siesta and do so afterwards. (Janetta pointed out that his conversation was a jigsaw of clichés.) The house was extraordinarily beautiful. Bacaloa Villa-fresca was its name, and I hope to remember at least the large tiled balconies and formal garden, the great ornamental water with its lake-house also lined with old tiles.

Drove on through lovely country to Tamar, stopping to pick hoop-petticoat daffodils and angel's tears. Janetta and Jaime want to dig up almost everything they see, even some plants that already grow wild but unnoticed at Tramores. Failed to get into the Pousada, but had an enjoyable night in a luxury hotel.

## March 25th: Tamar

Raining dismally as we went up to see the famous sight, and it went on doing so without pause, all day. Cold also. Our spirits weren't really damped, only our clothes and hair as we got out, obsessively drawn to further sheets and sheets of hoop-petticoats and angel's tears. Got to Càceres for the night and walked in an icy wind and occasional rain through its splendid streets of brown houses decorated with armorial bearings.

## March 26th

Woke early and went out into the cool air (dry, thank heavens) to change money and shop. But God, it's cold! I quite long for England's friendly warmth. A long tiring day, but driving through much lovely and strange country.

In Estramadura we traversed a road pot-holed with puddles reflecting the sky, lavishly bordered with little daffodils, full of birds, empty of houses, through a weird landscape sewn with smooth rocks like great tortoises. Stopped for lunch at Merida, and drove steadily as darkness fell and the procession of lorries began to advance wearing bows of light (like little girls do in their hair). Long after we had seen the lights of Seville we were still driving to get there. At last we arrived at the dear old Inglaterra and got the last two rooms with a bathroom between.

Revived by whisky, I recovered more life than I thought I possessed, and enjoyed our evening at a noisy, burstingly vital fish restaurant near the Macarena. The talk in Andalusian cafés and restaurants is cataclysmic, a prolonged and continuous explosion of chatter.

## March 27th

Tomorrow I shall be in England and I think of it with affection. Yesterday morning in Seville was *bitter*. Wearing a woollen vest, two jerseys and a coat I rushed out sightseeing by myself at top speed while the others shopped.

To the Alcázar, the cathedral, and the Convent of La Caridad where I read there were two pictures of corpses by Valdes Leal that 'made you hold your nose'. An ancient nun showed me round, babbling and sinking to her old knees and getting up again, telling me with apparent joy that *'Polvo somos y a polvo volveremos.'*[1] Here Janetta and I parted from Jaime and set off in her car via Ronda to Tramores, where Nicky came out to meet us: 'There is some bad news, I'm afraid.' The *tia* had left in a dudgeon and Luisa said she wouldn't stay either. They felt they were being suspected of stealing fruit or eating too much; they find it lonely and dull, and hate the old-fashioned way of life. Poor Janetta drove off rather crestfallen to cook dinner for the Fonda, Jaime's hotel. On the way from Seville she talked a good deal about her plans. She has cast in her lot very definitely with Tramores, Jaime and Spain. Georgie must make the best of Montpelier Square and plan her own life, as Janetta did at her age. I found a letter from Gerald, writing about Lynda like a happy bridegroom on his honeymoon, but one who is not allowed all the favours he longs for.

## April 8th: London

I arrived back in a miniature heat-wave; blue sky, temperature in the 70s; I tore off my Spanish clothes and for the first time for nights had no fire or hot-water bottle. A week later it was snowing, I have to admit. However, on the whole I find my old addiction to Spain slightly dwindled – as a place to *live* in, that is to say, and London more civilized, comfortable and stimulating. When I was in Dorset last weekend I compared that magical and flowery landscape with Spain's. Huge clumps of enormous primroses crowded every bank, mixed with tufts of violets, purple and white, celandine and harts-tongue ferns.

[1] 'Dust we are and to dust we shall return.'

102

## April 17th

Another slight brush with Julia has been – thank heaven – smoothed over, and I hope to learn from it to keep an even closer watch on my tongue. She comes to dinner tomorrow.

Mary said to me after finishing Holroyd's book, in rather an odd voice: 'By the way, I was always told that Carrington committed suicide because she had no money and no Ham Spray.' 'Nothing of the sort,' I answered. 'Lytton left her almost all his money, £10,000, and though Ham Spray was legally Ralph's he was only too eager to persuade her to live there.' I said no more, nor did she, and it was only later that I began to wonder who had 'told' her this, and thought 'Julia, of course'. For she has over and over again brought up to me a remark of Carrington's that she couldn't face life in a bed-sitter in Notting Hill Gate, and I have felt the latent hostility in this. No one who has been involved in trying to prevent someone from committing suicide and failed can help feeling it a sore place, and resent it being deliberately scraped. Then over dinner with Jonny and Sabrina, Julia and her 'nephew' Ian Angus,[1] I rashly or perhaps mischievously mentioned Mary's remark, but of course without saying I had any idea whence it derived. 'Oh, I think *I* may have been responsible for that,' said Julia. 'You see . . .' and she told the Notting Hill Gate story all over again. I rather hotly said this was a libel on Lytton and Ralph, and indeed Carrington herself, and then immediately changed the subject. I really did instantly forget the whole thing, for I caught the quick look of surprise on Jonny's face. The evening continued very jolly for several hours. Julia must have brooded, however, for she wrote a muddled little note, saying that she felt I thought she was accusing Ralph of meanness in not 'dishing out more of Lytton's bequest to Carrington' and she really always thought him very generous; and that she never knew what Lytton's will was and still didn't.

I wrote a fairly long and detailed reply, saying I was amazed at her last remark, because she had asked me a good many times what were the terms of Lytton's will and I had always told her. (They are also set out in full in Holroyd on page 629.) Then I repeated them all over again and explained that there was no question of Ralph's 'dishing out' Lytton's money, because all of it except Ralph's £1,000 was left direct to Carrington.

[1]   A librarian of University College, and a friend of Sonia's.

Is it absurd to have such feelings over things so long past? Yes, I dare say. Bunny, because he had been involved to some extent at the time, got my point at once and shared my indignation at the libel on all three – Lytton (for not providing Carrington with money), Ralph (for not handing over Ham Spray), Carrington for being moved by such materialistic motives. 'And it's *not true*,' he said. Afterwards he told me he had been pondering the question and thought Julia must identify herself with Carrington and have felt in some subconscious way that Lytton should have provided for her, Julia. I returned to London from Easter expecting a reply from Julia, and finding none I have rung her up. She was friendly and very apologetic, 'for letting things go in at one ear and out at the other'. So, thank goodness, another dangerous corner has been rounded.

Hilton for Easter – bitterly cold though sunny. I was very content to be with them all. The garden was ranged through by Richard's boys, three little cousins and Sophie, running around like a fairy on tiptoe, with her splendid little bullet head erect on its stalk, rosy-cheeked, excited by the company, bright as a button. She is fast learning to read and understands everything you say to her; she has a loving sweet character and adores Henrietta, though they sometimes swear at each other and even come to blows, like cat and kitten.

On Bank Holiday the amazing Nerissa arrived from a Southend Chess congress. Amaryllis, the apple of both her parents' eyes, is a sweet girl, but she's not so beautiful as the others. All three girls smoke like chimneys the whole time.

Henrietta was being very domestic, helping Bunny and making clothes for herself and Sophie. I do rather worry about Bunny, poor fellow. He showed me friendly but perhaps unimaginative letters from Angelica. There is a possibility she might come over in the summer, with Bergen, to sell her little Islington house and find somewhere else 'grand enough for him'. Bunny really dreads seeing her, as he told me in a voice that broke with suppressed feeling. His way of combatting despair is to fall in love with Magouche and her younger daughters collectively, and to work in the house with a frantic energy that betrays his restlessness. The girls helped a lot but he insists on doing the shopping and most of the cooking, all at the double, writing, entertaining his friends, tidying up.

On Monday evening he admitted to feeling 'dead tired' and I begged him to go and lie down. He fell fast asleep, but woke up with a start when it was time to have a drink with two old friends in the village. He looked so stricken and ill and anxious when he came downstairs, that I suddenly panicked on his behalf, wondering how to get him to take it easier without pointing that unpalatable moral: you aren't as young as you used to be?

What is left of Bloomsbury tends to treat the practical side of life in two ways – Bunny, Angelica, probably Duncan, Gerald, all have a curious liking for dirt and cold coupled with rich, home-produced satisfaction of other sensuous appetites (excellent food, drink, conversation, books, music); whereas the homosexual element – Crichel in particular – insist on their comforts and convenience but cannot lift a finger for themselves. Their food is therefore good only contingently on supply of good servants. The first group travels widely but in ramshackle style and never spends money on taxis or good hotels, nor do they worry so much about manners and grammar (the formal details of life) as the second, to whom both are of paramount importance. They also travel enormously but generally comfortably.

### April 18th

Dinner alone with Raymond last night at Canonbury. He had just finished reading Holroyd and said he had marked a lot of things he wanted to ask me about. Settled in the drawing-room after dinner, he sank far down into the sofa cushions, lit a cigarette and began looking up the page references he had jotted down to ask me about. One and all turned out to be minute points of accuracy, such as use of prepositions, mention of 'a small, neatly set out bridge table' (to which his comment was '*All* bridge tables are the same size, or nearly') and Lytton complaining in a letter of having left behind the stopper of his hot-water bottle. ('Surely he could have bought another?') Not *one* point that bore on anything thought-provoking. This mania for trifles is quite extraordinary in one of our major critics. He is insisting on reviewing a book on sixteenth-century Dutch history, instead of the Reith lectures next week. But I had a delightful evening with him; he's a lovable man and awfully pleasant companion. Just back from staying with Philippe and Pauline Rothschild, he had been lunching with Ava Waverley, aged about seventy and a widow, who suddenly said to him that 'Love was what all women wanted – at all ages.' He said he was seized by a strong feeling that she expected him to propose to her though they were mere acquaintances and met about once a year. I don't think he is at all inclined to boast, but it did sound unlikely!

I have read and reported on two books since I got back from Spain, the last despatched yesterday. Now, I thought, I shall have a bit of a holiday, and I don't *think* I shall worry about having nothing else to do.

However Miss Gollancz has just rung up to say I am almost certainly to do the Alejo Carpentier.[1] I have mixed feelings, and a desire to start at once 'in case'.

I told Raymond about Julia and Lytton's will. He reacted just as Bunny had done. 'But she'll forget, and go on saying it,' he said.

## April 19th

Julia arrived to dinner last night, unbuttoned a thick, black mackintosh and laid down an umbrella. (The day had been perfectly fine and rather hot but she told me she dials the weather every single morning before she goes out, to find out if there's a possibility of rain.) Sniffing the cooking smell, of veal and vegetables, she said, 'I'm glad it's meat as I had nothing but a chocolate bar for lunch. I *can't* eat by myself. I simply *won't* cook for myself, and I'm getting so *thin* [a rising note of hysteria] that my bones are literally sticking out of my body.' Then, as I began my usual exhortations and encouragements, she switched off with noticeable success.

At dinner she began telling me about a correspondence she had been having (by letter and in person) with Lawrence about Ingres and neo-classicism. Afterwards she read the letter, and a long fascinating conversation ensued, in which I most luckily saw the point of most of what she said. Ingres and the neo-classicists were to her mind shallow, and their defect was that there was no reference in them to what lay outside the picture space – the unresolved mysteries of the universe. She therefore found them smug, static and dead, instead of life-giving. Lawrence's letter was characteristically imaginative and interesting: he described a picture as being an entity in its own right, erected like a 'flag' or 'building', and having a 'sharp pride' in its own existence. He liked this phrase and repeated it as a sort of litany. The drawback is that only in theory can a work of art stand alone. The threads of association are made of unbreakable material.

[1]   Distinguished Cuban writer and diplomat.

Well, how can one record a conversation during which one has been absorbed in listening and considering? We agreed completely on our dislike of Egyptian art as sterile, dead and non-developing. Each of us understood the other's points if not actually agreeing with them. It was like a form of knitting in which the needles are held by two people.

## April 21st: Crichel

Basking in sun and happiness, the restfully stimulating and endearing company of Desmond and Julian, and unexpectedly beautiful weather. Birds keeping up a subdued chorus as intoxicatingly sweet as the scent of the flowering cherry, now at its perfection. An almost painful feeling that here are flawless days, whose idyllic beauty one had better gobble for they will flash past and very likely never return. The restorative effect of realizing that the possibility of real happiness has not gone. I have revelled in it these two days in this magical weather, in the music of Handel's *Hercules*, walks in the sparkling woods, jokes, fun, Julian's intensely vivid account of his Easter in Holland. He is reviewing Cynthia Asquith's diaries, and I'm delighted that he has responded almost exactly as I did when I read them among her uncritical adorers.

Not long ago Julia said that she thought one of Carrington's great characteristics had been that she was an 'impresario of quality', a Diaghilev who brought the best out of people. Both Julian and Desmond are this to some extent – Julian more than Desmond. It makes them exhilarating company, but in a way it is tiring having one's 'best brought out'.

Last night Julian dropped a suggestion that he would like me to appear on one of his telly programmes. A shrinking terror overwhelmed me. I think I should be absolutely panic-stricken and paralysed; possibly would get over it in the end, but by no means certainly. And to what end go through such torture? No, most definitely not.

## April 24th

Just spoken to Janetta on the telephone. She flew in last night, and I'm waiting in a slight simmer for her arrival. Summer prospects are opening their huge pink petals. As well as the plan to go to Vienna with Margaret and Lionel in June, I have now been asked to stay with Anne and Heywood in Cyprus in August. And I say to myself, 'Why not? How long is left?' and remember poor Frances Penrose[1] who is dying of cancer. Margaret and I are due to visit her this weekend.

## April 27th

Came down to Thorington with the Penroses last night, in preparation for our sad outing tomorrow. Janetta paid me a long midday visit yesterday, interrupted briefly by Amaryllis, Henrietta and Sophie. Janetta was charming to Sophie, the model of how an adult should behave to a child of four, drawn into her brick constructions as if she couldn't resist it, and inventing original pagodas made of teapots, bricks and cups – so that Sophie quickly sensed that she was as much involved as she was herself.

Alone, we talked long, forking the ground deeply, about all her three daughters, and her plans for letting Montpelier Square. She is 'worried about Nicky and Georgie', and Serge came in for a lot of criticism. Now that she works very hard herself, Janetta has become intolerant of those who don't, and Serge is one. She told me how, when she'd been criticizing the young to Julian for their desire to get what they could out of people while making as little personal effort as possible themselves, he had defended them, saying it was because they felt the world so awful. Yet she told me he had resented her attack on 'the awfulness of all the Piccadilly crowds, the hideousness and pointlessness of everything'. I ventured to say that the same process of vulgarization was happening everywhere – in Marbella for instance; also that London had life and a power to stimulate unequalled anywhere. London minds revolved and responded, and this made it an exciting place to live in, which is the reason why I don't even envy Janetta living in her beautiful valley.

## April 29th

The dreaded visit to poor Frances was not so bad after all. The picture drawn by Roland Penrose, and the fact of her telling Margaret on the telephone, 'Of course you know I'm dying,' may both have been exaggerated by evening drunkenness. A friendly lady

[1]   Widow of Alec, eldest of the four Penrose brothers.

received us (about seventy and immensely carefully dished up like a trifle, with dyed yellow hair, a thick mask of pink and blue maquillage and her elegant figure encased in bright pink slacks and jazz-pattern jumper). It was some time before Frances appeared, looking fatter and older, walking with a tottery step, her head shaking as she spoke, her utterance intercepted by long pauses. But what she said throughout our visit was to the point and sensible. If she is dying and knows it she is remarkably brave, and that is what I would expect of her. I have promised to go again, but I think for one night only. How can one possibly refuse? Roy and Billa Harrod also came to lunch, which was really quite jolly. Thinking of Frances and the possibility of death, I feel human beings as a whole *are* extraordinarily brave. Apart from the way they accept their various shocks and bereavements I can think of no one who has gone screaming out of life, as they have every right to do.

Another back-wash of Holroyd. Roy, tight-lipped, was saying that James had behaved in a dishonourable way, because after being allowed to take microfilms of Maynard's letters to Lytton on the strict understanding that they should not be published, he had let Holroyd do so. I flew to James's defence, but was I right? Or if I was, have I incriminated Holroyd, Noel Annan, or the librarian of King's College, Cambridge? The only thing I cling to is that the truth is always best.

### May 1st

The prig and the hedonist battle away inside me, but I don't see why they shouldn't co-operate. The prig responds to certain things in Bertrand Russell's scrapbook of an autobiography, particularly his feelings about the insane horror of war (1914–18 in his case). I admire him too for being able to analyse this with such detachment, singling out the strands of his great love for England and his desire that the Germans shouldn't win from his utter rejection of the war-frenzy and desire for instant peace. What's more he never stopped acting on his beliefs, however futile these efforts may have been. He went to prison for them, and made the best of it uncomplainingly, continuing to read and write philosophy there, though it can have been no joke. E. D. Morel, who did likewise, came out a shattered man with snow-white hair. Another thing to give one pause is that both Russell and Wittgenstein, two of the most brilliantly clever men of their day, gave away large inherited fortunes because they felt they had no right to them.

## May 2nd

Lunch with Janetta, Julian, Cyril and Jennifer Ross. Cyril came in beaming, and seating himself in an armchair like an egg in an eggcup, began at once: 'I have three things to say. I moved to Eastbourne yesterday. I adore it. I'm flying to Tanzania tomorrow.' He then entertained us with an amusing fantasia – a conversation in which he tried to wheedle letters and books out of Hemingway's son who lives in Africa. Very funny, and we all showed our amusement and made an excellent audience. But why *want* Hemingwayana? It really seems very odd.

## May 6th: The Rectory, Ham[1]

I drove Ben Nicolson down here for the weekend. The journey was made interesting by his giving me a dramatic account of the discovery of a remarkably outspoken diary of his mother Vita's, and the discussion between him and his brother Nigel as to what was to be done with it.

Robin has been genial and not uninteresting to talk to; Ginette is rather too flattering but attractive and pretty. Pat Trevor-Roper didn't arrive until Saturday, along with Joy and Den Craig.[2]

My first night I felt and knew where I was by means of thousands of nerves that penetrated the surrounding green fields and little woods in every direction making an invisible network in my brain, so that I couldn't sleep. Next morning Robin dropped me on top of Ham Hill; I walked there for a bit and then back. On Sunday, hearing that poor Mrs Elwes was in hospital, I walked up to Ham Spray and explored the garden. What *did* I feel? I think I had deliberately put a mute on my strings, so that everything was muffled. I saw with sadness how the dear face of the house had been ruined, as with a false moustache, by that hideous porch and the removal of the verandah; I noticed the loneliness of the ilex tree, and the melancholy jungle round the swimming-pool, and that the dogtooth-violets I had

[1]  Staying with Robin and Ginette Darwin, a stone's throw from Ham Spray.
[2]  She had been married to Beakus Penrose, beloved by Carrington.

planted under the beech tree had flowered recently. Then I walked back, feeling a little bruised.

I shouldn't have gone to Ham at all. I forgot that when one is a guest one has to try and be pleasant.

Two quotations from books that have pleased me – Henry James when death was approaching: 'So here it is at last, the distinguished thing;' and Bertie Russell: 'All my life I've been convinced of the value of two things – kindness and clear thinking.'

Julia has formed a project of writing something about Carrington, based on C.'s letters to her. I encouraged it, as I do all her plans. She rang up yesterday to say that on reading the letters she had been dismayed and amazed to find how 'flirtatious' and 'sexy' they were, and that she thought them 'too personal and private'. She felt Carrington must really have been 'in love with her'. So I'm sure she was in a way, though perhaps it was partly fantasy. And she had a special way of talking to Julia as if she was a princess which I think Julia enjoyed at the time.

Today she rang again. Did I know what other women Carrington wrote to in this style – with 'real lust and love'? I mentioned Henrietta Bingham, Catharine Carrington, Poppet and Vivien John.

## May 14th

Ralph Jarvis has had a new valve put in his heart, and Cony[1] asked me to visit him yesterday morning. Stepping inside the clinical austerity of a hospital clutched at my own heart. The anxious faces just inside the door sitting waiting for news perhaps: 'Will he live? Will he die? Save him!' written on their features. The coffin-shaped lift. Yes, of course it is also for stretcher cases, but the antiseptic air seems to call up a vision of corpses. Ralph looked anxious and a little feverish, but was on the whole philosophical and said it 'hadn't been too bad, but the first fortnight wasn't nice'. He bared his bosom and showed me that he had been sliced right down the sternum, a long, long seam, and there was a current of angst or even hysteria circulating in his large, grand room, with a Renoir propped up for him to gaze at. In face of such a crushing experience, I didn't stay long for fear of wearing him out. He had made a series of 'journeys to other places' while still remaining in his room: for instance to Ulster,

[1] Antonia, his wife.

where he had never been in his life. He was perplexed that the objects in his room and his New Zealand nurse went there with him. 'Write it all down,' I said, feeling I was ranging about clumsily in a sensitive area.

Last night to *Trovatore* with Janetta, Jaime and Julian. Julian has given up his Spanish holiday to take care of Kingsland,[1] though I was aware he had been wavering. One item that has swayed him is that he has become terrified of flying after a ghastly flight in a French plane when everyone screamed.

A glorious day with sun and blue sky has drawn me into the square garden. A hideous but somehow appealing tiny tot approached me, and later I talked to the negress in charge, who had the sweetest smile. I mean to see no one except the rest of my orchestra, and plot out my summer with pencil and paper.

### May 15th

I was invited by Sonia to a farewell dinner for Janetta and Jaime, and it has quite knocked me out. All today I have felt limp and apathetic. What was it? Sonia's overexcitement and fuss (not nearly as bad as sometimes), or simply the feeling of *too much* of everything? Certainly too much drink – Champagne before dinner (and choosing whisky I was given a stiff tumbler-full), hock, claret and Château d'Yquem. Quantities and quantities of excellent food. Conversation rather stimulating and good. The sympathetic pear-shaped face of Francis Bacon was crumpled into general geniality. The white and black cubistically-designed head of Lucian Freud was very much less sympathetic, and Julia was indignant because he talked to her about the responsibilities of marriage, as if he had ever shown the faintest awareness of them. Poor Julia looked frail and tottery, as if she hardly knew how to bear any of it, and indeed told me on the telephone next day that she had 'hated every moment of it'. I sat between Jaime, who turned his sparkling gaze often towards Julia, and Sonia. Towards the end of the meal her gasps and unfinished sentences and overemphasis began filling the room with invisible steam.

Immediately after dinner Lucian and Francis went off to meet Princess Margaret at Anne Fleming's, so they said, and Julia set off

---

[1]   House of his grandfather, Hilaire Belloc, in Sussex.

home. Janetta, Jaime and I prepared to settle for a gossip with Sonia, but she showed us in no uncertain terms that she wanted us to go. So go we did.

## May 21st: The Slade

The horrible wintry cold has literally preserved the incredibly fresh greenery as if in a frigidaire; as Julian said on the telephone it looks like 'green snow'. The famous view from the Slade made one gasp with its brilliance, the green elms in the foreground, backed by the tender brown oaks and a mist of bluebells in the woods. Clouds were driven through the pale forget-me-not sky by a shrivelling north-east wind.

We gardened feverishly. Eardley and Mattei returned from a shopping expedition with boxes and boxes of plants and shrubs, so that new beds had to be quickly dug by Eardley, and the white roots of creeping buttercups cast aside, while I followed him, hastily hurling the wretched little plants into the inclement earth. I felt like a murderess, and thought of them as refugees.

On Sunday we lunched with Charlotte Bonham Carter, whose ugly grey Gothic house stands on the brink of a beautiful and dramatic valley. She had collected quite a lunch party – the deaf man on my right turned out to be George Wansborough; we talked of Cambridge and many mutual friends. I had also a very unprepossessing female magistrate with a passion for opera, and a Polish lithographer with a beautiful silver-haired wife. Before lunch we circulated like characters in a dream in the tall, dark, cold drawing-room, admiring the flower arrangements, and were then shepherded on to the terrace. Charlotte Bonham Carter is said to be very rich, but mean; thimblefuls of sherry stood all ready poured out and a cold collation followed. She expends herself, however, in friendly enthusiasm – 'My *dears*, isn't this nice?' she keeps saying in a tone of incredulity; and one can't help admiring her dauntless courage in going off to Turkey all alone, travelling in buses and sleeping in cockroach-infested and filthy inns. If she is slightly absurd, she is also a character, and full of spirit.

## May 23rd

Janetta's departure day. I am glad for her sake; she is longing to get back, and says she has hated London.

Julia came last night bringing Carrington's letters. Oh, the muddle

113

she's in! Her attempt to sort them had not even reached the stage of putting pieces of the same letter together, much less getting them in order. The drawings chiefly of cats and Carrington herself in varying moods and attitudes are simply delightful. I tried to encourage her, but felt all the time she would never do it.

## May 25th

8.15 a.m. In my small snow-white bedroom at Kitty West's, breakfast eaten. Outside in the luscious, bright green garden are festoons of clematis, and apple blossom in its charming prime, but all swaddled in damp mist from last night's heavy rain. Through it comes the tentative chirrup and whistle of innumerable birds.

Waking at five, I was carried away on a stream of confused and unhappy thoughts. Oh brutal abstention of sleep, when one desires its poultice so passionately! I put on the light and read about Tolstoy – the torments of his life didn't assuage my own rather Russian feeling of pointlessness and precariousness, nor my seeing very clearly like a tiny picture at the wrong end of a telescope the utter spuriousness of life without mutual love and companionship. I can't and won't admit friendship to be base currency; it is as good as gold. Only, only, only – to live on it alone is like trying to live with money in one's pocket and no food to buy with it.

Only Kitty and Caroline are here. I looked at Caroline last night, as she sat by the fire folded up on herself like some elegant insect and with her small, finely-sculptured head shaking slightly as she talked, and longed to make contact with her.

To drinks with Jimmy and Tanya Stern and on to dinner with Billy Henderson and Frank Tait. Jimmy Stern is a professional talker; he was allotted to me, and we both I think enjoyed our *paso doble*. In Billy and Frank's cottage, china and glass ornaments stood in serried rows on every shelf among vases and vases of flowers, wild and tame, whose petals kept falling with a gentle plop in the warm room, while an argument began about violence – protagonists Frank and me. I always see the other person's side afterwards when the light of battle has died down, so that I think such arguments are valuable. At the time I thought it unreasonable of Frank to see no difference between the present cult of physical violence (in films, books, crime, etc.) and the violence he sees in the fact that there are still people being 'obliged to' do so-called 'menial' jobs. Indeed I don't see why cleaning shoes, which he took as an example, is more violent than translating. And I do not think it is violent of the Spaniards to allow men to earn their living being *limpia botas*.

## *May 27th: London*

A long talk about France[1] on the telephone with Robert who has just been there. He found it depressing on the whole. The students and the workers really hate one another. There seems small doubt that de Gaulle will get a *non* next month, but meanwhile what? Robert had talked to a lot of students; some talked sense, some complete rubbish. They have fitted up the Odéon as a dressing-station, with operation tables ready for the next riot. I am aware of a certain excitement at the thought of ideas and ideals suddenly becoming more important than everyday money-grubbing, but it does look as though (just as in 1789) idealism will soon give way to personal greed and this awful, awful thirst for violence. Why do people resist the idea of there being 'waves' or phases of such things as violence? Human beings *en masse* do not develop at a steady pace and crowds are as moody as individuals. States of mind are as infectious as measles.

It is hot. Summer has suddenly arrived. I have been dropping and breaking things all day, and feel humiliated. As Gerald says in today's fat letter, 'Any day may bring disaster. One is threading the minefields all the time.'

## *May 31st*

My dropping and bungling produced in the end a reasonably good dinner for Wynne, Kitty and Julian (the Kees backed out). And conversation didn't flag. Julian stayed on for a few minutes and described the way he spent his time and the exhaustion it produced. For talking is an immense expense of energy and he is becoming an almost professionally brilliant talker.

[1]   Season of serious student riots.

News from Bunny that Angelica has arrived in London. 'How did she seem?' I asked. 'Very friendly to me personally, but somehow *cold* – an ice maiden. It was what happened to Vanessa, but much later in her life. She's completely submerged in her feeling for George [Bergen] and has taken on all his views and values *en bloc*. Yet she says he may well "not want her back".' I asked Bunny where Henrietta and Sophie were – he didn't know.

## June 5th

The eve of departure for the new world of Austria. Packing and heaping are soul-destroying forms of pseudo-organization.

Last weekend I was at the Lees-Milnes. It was a relief to arrive into the beauty of grey stone and green countryside. Jim has achieved what he most desires – I could see no sign anywhere of the modernity he detests. Not very good news that L. P. Hartley was coming to dinner – I had just been reading a letter of his, almost obscenely attacking Leonard because he had written a fairly crushing review of Cynthia Asquith's diaries. Hartley suggested that Leonard was 'senile' if he couldn't appreciate her brilliance, pitched into all Bloomsbury for being malicious and pacifist among other things, and ended with complete irrelevance that Virginia was a crashing snob and had neither wit nor humour but a certain effective cruelty in conversation. 'As Lord Oxford justly said, *The Voyage Out* is a second-rate novel about second-rate people.' This letter made me feel reluctant to see him again. Alvilde later contributed a story of how he had told her, 'giggling and squirming', how he had murdered a swan which behaved aggressively to him when he was taking his forty-minute daily row, given it secconal in pellets of bread and finally buried it alive. I can hardly believe this, but I must say when taxed with it he didn't deny it.

Tea on the lawn as in a past age, silver kettles, swooping white doves; Alvilde's garden is a creation of great beauty and permeated by her love and care for her often rare and unusual plants. With Hartley came a whimsical and ageless spinster who had lived and worked with both Cynthia Asquith and Vita Sackville-West, and was ready to quote Verlaine at the drop of a hat, her brown eyes shining with excitement. Leslie was not hostile to me as I had half-expected, quite the reverse. But I felt his '*Dear* Frances' and two-handed grasp were insincere, and that there is both malignity and cruelty inside that shapeless organism. At dinner Jim was asking me about Holroyd and discussing the exact social status of the Stracheys – upper-middle, or lower-upper class. (What does it matter?) Hartley weighed in about his letter attacking Leonard. I thought I'd let him know I'd read it, and said (I think), 'Yes, you *were* pretty fierce.' He returned to all his points with a look on his face like a savage old dog mumbling a bone. I said: 'I wonder if you'll get an answer out of Leonard?' LPH: 'Well, I've kept one shot in my locker; I shall say "at least he ought to know what it's like living with a maniac."' F: 'That, it must be said, is something Leonard has never shirked facing with the utmost reality and dignity.'

Through the weekend we had sweet, drowsy, bumblebee weather. I walked round and round the garden, sniffing at newly-opened roses, looking at the enormous blooms of the tree peony with its great single pinkish-white petals, blotched with black.

Yesterday I rang up Angelica and had a long conversation. I asked her if she could come and see me; no, she said, because she was cleaning out her studio. How long would she be with us? She didn't know. If George [Bergen] joined her she might stay longer, but this wasn't certain, and if he didn't she would go back. In a rush: 'He's the most extraordinary person I ever met in my life, and totally unlike anyone else.' I asked her about America. 'Oh, you ought to go, Frances; it's really amazing. In many ways I like it better than England.' F: 'What excites you about it so much?' A: 'There seems to be a fresh wind blowing through it all. Here it's so stuffy. Even the air and the climate are better. And then New York is so beautiful. Of course it's less civilized, but I don't know how much civilization matters.' I said I gathered there was a good deal more violence, and I didn't like the idea of that at all. She admitted this, and mentioned two cases of violence towards blacks.

## June 6th

Writing in the air terminal, sitting on a black leather Goebbels sofa, trying to breathe deeply. I am agitated at having failed to get any reply from Julia on the telephone last night or twice this morning. Also because Robin Campbell gave 'a very bad report' of her Whitsun weekend with them. He said, 'She's almost mad with fussiness and pills. She must pull herself together, Frances!' accusingly – a new line from him.

Yesterday evening Julian, Georgia and Henrietta came to dinner. I give the prize to Georgia, whose appearance and talk were simply splendid. Julian, perhaps tired by the end of the evening, struck me as more irrational than usual, and when he said that parents '*must* love *all* their children', all three females pounced on him and said this couldn't be done to order. Julian: 'Then why did they have them?' Henrietta: 'To give tangible expression to their love for their mate.' All this arose out of Tolstoy. I'm left by Troyat's book about him feeling that he was a volcano ceaselessly erupting torrents of lava, which might take the form of masterpieces or of absurdity. But I do not feel that the tragedy of his marriage was all his fault.

Talk of violence followed naturally on the horrific news of the shooting of Robert Kennedy. Serge had been talking to Julian in praise of violence, and amalgamating it in his philosophy of life. A friend of Julian's saw Hartley's letter attacking Leonard in the *Listener* office and said, 'You *can't* print that – it's the letter of a madman!' Leonard has written an admirably restrained reply. Georgia had stuck up for Bloomsbury standards against the aristocracy in a house full of them (including Diana Cooper). I felt too disintegrated by departure to take a strong line in the conversation, and sat back enjoying the enviable vitality of youth.

(Airborne) I met Margaret and Lionel in the inferno of the airport. They only just got there in time and Margaret described to me how Lionel had had a worrying symptom – 'an artery in his leg partly blocked'. He is going to meet his Polish girl before he joins us in Vienna, but at the last moment blamed Margaret 'for not refusing to let him'. Robert Kennedy has died – a good thing, as he was terribly damaged, poor fellow. We have put down at Munich – very hot – but remained on the tarmac, and are now off again through dense cloud to Klagenfurt, where I suppose I shall suddenly awake to reality, whatever that may be.

## June 7th

Our Vanguard banked steeply into the green valley of Klagenfurt. Then we were down and it was a warm, faintly sunny afternoon, with no wind and signs of recent heavy rain. A young man in a car (the hotel chef it seemed) met us and drove us thirty-five kilometres to our destination. Coasting along the opposite shore of Ossiachersee, he pointed out our pension peeping coyly from between two curtains of conifers. These enemies are everywhere, dense, stifling, with tall straight trunks. The moderate-sized mountains are blanketed and woolly with them, and with villages like the toy sets you buy at the Christian Aid shop in Sloane Street dotted below, made up a tame, smugly domestic landscape. Where is the wild and beautiful Carinthian country spoken of by visitors to the Bromovskys? It's not at all what I like, but I feel friendly towards its soothing, unfrightening peace and even its slight absurdity. The lady of the hotel speaks excellent English, and my dread of not having a room to myself was unnecessary. We have two single rooms. Mine is a tiny cupboard, reached by a rustic ladder at the back of the house; it has no window at all, so one must either keep the door open, or shut it and breathe through the slits in it, as I do at night. Except for a Canadian in the adjoining cupboard, all our fellow guests are youngish, jolly, Austrian married couples with good cars. Margaret came back from wandering among the pines, saying she had found an orchid, and the bathing place just below the hotel (whose lawn slopes rapidly to the lake).

After the rain the pines give off a wonderful smell. Aeroplane whisky, a good dinner and early to bed in a state of placid relaxation, as I thought, but not a bit of it. Electric antennae seemed to be radiating from my brain, piercing the woods and going right across Europe to Munich and London. Cars came noisily home and parked under my 'window'. After that the nightingales got going and I remained tortured with wakefulness for many, many long hours.

### June 8th

When we arrived we felt the water of the lake and it was so warm we thought of bathing. I wish now we had, for next morning low clouds were straggling in the wool of the mountain, and though breakfast was laid on the terrace, big drops began to fall. A hideous, dark, damp Alpbach day. We set off to walk to the village of St André. At times Margaret talks compulsively about her matrimonial situation: Lionel rang her up last night. Dunyusha[1] is taking him to some mountain place, a sort of Polish St André. No mention of her husband. At dinner poor Margaret asked me: 'Would you call what

[1] The Polish young woman with whom Lionel was having an affair. He was to visit her while I kept Margaret company in Carinthia.

I'm feeling jealousy?' After lunch we struck up a *wanderweg* among the pines in intermittent rain. The red spots on their trunks looked like fresh grazes on a child's knee, and the pleasure in following them is very childish too. The vegetation was exciting and I brought back a harvest of flowers. Our walk took us to one of the landing stages further up the lake, whence we chugged delightfully back in the little lake steamer.

As usual after only a couple of days I can't help trying to sum up this Austrian ambience and I do not really like or anyway greatly respect it. There's something too smug, simple-minded and childish in their attitude to life, their wooden houses, their uncritical jollity, their stupid way of going about in low-necked, cotton peasant dresses with puffed sleeves when it's cold enough for thick sweaters. Reading about Vienna in Ilse Barea, I learn for the first time about 'Biedermeier' and recognize it. Yet this sweetness must all be too good to be true, for nearly every famous Austrian in her book seems to have committed suicide; so there is obviously some desperate non-facing of the black side of life. I'm sure they are sensual, but in a healthy Bedalian sort of way. As it is cold, a roaring fire was lit last night under the hunting-horn in the dining-room. Afterwards tables drew together and there was noisy talk, loud laughter and card-playing. Margaret and I retired to her room. She told me this morning that she sat up until after four last night writing a not-to-be-posted letter to Lionel in an attempt to discharge her feelings. 'Were they feelings of anxiety, indignation or just pain?' I asked, and I think she said, 'All three.' She returns to Lionel's rankling remark as they parted: 'Why didn't you prevent my going?' I told her it was just a magic ritual – like throwing salt over one's shoulder – to get away from guilt by throwing it on to her.

### June 9th

I didn't quite realize to what an extent I was once more in for a propping-up operation (I only hope it is effective), nor how profoundly rattled Margaret is by this escapade of Lionel's.

I was woken this morning at seven-thirty by torrential rain beating itself into the ground, and it hasn't given me cheerful thoughts. At the moment I really hate this ugly, demure, cold, wet country.

Yesterday we took a *wanderweg* that winds steeply uphill through the close-set bars of the conifer trunks to the ruined castle at the top where there is a bar and restaurant. My travelling companion is extremely good-natured and easy-going, but slightly competitive about the German language and walking, at neither of which she shines. Today I thought of Julia's description of her 'stumping rapidly about with a perfectly blank face'. It was indeed blank today, with misery and preoccupation and the hangover from a sleeping-pill. I feel dreadfully sorry for her.

### June 12th

Today we go to Vienna. Margaret is worrying desperately about Lionel, who has been in Poland five days now, and regulations don't allow more than ten – 'half-time' as she says. But she's a prey to gloomy forebodings, and veers from the belief that Dunyusha is madly in love with Lionel to the idea that it is all some fantastic political plot. 'What does he *see* in her, I want to know?' Her outpourings are repetitive but also truly pitiful, and I listen and listen and listen, and try to think of something comforting to say, such as reminding her that he has telephoned once and sent a telegram since he went. She thought the telegram 'might have been sent by Dunyusha'. I've been wondering whether I ought to say that Lionel is behaving monstrously, but though I am deeply sorry for her sufferings – and they are worse than I expected – I don't really think he is. She says I'm more 'detached' than any of her friends. Given the opportunity, I would, I think, be prepared to tell him how very much she minds, but she is in a state not far from persecution mania.

### June 13th: Vienna

7.30 a.m. in my large double room.

It's much warmer here, clear blue sky. But when we arrived, there were no letters or messages from Lionel. Margaret exploded. I'm by now too bewildered to know whether her fuss and outcry is justified; but one might as well say: 'Is a person justified in screaming when his leg is broken?' She's in agony. 'How can he do it? I can't understand it! He must be a *fiend*.' Or 'What's she up to, I want to know? I think she's a bitch. Yes, that's what she is I believe, a *bitch*!' Her irrationality at those moments is rather a surprise and leaves me at a

121

loss how to respond. To a Mozart concert in the courtyard of one of the houses where he had lived. A sunny fresh morning – *great* pleasure.

## June 14th

Got home from the concert to find Frau Professor Weiniger, an elderly female anthropologist, deafer even than Margaret, with a level, pale blue gaze that reminded me of Alix. She had come to settle about Lionel's lecture, and came with us to one of the old-style Viennese cafés, where most people were reading the papers or drinking small cups of coffee. One can get all sorts – I like *Mocca braun* which is strong with a little cream. Margaret characteristically plumps for wishy-washy *mélange*. As she says, 'Our tastes in food are different.' She is violently attracted by the tinned soups and plastic plates of egg or tunny salad soused in vinegar to be got in the self-service establishments. I can hardly swallow them and am longing for a meal of hot meat and two veg.

On to look at the Karlskirke, and on our return home found news – hurrah – from Lionel that he will return on the Sunday aeroplane, or 'by the night train if there is fog'. Margaret snoozed out of sheer relief until it was time for our evening's outing. A great deal of walking through the old town and past the university to the Maria Treu church for another concert. I find that my plastic meal can be humanized by a *viertel* of red wine, always quite good. I sat gazing into the high domed roof painted with swirling figures among clouds shaped like diving hippopotami and upside-down cupids, while the organ filled the vast space beneath with booming Bach, Telemann and Frank Martin, supported by a flautist. I have never liked those liquefying, overlapping reverberations of sound made by an organ, specially in so large and resonant a building, and I wasn't greatly moved by the music. We walked home past the floodlit buildings of the Ringstrasse – the two museums and the House of Parliament. The delightful feeling of getting to know Vienna is now well under way.

What will it be like when Lionel joins us? When I said to Margaret that I was longing for a 'hot meat meal', she replied, 'We'd better have it before Lionel arrives; he doesn't like meat.' F: with some indignation, 'Well, *he* needn't eat it!' I'm keeping an entirely open mind as to whether or no I go on with them to Prague, according to how our triangular stay works. If I don't go with them I think I'll stay here bravely alone over the weekend as an experiment and then fly home.

## June 15th

Margaret often describes herself as a manic-depressive and Lionel as a paranoic, but I don't really accept this glib classification. Brilliant weather and hot; we took a tram to Schönbrunn and spent most of the day there – very, very enjoyable. The only trouble was getting away from the terrible red-faced tourists, who surged through the enormous rooms and could be seen advancing on the palace, wave after wave of them, like an army assaulting a citadel, through the main gates and across the vast courtyard. How little remains in the mind! The Duke of Reichstadt's rooms, the iron bed in which Franz Josef died, were human and literary sights, but certainly best of all from the visual point of view was a suite of rooms on the ground floor, painted with birds, flowers and fruit, and as charming as anything I ever saw of the kind; almost empty of tourists, too.

*Trovatore* was on at the opera house that evening. Should we queue for possible returns? Here we had a bit of luck, for when we were scouting round to see what hope there was we met a stout lady trying to sell two quite good tickets in the front row of the balcony. McCracken was Manrico as at Covent Garden. Pitch dark pretentious decor. I find that Margaret lives in terror of dropping asleep on such occasions, but she didn't, and I think was interested but slightly appalled. As we came out she said: 'So you like that sort of thing better than Mozart?' 'Of course not!' I said, irritated by this form of eclectic idolatry which allows one star only in the artistic firmament.

## June 16th

Yesterday began badly. Poor Margaret came into my room waving a telegram and saying in a quavering voice that Lionel was *not* coming by air on Sunday after all (he had his ticket) but on the night train, thus missing Haydn's *Creation* on Sunday evening, which he loved and had been particularly keen to hear. She had wired to him that we had a ticket for him. She was hysterical and distraught. 'Shall I wire again?' F: 'But what could you say?' 'Simply "You bloody old fool"?' she said with a laugh, but then fired off all the explosive charges she had in her locker. 'What does he *see* in her? He's just a silly old *man*. He's *seventy*!' The mention of fog in his previous telegram aroused Margaret's suspicion at the time, and I do now see it must have been some sort of preparation for this delay, for the weather maps indicate that there's as brilliant June weather in Poland as here. Vienna is having a heat wave, brilliantly sunny with a light breeze. It has really been awful to witness poor Margaret's agony. She laughed as she told me that she once before, in the middle of the night, sent him a telegram saying, 'Silly old man'. I tried to persuade her it was useless to send off any more telegrams, for it would be too late to alter his plans. He should now be back at crack of dawn on Monday (tomorrow).

All day yesterday she was a prey to sudden glooms and hysterias, rushed to the whisky bottle, finished it off, bought more, rang Frau Professor Weiniger to see if she would come to the *Creation* on Lionel's ticket and failed to get her. There have also been letters and telephone calls from the Czechs who want him to lecture in Brno and Prague. I suggested she left Lionel to sort this out himself, and perhaps reap the reward of his delay, for his professional life is very important to him. I try all the time to reassure her, but persecution mania is very infectious and I begin to feel doubtful of my power to judge the true situation and am secretly terrified of something going wrong when I should have a serious case on my hands. Still, I do really believe he will turn up safe and sound tomorrow morning.

Later to another church concert – Haydn's *Nelson Mass*. As we sat in physical agony in the torturously uncomfortable pews, with our backs to the source of the music in the organ loft, we seemed like a bed of reeds through which a tide was flowing. It gave me a fellow-feeling for the man sitting beside me to see that he was gently swaying or shifting in that tide. (I'm not really drawn to those who take up an austerely motionless position when listening to music, nor yet who sit as if cogitating a problem.) Then he made a silent but pretty bad fart, and at once took off his spectacles, as if with an impulse to disguise himself, which I could easily understand. If Lionel doesn't arrive tomorrow, what then? Margaret is getting up to meet his train at 7.40 a.m. at the station. All her obsessions on the subject have been repeated so often today that I could think of nothing new to say in reply.

We've had a very hot Sunday. In the evening the magnificent *Creation*. We were in the front row just above the orchestra and had a splendid view of Joseph Krips's fat face coaxing what he wanted out of his soloists, with an expression like someone trying to cajole a smile out of a baby in its pram.

## June 17th

8.15 a.m. I heard Margaret's voice shouting loudly to the girl receptionist. With my breakfast came a note she had left for me that has left me simply gasping. She wrote: 'I'm so afraid Lionel may not be on this train. Perhaps someone used his passport on the plane yesterday. One of us should go to the embassy. Just *supposing* I am prevented from coming back here from the station . . .' and she went on to give dates and numbers of passports and visas, addresses of friends in Warsaw, etc., and ends, 'Here are the two phoney telegrams.' Why phoney?

9.15. Lionel has just arrived looking bronzed, happy and not a day over forty-five. He was delayed by a slight collision on the Polish railway. Goodness, it might easily have been worse.

## June 18th

Not only did Lionel's arrival give the lie to Margaret's different fantastic theories – I see her wild letter was written at 5.30 a.m. – but he is entirely in command of everything, and has rung up institutions and fixed lectures and seminars with complete efficiency. (Margaret had told me she always had to do this, and that he was entirely dependent on her. She also said that she had to do all the German talking, but Lionel speaks quite well and Margaret is almost worse than I am, with only two sentences: 'Bitte, wo ist . . .' or 'Bitte, haben Sie . . .') Lionel has obviously been rejuvenated by having a wonderful time with his girl, whereas poor Margaret is exhausted by jealousy and persecution mania and looks quite done for; she almost dropped asleep over lunch in the Café Mozart, and briefly did drop off in the opera last night. I commented on Lionel's efficiency. 'Oh yes, he always gets what he wants.' But he has of course been lively interesting company, and is full of stories about Vienna in the 20s, when he was here with Frank Ramsey,[1] Adrian Bishop and others, and wants to do what they all did then – eat *eierspeize* and drink beer in cafés and go to the gallery of the opera house.

[1] The Cambridge philosopher.

I thought I'd leave Lionel and Margaret to settle down together, and went off alone, bought a nice pair of yellow sandals, and booked my ticket home today week. I've definitely decided not to go with them into Czecho for those few days.

Now Lionel is here I lose the heavy feeling of responsibility for Margaret and return to a pleasant lone-wolfery.

*Don Carlos* last night – adored by me, interesting to Lionel, and confusing to Margaret.

## June 19th

It gets hotter and hotter. I can go stockingless in my new sandals and wear a thin cotton frock. Penroses still deep in plans. This morning I told Margaret I was going to the art gallery and she met me there. Among the superb collection of Titians, Velázquez and Rembrandts, I was moved to see Ralph's 'favourite picture in the whole world' – Tintoretto's *Susanna*. I lunched alone out of doors in the park, having the almost invariable meal of omelette and salad, with *apfelsaft*. Omelettes are specially good here, *baveuse* within and crisp without, stuffed with pieces of bacon.

Afterwards I walked and walked in the heat – how one walks in this town! I wandered through the Hofburg and its library, and into a church where I found myself gazing at the row of pewter mugs containing the hearts of the Hapsburgs – the Duke of Reichstadt's is a very small one. I am trying to get a seat to see Jurinac as Mimi in *Bohème* on Sunday night.

In the evening with Margaret to hear Lionel lecture to a learned and deeply interested gathering about chromosomes. Enthralling. It seems that a man who has two or more, instead of only one X chromosome, is definitely more prone to violence and aggression than normal men, while a woman with two or more X chromosomes is merely stupider than usual. So masculinity = aggression, femininity = stupidity. He showed us slides of abnormal ridge-formations on the hands and soles of the feet, associated with genetic aberrations like mongolism. The lecture hall was electric with attention and with loud creaks from the wooden benches, when anyone shifted their bottom. A Japanese (or Chinese?) sat in the front row taking notes assiduously. Vienna is full of them. Afterwards questions were asked. When all was over people crowded round Lionel.

Margaret touchingly said today that she wanted to pay for the seats she had ordered from England 'because I'd been so kind'. Of course I won't let her, but it makes me regret my criticisms of her. This morning in the art gallery she explained her delusions – as they now seem – about Polish plots, by saying: 'You see, it's such a relief to me if I can think Dunyusha is plotting and scheming. I'm sure you can understand that.' And of course I could.

After the lecture we went to look in vain for Freuα´s house in the Berggasse. Later, an enormous walk in the dark to places connected with Lionel's early life in Vienna,[1] all round the old town, through streets of portentously tall houses, under bridges, up steps. Lionel was being psychoanalysed at that time for bed-wetting, so Margaret told me later. Having heard this I naturally saw the course on which he led us in symbolical terms. Down a deep sunken street called Tief Graben (Deep Trench) under a bridge and towards the Hohe Market. 'I'm always dreaming about Vienna,' he said as we walked along, 'and in my dream there's always somewhere I'm trying to get to. Now I realize that it's here.' When we found a large fountain in full operation in the middle of the marketplace, it seemed too good to be true. Lionel is very much in the saddle, and, far from expecting Margaret to make all the arrangements, a little inclined to criticize hers.

### June 20th

The Penroses bicker a good deal. I dare say it is the mere easing of surface tensions, and better ignored. This morning's plan (Lionel's) was to go by tram to the little spa of Baden, where there were associations with Beethoven and Mozart and pleasant woods to walk in. We were to meet at the hotel at eleven. Lionel appeared but no Margaret. Later she too turned up and all day long they were both referring to the monstrous way the other had gone off and got lost without a word at the Mozart museum. Margaret said to me: 'You see how he goes on as if I didn't exist? Just as he only got one ticket to Cornwall when we were both going.' Yet on the other side I've suffered more than once from Margaret's habit of vanishing suddenly and without a word at lightning speed, like a billiard ball rolling across the cloth and disappearing into a pocket. Apparently

[1]  Where he had come to be psychoanalysed – by Freud, I believe.

Lionel accuses her in the middle of the night of wanting him to die, so that she can be a merry widow. I hesitate to take the conventional Freudian interpretation of this – but whatever Dunyusha is like, she certainly makes him happy. He looks much older as well as more harassed and unkempt since he got here. It's true that he often treats Margaret as if she were an imbecile; I think her deafness is partly to blame and this is one reason why I urge her to wear her hearing-aid. She is loth, but makes valiant efforts.

At last we got off to the Baden tram and trundled pleasantly out of the suburbs. It is a charming, unspoilt spa, with a lot of pretty Biedermeier houses, innocently encrusted with curlicues, caryatids and lion's heads. We ate under a sun-umbrella outside one of the sulphur springs.

After lunch we walked up a wooded hill to a café with a view. When we descended it was music time, and in a bandstand where Johann Strauss was once conductor, a string orchestra was playing delightfully in their shirt-sleeves because of the heat. The elderly cure-takers were sitting with programmes, clapping the music under the trees. For once I thought I saw serenity and peace in this picture of old age.

In the train home the heat was ferocious but the country we passed through was bathed in golden evening light, the cornfields like floss silk and the small lakes full of enviable swimmers. I take my fan everywhere and am glad of it.


## June 22nd

Disgustingly wet day. Through the rain to the Harrach gallery, where the only interesting pictures were, as Lionel said, obviously by a lunatic, and toiled up a winding stair in Beethoven's house. Then home to change our wet clothes. Lionel's second lecture was to be given in the evening and Margaret and I had planned a frivolous outing to the Volksoper to hear *Der Zigeuner Baron* by Johann Strauss; this was tremendously jolly and enjoyable, put on with hilarious gaiety and a lavishness that would have livened up *Don Giovanni* (seen last night, seemingly set in a Durham mining village). There were papier mâché elephants and circus animals, wild Hungarian dancers and a whole army advancing on horses that rose and fell like those in a roundabout. When we emerged into the suburban darkness we were amazed to be caught by a slightly tipsy and gay Lionel, swept off to a car and told we were to join the scientists at Grinzing for supper. Our hosts were a very handsome young doctor with dimpled cheeks and his charming wife who had brought a cold collation to eat with the *Heurige* wine. This was served in beer mugs, very cold and delicious. Frau Professor Weiniger levelled her pale eyes at me and sang into my ear some tunes from *Der Zigeuner Baron*, quite inaudibly because of the general hullabaloo that was going on – everyone in the long room was shouting and laughing for all they were worth, some young people holding hands in a ring round their table, swaying and singing drunkenly. The young dimpled doctor admitted that Freud was thought much less of in his native town than in England, and psychoanalysis as a form of therapy was out of favour. I'm much struck by these charming civilized Viennese scientists.

## June 23rd

I have been alone here in Vienna since lunch-time yesterday, when the Penroses took their bus to Brno. I wondered if I should start swooping into that dreadful spiral of loneliness. But no, thank heavens, nothing of the sort. Yesterday morning Margaret and I went to the Spanish Riding School, where a training session of the white horses was going on. All the horses that draw Viennese cabs are white or grey, so I imagine they move on when too old for this highly-skilled performance. I took the opportunity to tell Margaret that I thought she needn't really worry; that Lionel was deeply devoted to her *au fond*, and quite incapable of dastardly behaviour. Also that I thought the well-meaning friends who tried to alarm her about Dunyusha's schemes were not doing her a service. I saw them go with sadness and great affection. Then off to my room to plan the rest of my time. A sort of intoxication came over me at being on my own in this capital city. I can manage the language sufficiently well to get by, and feel I now know Vienna rather better than London. The fine weather has returned. To Prince Eugen's two splendid baroque palaces – the Upper and Lower Belvedere, joined by a sloping garden of fountains and statues. Both house collections of paintings and statues in their magnificently ornate rooms.

## June 24th

In the morning I walked for hours, right up to the Danube canal, back to the old university, and several churches and Prince Eugen's winter palace.

My seat for *Bohème* was in the front row of the gallery rather at the side. I laid my head on the red plush rim and saw pretty well and shed tears at the end. Next to me was a young man helping repair his girl's make-up, as I walked off to Sachers for supper and a slice of their famous *torte*.

## *July 8th: London*

The months ahead stand like a lump of clay waiting to be moulded into something tractable. I think I shall go to Cyprus with the Hills, but not to Majorca with Mary and the Tycoon nor to the South of France with the Jarvises. This evening Tom[1] rang up to ask me to the Lakes: of course I am gratified by these extremely kind offers. There being no valid reason why I shouldn't accept them all makes it more difficult to decide. Yet I don't want to rattle to and fro like a ping-pong ball.

Henrietta and Sophie have been twice to see me. They were in London to visit Angelica. Sophie looks tall, a little thin, composed. The first time she came she was very good and absorbed herself in various activities. The second time I was harassed by work and a migraine, took them out to the café next door, and she was fractious and whiney. But on the whole I think the extraordinary life they have been leading is fairly all right for her, and certainly it makes Henrietta happier. She talked a lot about their caravanserai[2] and the principles they live by – four young men and Henrietta and Sophie in a big tent, with five horses and a cart. They move about, dressed in romantic clothes, cooking on wood fires, looking after their horses, a goat and a dog. They believe in non-violence, 'being good and kind' (hurrah, I said), are *almost* vegetarians. Things began to acquire pluses and minuses as I talked to her: animals and nature plus; cars minus; spirits minus 'but I've introduced them to wine'. What about marijuana? I expect so. Thank heavens flying saucers, and attendant mumbo-jumbo is out for Henrietta at least. She wanted to talk about

[1] My brother.
[2] Of hippies, headed by Mark Palmer.

Mark Palmer's extraordinarily gentle and sweet character, 'he's as near a saint as anyone I've met.'

Last weekend I went to see Alix and collected Carrington's last diary from her. She had just read it and thought Noel should do as he liked with it, 'because it reflected nothing but credit on her and on Lytton'. I would have loved to have stayed longer at Lords Wood – there's always so much to talk about with Alix. Then on to the Carringtons, where Noel, Catharine and I all read it. I found I remembered it pretty well. Catharine was so upset by it that she had a sleepless night twenty-four hours after reading it. I wondered if it was partly the shock of finding herself coldly described, as 'dim'. But of course the finale is desperately moving. There can be few descriptions so lucid and so harrowing of committing suicide, yet she wrote it all faithfully down; then came the horrible return to life to see Lytton die, and then the no man's land shadowed by her obvious determination to do it again. Noel came down to breakfast on Sunday with the plan that a collected edition of her letters should be published. Would I do it, he went on to say? I made a number of excuses, and then said I couldn't face plunging into the past for several years. He understood this and accepted it, saying he felt the same. He suggested Bunny, and perhaps that's a probability.

Reading about Beakus Penrose and the pain he had caused poor Carrington by his wooden insensitivity, telling her for instance, 'You see, I don't find you sexually attractive,' when she was in despair because of being older than him, I remembered him as he was, 'just a Figuerhead [sic] after all' as she wrote, not the intelligent and charming character Lionel and Margaret like to make him out.

### July 10th

Under a pitch-black sky to the private view of a huge Matisse show at the new gallery on the South Bank. Their confidence, simplicity, and concentration gave my spirits an enormous lift. They intoxicate and overwhelm, yet so completely focus his view of the world that painting seems to be something entirely for the painter and not the looker. After talking to Cyril, Robin and Susan, I came face to face with Angelica looking radiant and beautiful, and she has promised to come and have dinner with me.

Since coming back from Austria I have been translating under

131

more and more pressure, aware that everything else was getting forgotten and pushed aside.

## July 15th

My work is packed off. I've bought my ticket to Cyprus. I feel too idle to think or write. Last night Angelica came and we had a delightful and most interesting evening. Would she mind, I wondered, that I'd asked no one else? Would she think I was trying to 'pump' her? I took the bull by the horns therefore and said I found one never talked to anyone if there were a lot of people and I had very much wanted to see her. Then we started off on various impartial subjects, Matisse, etc., thence to Henrietta's plans and only over dinner did we come round to Bergen. (Bunny barely mentioned, as it were *en passant*.) She talked most freely and humanly, and I was much touched, as one always is by that generosity that opens and reveals a person's inner feelings. And I take back everything about ice-maidens. I even think she has lost some of that disturbing quality in the furnace of her affair with Bergen. The training given by a pure Bloomsbury background – a training I would say that ultimately conduces to honesty, directness and of course utter disregard of *idées reçues* – has stood her in good stead, even if it sent her blinkered into the sort of annexe to Bloomsbury that Hilton was. I was again astonished by her courage in going off to Bergen. She seemed to be amazed by it herself. Said she hadn't known him at all; he was a perfect stranger. I tried to detect some antibodies to his influence produced by return to England – I don't think there are any. She says she will stay till October, 'perhaps longer'. She wants to go back to New York, loves it, and yet, and yet, she talks of getting a separate studio from Bergen so that they shan't live on top of each other. She is clearly still under his spell, thinks him an 'extremely remarkable person, who has in some way been torn apart by his mixed blood' (he is part Russian, part Spanish). 'Unhappy?' I asked. She weighed it. 'Yes, certainly unhappy.' I have strongly the feeling that being a realistic and intelligent person, she has not in the least been warped by this disturbing experience. It has merely had the effect of causing her to go through a delayed process of maturing. Although she is fifty, her hereditary and acquired characteristics have enabled her to weather it without getting embittered.

### July 17th

The training given by Bloomsbury – I think about it a lot. It has indeed come rather into the public eye as a result of a number of things. Miss Hamil[1] came to see me the other day and I gave her Lytton's letters to Ralph; also a list of people I had letters from asking her which might be worth keeping. Her reply was 'All.' There's something disconcerting about this conversion of human contacts that one has actually been the recipient of into money – flesh and blood into metal. I don't know if it is unrealistic or even sentimental to be disgusted by it.

### July 18th

I think a lot about Cyprus, and slow threads of anticipation like the anchorage of a spider's web seem to be forming.

Just returned from the Kew Herbarium and Mr Meikle the expert on Cyprus – a perfectly charming Irishman, quite young, soft-voiced. He and it beguiled me utterly. The Herbarium, like the Botany Department at South Kensington, is aloof and hermetic and brown. Doors must be unlocked; porters come. Has one an appointment? Will one sign the book? The chief Kew men carry little bleepers in their pockets so that they can be summoned when wanted, but Mr Meikle had gone off without his. Surely these people concerned with adding to human knowledge rather than putting it to practical use are the happiest and kindest of men. Mr Meikle's face was as radiant as Noel Sandwith's used to be. Then what kindness to me, an amateur intruder. While I was waiting, another professional botanist led in a party of visitors, his face wreathed in the almost imbecile smile of distinterested curiosity. But *goodness*, I like, envy and admire them all.

### July 22nd: Thorington Hall

Whence I came on Friday evening with Julia, Lionel and Margaret. All appeared to be going as smoothly as silk, and then, suddenly on Saturday night Julia rounded on me with a swift venom that (temporarily I believe) dissipated my goodwill. She made me aware

---

[1] American dealer in letters etc.

that I must have been appallingly on her nerves *without knowing it* – that is perhaps what is so humiliating. The circumstances are almost too absurd to write down: Julia had spent about three hours of Saturday afternoon behind drawn curtains, lying on her bed, and I took her a cup of tea. She came down about seven with her face very carefully made up, but I think under the influence of her pills, so that her remarks were wider of the mark than usual. Watching the telly she was very irritable with the Penroses for not understanding their own set properly or being sure which network they were on, and I could see that she could hardly sit still, her exacerbation was so great. A tiny thing occurs to me – Margaret and I sat side by side with legs outstretched on the sofa to watch a programme recommended by Julia and enjoyed by us all. Twice Julia got up from her armchair and said, 'Do sit here, Margaret; I like a stiff-backed chair.' And twice Margaret said good-humouredly, 'No thanks, I like having my legs up.' Then she drew our attention to an odd face in the background of the telly screen and I said, 'Oh yes, I see; he has got a very low forehead.' Whereupon Julia shot out of her chair and with a really viperish glance almost shouted at me: 'Frances, you're *always* talking about low foreheads.' I said feebly, 'I haven't mentioned them once this weekend.' 'No, not this weekend, but you *always are*.' After a pause, 'That was meant for a joke.' This totally unexpected repetition of an attack she's made on me before (saying that I repeat myself, i.e. am a crashing bore) had a traumatic effect on me, I don't know why. I went to bed but couldn't sleep for love or money. I tossed and turned in more senses than one. That is, I felt like a worm that was at last turning, that could take no more. In the course of my tossing I detached myself from my sense of responsibility for her to such an extent that when morning came my chief idea was to keep out of the way of someone who found me so maddening. I therefore left her and Margaret to go for a walk alone together. And on Monday morning I was forewarned and able to deal with her momentary hostility without the smallest pain. In a second incident, over the breakfast table, Julia asked me a question when my mouth was full. When I answered she said, looking at me sharply: 'I can't hear what you're saying.' 'Perhaps you're getting a little deaf?' I said, having noticed that she was, and heard her say so. 'Oh no, I think it's that you're not talking distinctly.' 'Well, I'm famous you know, for my loud penetrating voice,' I said, and was backed up by Margaret from the larder with 'Frances is the only person I can always hear.'

What interests me is that as I had been so hurt by her Saturday night onslaught I had assumed she must have noticed it. If so she presumably felt I needed a little more correction. I realize that I was absurdly sensitive on the first occasion, but I made up for it by not minding the second in the least.

During my wakeful night I thought of the relish with which she has repeated to me her own bloodcurdling rudeness to Susan Campbell or Cynthia or Philip Toynbee. She is so honest that she admits the pleasure unmixed with guilt this gives her. Reflections resulting from all this: with Julia one must wear some sort of armour. It isn't enough just to keep a guard on one's own tongue as I've tried to do ever since Rome. One must carry about an antidote to snake poison. Of her other victims, how many mind? Cynthia told me the other day that having Julia to stay for five days after Christmas had finished her off. Susan admits she gets a battering but says, 'I give as good as I get,' which is probably the best way to deal with it. Surely she herself must feel poisoned by this heartburn rising within her?

It was a delight to be with Margaret and Lionel and in particular to see Margaret with her round face cloudless and shining. She was quite unpreoccupied and full of talk and fun.

In spite of this miniature crisis the weekend provided a great deal of pleasure – talk, music, jokes, lying on the lawn in the sun. I had a walk with Julia along the charming little stream covered in yellow water-lilies and fringed with willows and tall rustling plants, through which one or two anglers prowled like tigers. She was appreciative of it all, and projected herself into every riverside cottage or village inn. J: 'It's so awful the way one gets no fresh air in London. I can't open my window because of the noise. And I can't bear to go out walking alone.' F:'Couldn't you take walks like a sort of medicine – unpleasant things which make you feel better?' J: 'Oh no, because I've no desire to go out, you see. And then if one goes out alone – or when one used to go out alone – men tried to pick one up.'

While I was sitting reading Anthony Storr on aggression in the lion's roar of the sun yesterday morning, enter a lady doctor aged eighty, wearing a remarkable hat made of thousands of exotic feathers, and warming me by the way she clasped my hand in both hers with spontaneous friendliness. She had come from officiating at an adolescent brains trust, and we sat talking for some time of the young, violence, war, the cosmos. She went to Thailand and Angkor Wat last year, has six children and is a Quaker and a pacifist. 'I might perhaps go to Japan next year.'

## July 23rd

I got home to find four truly welcoming letters from the Hills, pleased with Cyprus, and obviously really keen I should go. They acted as Elliman's embrocation on the bruise left by Julia's nipping beak. So *avanti*. Henrietta and Sophie to lunch, both very sweet, well and brown. Henrietta described how four of them, with horses and cart and Sophie and four dogs, arrived at the house of a perfect stranger at tea one evening, and let loose their horses and dogs on his land before they could find him to ask his leave. His rage seemed incomprehensible to her (he had dogs of his own). 'I must say I wasn't expecting a visit from *four* J.C.'s,' he said (the men were wearing burnouses and beards). 'The devil's more in my line.'

## July 27th: In the aeroplane to Cyprus

Met at the airport with the dreaded words, 'Two hours' delay', and the crowds were appalling. I queued to send a telegram, then among desperate women and children for one of only *five* smelly apertures to pee in, and this only just gave time to queue at the bar for a whisky one minute before it shut. The queueing, excreting, ingurgitating hordes, of which I was one, seemed like souls in hell, yet without any looks of torment on their faces, oddly enough.

Now, aloft in the sky, I am in heaven. The aeroplane is less than half full; little boys are prattling behind me and a baby bouncing in its cot affixed to the luggage rack. The great thing is to realize the complete passivity of flying, and thank God for this inactivity. The voice of our captain keeps hoping we are enjoying ourselves and will have a pleasant holiday.

## July 28th: Kyrenia, Cyprus

Writing next morning I look back on the flight itself as pleasant, easy and dreamlike, with moments of near rapture. Then we were down at Nicosia, among voices jabbering, in Greek? or Turkish? and there was Anne, looking about her from within an unusually long mop of white hair, and Heywood bronzed and beaming, leaning back slightly as he advanced. There was a post office strike, so of course they hadn't got my telegram. Also two of their three servants had left, which sounds like an unmitigated blessing. We drove through the darkness; stopped by a polite Turkish patrol, and soon afterwards we were turning into the gate of Kasaphani House. Anne wanted to postpone every subject so that we could go into it *properly*, a good reason and one I appreciate, but I began to fear they would all be shelved for ever.

## July 30th

Our servant Paraskevi is a nice middle-aged women, swinging a colossal bottom as she walks and carrying a small, neat head proudly erect. I admire the way that without even knowing the Greek alphabet, Anne plunges manfully in, with the aid of notebooks and phrasebooks. Paraskevi only has a few words of English. This interest in the language had infected me, and is part of the absorbed curiosity I feel in a new place. The history – yes, I want to find out about that too, and also something of the Graeco-Turkish situation. On Sunday evening we walked up the lower slopes of the range of tall hills behind us, as far as the first village. One woman replied with a rather reproving 'Gùnayden' (Turkish) to our 'Kalymera' (Greek). I feel despairing of botany as everything is paper-dry and brown, and literally nothing in flower except quantities of the tall, blue, round-headed thistles we used to grow at Ham Spray.

Yesterday, Monday, we went shopping in Kyrenia, a very attractive little port with a huge, pale golden castle sprawling beside it like a Trafalgar Square lion. No Greek–English dictionary to be bought in any of the bookshops! 'We have never been asked for one.' Most of the shop-assistants talk good English, but Cypriots look as if they didn't do much thinking. Looking into the bright grey-green eyes shining startlingly from the faces of George (the travel agent) and his brother (who sells postcards next door) however, I couldn't help feeling they could if they wanted to. There are a good many United Nations soldiers in pale blue caps, blond Canadians or Scandinavians, handsome on the whole but with the consciously virtuous air of school prefects. What must the Cypriots feel about them?

After lunch I sprawl naked and face down on my bed, turn on the electric fan and generally sleep for a short while. Life begins again about four, and the indoor thermometer seems to remain steadily between 80°F and 90°F day and night. Heywood has hired a car from George, the travel agent, and yesterday we drove up to the village of Bellapais and went over its noble abbey. The vast refectory rises sheer from the mountain side and all its windows open onto the plain and sea. Strolled through the charming upper alleys of the village till we got onto the tufted aromatic slopes above it. Women seemed to have clustered up here in their gardens (leaving men as usual in the cafés lower down) and were embroidering and chattering. Children all call out 'Hullo' or 'Bye-bye'. A very handsome Cypriot woman took us onto her roof to admire the view and we longed to know how to say 'How beautiful! How marvellous!', both of which we looked up as soon as we got home. One is impotent without such phrases.

I'm re-reading Durrell's *Bitter Lemons*, between scurries into Greek phrasebooks, English newspapers, guidebooks and postcard-writing.

### *August 1st*

Here we are launched into the month of perhaps most terrific heat. Impossible not to think of it as an enemy, and there was a moment yesterday when I began to dissolve and weaken in it. At the least effort one's body streams with fortunately scentless sweat, and if the car is left in the sun it becomes a red-hot furnace. Our routine is to bathe before breakfast, staggering from bed and returning hardly less dazed to eat bread and black cherry jam and drink Nescafé. If I wake late and bathe during the morning there are other people inhabiting our little beach, and patches of the sea have become actually hot. This absorbs the morning, just as yesterday morning was absorbed by my going with Anne to shop in Kyrenia. The market is cool with fans and far from crowded. Only the English seem to shop there. Where do the peasants buy their food, I wonder?

Paraskevi is delightful, and quite obviously charmed by Anne's friendliness and loud rumbustious laugh. One hears them in the kitchen slowly enunciating words in each other's languages fortissimo as to a deaf person and then suddenly breaking into a gabbled duet in their own. When Anne says 'ξψχαριστώ' ['Thank you'] Paraskevi lays her hand on her bosom and says with feeling, '*Me* ξψχαριστώ' ['*I* thank *you*']. Then there is our comic dog, called 'Pooch' after Mr Behrens[1] although it is female. She is a ludicrous animal, with eyes hidden by fountains of black hair and a crooked smile of apparently false teeth. After making water she points her leg backwards like a ballet dancer.

The thunder-shower has freshened the garden and I went out in the afternoon to pick roses, geraniums and jasmine, but the mere effort of cutting off the dead leaves and arranging them in a vase produced waterfalls of sweat. Later we drove off westwards through Kyrenia and along the coast to the monastery of Lambousa standing alone on the rocky shore. The Byzantine church had an innocently cheerful iconostasis and rickety pulpit.

## August 5th

A gentle day yesterday, ending with supper in a roadside café, off-white Aphrodite wine and a splendid selection of *mezès* (hors d'oeuvres).

On the way home, reeling through the dense thrumming darkness between the headlights of cars, we talked about the sadness of always seeing strong young men in the cafés, in their clean white shirts, tapping their feet to the insidiously sexy music, and no girls. Then Anne, shouting slightly as she endearingly does when drunk: 'But really I think there's something to be said for the system, my dear. The girls are protected and secure, and suitable husbands found for them. I really think Lucy[2] would have preferred it, my dear.' Heywood and I teased her, but not very seriously. Yesterday evening we drove up to St Hilarion castle perched on the highest peak of the range. I wasn't prepared for the state of frozen warfare subsisting up here. The castle and a large part of the range is 'held' – whatever that means – by the Turkish Cypriots, and no Greek is allowed through except if escorted in a convoy by Land Rovers full of UN troops. These tall, handsome, bronzed athletes from Canada, Denmark or Sweden are to be seen everywhere in great numbers, walking or driving about in their pale blue caps. As we climbed to the pass a notice said, 'Welcome to the Free Turkish Zone', and a new sort of

[1] The owner of the house.
[2] Her younger daughter.

face and figure let us through the barrier to the castle. Instead of the very square, strong, black-haired Greeks, these were tall, lazy figures with gentle, amorphous features. Such a one showed us over the sensational Andrew Lang-Gothic castle straggling over the crests. Up steps and steep slopes we panted behind his strong, booted legs, and looked down through light, drifting cloud to Kyrenia far below. On the way home we tried to take a side road to Bellapais, but two talkative UN sentries stopped us, both telling us there was a Greek post there and they wouldn't let us through. They encouraged us to try; tourists could help break down the barriers, and we did, but two very young Greek boys, waving rifles inexpertly and sheepishly, turned us back. I felt outraged by the sheer silliness, and the friendliness of the Turks makes me prefer them to the Greeks.

We plan an excursion to Salamis tomorrow and a night at Famagusta, and this evening we are going to call on a friend of Eddie's[1] at Lapithos along the coast.


### August 7th

Eddie's friend, Dr Paul Wilkinson, wrote that he lived 'the life of a recluse in a shabby old house'. Out to greet us came a lean bearded man, looking like an explorer, with a strong, manly handshake and a prissy, pedantic voice. His house was old, not at all shabby, and very romantic. Low pointed arcades surrounded the cool patio full of plants and a pool; his living-room walls were lined with a magnificent library. We exclaimed and admired and peered at the shelves. He began to bring out rare editions of the classics, incunabula and splendid bindings ('That's rather fun'). 'I was once a bookseller,' said Heywood in his small, soft voice. I thought at first Dr Wilkinson hadn't heard, but he let out later that he knew the shop well. He didn't possess, or anyway would have died rather than reveal, any interest in other people, and resisted our attempts to steer the conversation or get information on subjects like the Graeco-Turk situation. 'Oh yes, it's very tender just there,' he said of our being stopped on the road to Bellapais, and then changed the subject, leaving me with the feeling that he was much more involved than he cared to say.

[1] Gathorne-Hardy, Anne's brother.

## August 9th

Back last night from a much-enjoyed two days' tour, dusty and tired, streaming with sweat and longing for a bath and hair wash, we found a telegram from Sheelah Hill[1] asking Heywood to ring her up that night. Their Aunt Dorothy has been very ill, is over eighty, and we all supposed she had died. Anne and I tried to persuade him not to agree to go home, feeling this was all too likely; but as a result of his angelic kindness and anxiety for Sheelah he returned from the telegraph office in Kyrenia having got through quickly and saying it couldn't be helped: Aunt Dorothy was dying and had asked for him, and John and Sheelah wanted him to fly back at once. He has booked a flight for 1 a.m. tomorrow, only hoping that in the intervening time (today) news of Aunt Dorothy's death might make it unnecessary. While he went to telephone, Anne talked to me about her mother's death in a jerky and deeply felt way. She told me how when she was sitting beside the semi-conscious and slightly restless old lady, she had suddenly sat bolt upright in bed and cried aloud, 'My life! My life!' conveying an anguish at losing it that was acutely painful to Anne. She clasped her mother in her arms and kissed her continuously, saying urgently, but she felt unconvincingly, 'It will be quite all right!' 'But do you *know*?' her mother kept asking. This shattering episode broke poor Anne down completely, but luckily the doctor arrived and took command. Anne retired in floods of tears to sit with Anthony and Eddie and though she heard 'shouts' from her mother's room this was nothing out of the way – she always gave tongue at the least thing. The relief of the whole family on hearing she was dead was very great. All this came out with a characteristic expression of groping among her feelings and memories with a desperate honesty I found extremely touching.

Our two days' tour: early start after seven o'clock breakfast, eastwards along the coast, till we turned south across a desolate, treeless plain bleached white as bone by the heat, and then to the Monastery of St Barnabas where three ancient, rosy, happy priests with long, snowy, fluffy beards were busy painting hideous icons, and reacting like prima donnas to the admiring tourists. They evidently liked having mini-skirted girls bending flirtatiously over their easels. Salamis was only a little further on, and exceeded all our expectations, with its magnificent situation on a wide bay, the

[1] Heywood's sister.

completeness of the Roman theatre and palace, two large and perfect pieces of mosaic and some headless statues with flowing white drapery. The beach was close by, so we bathed before lunch at the outdoor restaurant: Ouzo, quite good white wine with a salty taste, omelette, melon and figs. Local cheese has the consistency of plastic or indiarubber.

It's hard to explain why the old town of Famagusta is so exciting and impressive, for it is in a state of near collapse and might easily seem grim and depressing, entirely enclosed as it is in its medieval mud-coloured walls and bastions. From Othello's tower we watched a display of Turkish wrestlers, looking like marionettes on jerking wires. Nearby a large Venetian lion in golden stone, its smiling face blurred with age, lay like a tame dog at the foot of the wall. Everywhere were the familiar Turkish fatalism and lethargy.

Back to Nicosia, where the division down the middle between Greeks and Turks made a sinister impression. When we began to head home a Greek armed patrol stopped us. We were asking how to get onto the road to Kyrenia and they were trying to tell us in inadequate English, when I suddenly saw by my left elbow a UN man standing with a look of abject terror on his face, pointing his rifle vaguely towards the Greeks. I asked him the way to Kyrenia but he was a Scandinavian and made no reply. I think he believed he was 'protecting the tourists', but his non-comprehension of any valid language made him speechless. Another, when asked the way to Kyrenia, had never even heard of it. These frightened UN men seem more likely to provoke than prevent incidents. I was depressed by the message that all these patrols, sentry-boxes, Turkish flags and Greek flags, betokening the horrid, silly, little-boy war-game might any moment become murder in real earnest. And it was *too* hot.

### August 10th

No telegram announcing Aunt Dorothy's death. As the day drew on, Heywood's expression grew more miserable and resigned, and I began to feel guilty for not having bullied him sufficiently to stay. But what right had I to do so? Yet I'm sure that though doomed by his own kindness and responsibility, and the offers of help he had sent to Sheelah (in the confident belief that she would reject them) he would have loved to be kept back by his coat-tails. I said something of the sort as we sat on the loggia in the darkness and he said, 'No, my dear;

*Left:* Henrietta on the lawn at Hilton

*Above:* Sophie at Hilton

*Below:* Anne and Lucy at Cadgwith

*Above:* Rosamond Lehmann in the cloister at Monreale, Sicily

*Left:* Mary and Nicko Henderson at Mijas, Spain

OPPOSITE
*Above:* Janetta's Spanish house, Tramores, takes shape

*Below:* Rose and Janetta by the Tramores swimming-pool

Rose, Susannah Phillips
and Julian Jebb at
Tramores

Janetta in her kitchen at
Tramores lined with old
Spanish tiles in green
and white

Janetta, Jaime and Rose eat lunch outdoors with Robin Campbell and his two boys

*Above:* Lynda and Gerald in the mirador at Churriana

*Above right:* Nicky and Rose knitting for Nicky's baby clothes

*Right:* Lionel and Margaret Penrose lunching out at Baden, Austria

Robin, Arthur and William Campbell preparing for a sail on the Solent

Pat Trevor-Roper, Desmond Shawe-Taylor and Raymond Mortimer at Crichel

*Above left:* Bunny and I drive to Tuscany; just through the tunnel

*Above:* Bunny and Magouche: a Tuscan picnic

*Above:* Eardley Knollys, Mattei Radev and John Malet at the Slade near Alton

*Right:* Jean-Pierre Martel and Georgie's wedding, with Alexander and Sarah Kee as attendants

*Above:* Bathing at Cape St Vincent: Robert, Cynthia, Alexander and Sarah Kee

*Right:* Frances Partridge making a sand sculpture, Portugal

*Below:* Dadie Rylands at Alderney

thank you, but I really must go.' Like Janetta, Heywood cannot speak loudly or forcefully. But this doesn't mean – any more than with Janetta – weakness of character. When the time came we all drove through the moonlit night to Nicosia airport where a vociferous Levantine crowd were milling around, and off went poor Heywood through the door of no return.

## August 12th

The second day that Anne and I have been alone together. We get on very well. Talk ranges everywhere – gossip, history, archaeology. We've had giggling fits over Pooch, and on the way to Nicosia an argument about Gibraltar became quite heated. Anne upheld the Gibraltarians' 'right of self-determination', 'saving the English from fascism', and I had a job to get a word in edgeways. We were supposed to be meeting Lucy on her return from Turkey, but (not at all to my surprise and hardly to Anne's) she was not on the plane. Anne took it very well and probably worried less than I worried about her worrying.

So we sit here, awaiting telegrams from both Lucy and Heywood, and this evening we shall go to Kyrenia and send several more. The wind has completely dropped, making the heat seem more tremendous than ever. It was frightening yesterday: the plain round Nicosia is a blinding white desert under merciless and constant attack from the cloudless sky and the fiery ball of the sun. We had to get there in the full heat of noon, so as to see the museum. It was relatively cool and full of lovely things, but after five minutes there I began to stream with sweat and feel so weak I thought I would faint. Then I recovered and we spent nearly an hour happily absorbed. Snack lunch in the air-conditioned airport and the long wait and watch for the arrivals from Turkey, who didn't include Lucy. Coming out of the airport was like braving the hot breath from a furnace-room.

## August 15th

Second visit to the extraordinary Dr Wilkinson.[1] This time I was struck by the expression of vulnerability in his eyes. When we arrived he didn't come out to meet us, though we knew he could hear us from

[1] Poor Dr Wilkinson's end was tragic. In a subsequent eruption of violence he was tortured and murdered by Cypriots, although he had done much to befriend them.

his patio. Poor fellow, he waited for us to come in and then started up from his table, pushing aside his book and chess problem with feigned surprise. For a moment I was deceived, and thought he had forgotten we were coming. Very far from it. Almost at once he led us excitedly to his large writing-desk where he had laid out an exhibition of books, photographs and souvenirs of St Helena. Did I say that he told me on our first visit that he had spent three years there and loved it? I mentioned that I had been translating a book about Napoleon's stay there. He hardly responded at all – very characteristically. His reactions have to wend their way underground and come out in such curious forms as this grand exhibition laid on for my benefit with infinite care and obvious pleasure. I felt nervously anxious to do it justice, and was really touched especially when he said, 'I thought of it in the middle of the night and was *so excited* by the idea.' He even showed me an advertisement of my translation in the *Times Literary Supplement* saying 'I think I've pin-pointed you' which pleased him even more than it did me.

### *August 18th*

Drove to Nicosia in time to see what was once the meeting-place of the Whirling Dervishes, and walk thence through the Turkish quarter to the chief mosque, Santa Sophia, through which we were led barefoot by a Turk in a Delacroix turban. Back to the airport to meet Heywood. Anne is so terrified of flying that she now refuses to do it, and in order to get here she and Heywood spent five stifling hot days and nights on the Orient Express and as many more in a stuffy cabin at sea. I asked her if she felt nervous when her nearest and dearest were flying. 'Not in the least, my dear,' she replied with complete honesty. 'It's just that I find the particular *sort* of fear I have when flying unbearable.'

Heywood was the first to stride out from the aeroplane ('He always does, my dear!'). Aunt Dorothy is not dead yet.

Now I'm in the airport at Nicosia myself on my way home, and a rumour of one hour's delay is going round. A feverishly keyed-up young man beside me keeps leaping up and striding to and fro. The tune of the soprano solo in Fauré's *Requiem*, which both Heywood and I had been frantically and unsuccessfully trying to remember since last night, has just swum effortlessly into my head, perfect in wind and limb, and now repeats itself there *ad nauseam*. Strange are the workings of memory. So here Fauré and I sit together and shall sit for another forty minutes, inextricably amalgamated. I shall now relax and recapitulate the last two days.

I had made a provisional plan for a day's outing for Friday, but feared that Heywood might be too tired for it. In the morning he swore that he was not, and had 'slept like a dog'. So we set off, and had one of our best days. Not too hot either, with a refreshing breeze. Skirting Nicosia we made west across the middle of the island, stopping to look at another Byzantine church. I grow fonder of the landscape, and today we drove through lush and varied land, with red soil, plantations of citrus fruit, bananas and palms. I could wish for some camels. Then turning off our fine tarred road we bumped up into the lower slopes of the Troodos mountains to see the famous little church of Asinou. We had to pick up the priest in the last village and at first he couldn't be found, in spite of a helpful Cypriot with very little English talking about the 'Pub' or 'Papa', or was he saying 'Papa was in the pub'? Hard to say, especially as he answered 'Yes' to all our questions out of desire to please. At last a noble figure with a tiny bun appeared and got in beside us. He also spoke no English. The church was extremely small, but inside was entirely covered with paintings in brilliant colour, in the strongly outlined, stiff but lively Cypriot Byzantine style. St Mamas rode on a grinning tiger, the naked damned bled or were coiled in snakes in hell. When we dropped our priest he raised a hand in blessing, and Heywood forgot himself and did the same to him. Onwards towards the classical site of Vouni, an astonishing place, chiefly because of its staggeringly beautiful position on the top of a conical hill whence one looked in both directions along the coast and over the royal blue sea, from low walls, all pale cream-coloured; the guide told us with his brown face wrinkled in delight and his strong white teeth showing in a grin how he had himself dug up various objects we had seen in the museum at Nicosia. He pointed along the coast to a Turkish village, where they had shot at him, 'pip-pip-pip', when he tried to dig up some remains on an islet. We were tempted to go further west, by the beauty of the coast, but a UN checkpoint stopped us, and a man speaking with an Ulster accent asked, 'Do you know the rules?' 'No, what are they?' 'No stopping for the next two miles.' 'But we wanted to go to that village along the shore and bathe.' 'Well, I'm afraid you can't.' 'Why not?' 'It's against the rules.' We hesitated. 'It's a Turkish village, isn't it?' 'Yes.' 'Well, we've always found the Turks extremely amiable to us.' The UN man went off again, returning to say, 'The sergeant says you can go on, at your own risk.' Heywood and I were keen to go on. Anne said that the man was only doing his duty, and the UN were a splendid and highly valuable force. So they should be, indeed, but I now realize what extraordinary tact as well as other qualities they need. Perhaps they sometimes help keep the bristles erect on the backs of the two hostile packs of dogs; perhaps they maintain the very situation they are supposed to be calming down by emphasizing the barrier between the two races. We *did* go on, at any rate, feeling rather dashing and wondering exactly what 'our own risk' meant. We reached the shore and bathed from a row of ramshackle huts mostly without doors, returning intact from our dangerous incursion among the Cypriot Turks, and feeling very much in their favour.

I have now been ushered on board an Olympic aeroplane. During the flight I read in my *Sunday Times* an interview with Mark Palmer about his 'tribe', which filled me with dismay. So this is the ideology which rules poor Sophie's life! It was a fearful shock to see how thunderously silly it is:

'We really are on the path to the Kingdom of Heaven,' he says. 'Any bad scenes we have to go through we are grateful for. One can only benefit from the divine wrath – indeed it is an honour to be the recipient of it, and we all need to learn a great deal of humility before we enter the Kingdom of Heaven.'

'What is the Kingdom of Heaven?' asks the reviewer. 'Well, we have glimpsed it through drugs, which we believe were sent from above and are part of the divine plan. They prepare us to meet our God by widening our minds into the infinite mind. They show us a glimpse of the divine love. We act from the heart, not the mind – and we're developing now up from the lunacy stage into another kind of, well I suppose you might call that lunacy too. A sort of holy lunacy.'

### August 20th

Can I really have been back only two days? My arrival was misleadingly quiet and easy. A telegram from Janetta saying she was arriving tonight; could I dine with her? Before that I saw Julia looking better than I had expected. She ate nearly all her meal and was amusing about her weekend at Crichel. 'They are sweet fellows, but terribly far away somehow. I couldn't help feeling a lot closer to Moses. What a delightful dog! Then the worst torture of all befell me. You know how I loathe Benjamin Britten's music? Well, out of sheer politeness I had to listen to the whole of *Billy Budd* played with deafening loudness.' At the end she admitted she had hated it, and the logical-minded Desmond couldn't understand why she had let herself in for it. Nor could I.

Today I've had Bunny to lunch, and hope for Janetta tonight.

### *August 21st*

And got her, none the less welcome for being delayed, and oh the pleasure of making contact so swiftly and completely. We ate salmon trout and mayonnaise and drank Bunny's white Burgundy. She has left Henrietta and Sophie at Tramores, though this didn't come out at once, curiously enough. She gave me a careful report on Sophie, partly very good – Henrietta is sweet and loving to her, Sophie looks well; Rose and Jaime had had long talks to her and reported that she was 'very bright'. But the bad is that the life of being trailed around in a cart behind Henrietta and Mark Palmer has obviously given her an uncertain feeling.

But how for a moment can I set aside the horrifying morning news that Russia has invaded Czechoslovakia? Robert rang up this morning to say he was flying out there at once for television, and his voice was electric with the half-excited sense of emergency. Though my heart has plummeted to my boots and beyond, and the familiar thoughts of 'it's quite enough; time to go' return, I notice with alarm that the very muscles of panic are tired.

### *August 25th*

Packed days turned to brawn by Miss Gollancz ringing up to ask me to translate the Carpentier at once. Janetta almost every day, Julian. Janetta was serene and poised; and I felt she was happy and confident about her own life.

### *August 28th: Cranborne, with the David Cecils*

I'm contentedly digging into my new translation and becoming more interested in it than I thought I would.

I love my fellow guests, Iris and John Bayley. On Sunday night, I remember among many conversations that took light and dashed away like forest fires rather an odd one about executions. If one had (like so many historical characters) to have one's head chopped off, would one prefer it to happen in public or in private? David and John said in public, we three females no – but David's enthusiasm for a public execution was what astounded me. With phrases like 'make a good end' and 'I would feel I owed it to myself', he pranced proudly about the room like some sort of heraldic animal, eyes aflame. Stranger still, he had no doubt at all that he *would* make a good end. I suggested that like other intensely emotional moments in life – having a baby, or making love – one would rather be in private, and that with the end of one's life so near, all paraphernalia would seem futile, and an efficient quietus would be one's sole concern. I think Iris and Rachel, after hesitation, joined me – Iris with the qualification that if one were dying for a cause one believed in, one might make an effective last speech. And so she would, of all people. One of the things I like about Iris is that she's not afraid of saying 'high-minded' things.

Almost Cypriot heat, sun, lovely walks, and this stimulating company. In the background the moving, agitating drama of Czechoslovakia, not over yet. It has been a near thing that passive resistance and high moral courage have not triumphed. As it is they seem to have saved awful bloodshed and resulted in a painful compromise. Russian Communism has been seriously discredited with other Communist parties and I am at times haunted by the dread that it is the beginning of some huge and grizzly campaign, or even of nuclear war. There's a horrible feeling of *déjà vu* about it, a reminiscence of Munich, and perhaps the noble Czechs have merely gained themselves and the world a few months' grace.

## August 29th

Gerald came to dinner last night, arriving so tired from a day's shopping that I perhaps overfortified him with whisky; Julian came too but very tactfully deferred his arrival so that Gerald and I might have a quiet time together. During this, we talked a little about Lynda, and whether Holroyd or Jonny or Julian should be his literary executors. He was curiously half-hearted and also vain about Lynda, saying more than once that she 'loved him at least as much as he loved her', that he 'was not in love with her', that he '*could* live

148

without her'. (What a change!) Also that 'she gained more from the relationship than he did' – rather strange considering that she is twenty-four and he in his mid-seventies! Further egotisms: he was pretty uninterested in Czechoslovakia, says he never reads the papers except the *Sunday Times* a week old, and clearly felt that the fact that Gamel had lost some of her family jewels was more important. He had taken them from the bank, and found that only worthless trinkets remained and he admitted this aroused bitter feelings in him against Gamel.

Each gap in our intercourse makes me forget what a stupendous egotist he is. But it was only after Julian arrived and we had sat down to dinner, and he had drunk a good deal of wine that he began literally to whirr like an alarm clock, and a buzz of words issued from his mouth. An attack on Shakespeare was perhaps the nearest he got to his famous coat-trail. He had written 'some of the worst plays in the language', and 'very little good poetry'. Dante, Homer and Racine could all put him in his place. I rose a little, but not much; Julian and I exchanged conniving glances and occasionally tried to head him off; when he got too exasperating we addressed each other. Julian was so amazed that he rang me up after he had got home to make sure Gerald hadn't ruffled me too much – an example of his great sensitivity. No, he hadn't, but of course it's in the same mood that he has enraged me by attacking Ralph and calling him a 'dolt'.

### August 31st

At the Campbells' cottage on the Solent, relishing the warm, salty, blustery air, and the striped landscape of green, grey and blue. Robin came to supper last night and drove me down here in the darkness and the Bank Holiday crowds. I've hardly ever been so frightened in my life. I think he's a good driver, but an extremely dashing one, and his powerful car flew past everything at a roaring speed. Being short of a leg, he has of course no foot brake, and the sudden application of the hand brake was often alarming. We nearly did have an accident as a matter of fact, for when belting down the fast lane of a dual carriageway we came face to face with a car coming to meet us that had got into our lane by mistake and couldn't get out. We were both haunted by the terrified stare in that pair of white headlamps, and I can't bear to think of what lay ahead of the driver, for there were many drivers hastening along more aggressively than Robin. But when at the end of our terrifying journey we turned into the home lanes, and our headlight lit up a Beatrix Potter landscape of low trees, densely peopled with wild ponies, foals and rabbits, its magic was potent indeed. Getting out stiffly, I received the strong tang of the sea in my nose, and thought incongruously of the hot, aromatic incense-like air of my arrival in Nicosia.

## September 8th: London

Robert invited himself to lunch yesterday. What a pleasure to indulge in two good hours of concentrated conversation, both on the personal level, and of course Czechoslovakia on the non-personal one. I was infected – though I had the disease already – by his great enthusiasm for the Czechs' achievement, and felt real excitement over the fact that the lesson they have taught the world is primarily a moral and a pacifist one. That he felt it to be this (as he obviously did, saying, 'You would have been tremendously excited') from his first-hand experience was a great encouragement to my native optimism. He described the state of Prague as being wildly exhilarating, even though some friends he has there were of course wondering whether they should leave the country. The first Russians who arrived were very young and inexperienced and completely in the dark as to what they were doing or even where they were. Some really thought they were in Belgium or Germany. They became demoralized so quickly that they were removed after four days and new, tougher troops sent in. The Czechs eagerly gave help to people like Robert who were smuggling out television films.

## September 10th

Gerald to dinner again last night. He's much better alone, and we talked for a long while without friction. He says he's so much excited by company that he always loses his head and is bitterly ashamed of himself afterwards. 'If more than two or three people are present I can't think, I just talk.' That's his difficulty – he goes on talking without thinking. I took it as a sort of apology, as I believe it was meant.

The Sunday papers have taken up the theory that equates aggression with activity, and try to prove that aggression is a good and vital emotion, by quite simply equating it with activity, for which there's not the smallest justification that I can see. They published a horrifying picture of Dresden destroyed by bombing. 'This is the result of aggression,' they say, 'but so was the original building of this beautiful city.' It was *not*. It seems to me a travesty of sense to say that creative and constructive activity equals aggression.

I feel bitterly about this, and that it's one of the fallacies hurtling us towards violence and chaos.

### September 12th

I have been very much enjoying my quiet trot along the uneventful road of my new translation and a life simplified by the fact that many friends and Henrietta and Sophie are all away, yet with an invitation to the country for every weekend, until the end of October.

My weekend alone with Raymond in the wet green Dorset countryside was peaceful, industrious and soothing. What Harold Nicolson says about him in his diary is very true: he is a 'good' man. And like Harold Nicolson I like good people. We got on very well together I think. The only subject of disagreement, and that not too acute, was Czechoslovakia. He apparently takes the cynical view that it is just a little trouble between Communists, mainly concerned with power, and refuses to see any ideology in the stand the Czechs made for freedom. Over and over again during the weekend he threw up metaphorical hands of dismay at different manifestations of the modern world. We had the Sterns over, and Rachel, David and Laura. I was struck by the casual way Raymond began a conversation about Joe Ackerley with the words 'before he died', just as he might have said, 'before he had breakfast'.

### September 22nd: Hilton

My pleasure in seeing Henrietta and Sophie again wasn't quite unmixed with worry. Dearly as Henrietta loves Sophie, she has naturally not recovered from the trauma of so short a while ago and now she is finding life hard, and unable to cope with. Meanwhile Sophie has become a fascinating little being with dark eyes and gold-tendrilled hair, affectionate, lively-witted and thoughtful. My heart is almost unbearably touched by her, and I also feel desperately sorry for Henrietta and that somehow we must find some way of giving her a rest.

There is also the sadness which fills Hilton itself, crumbling around Bunny, who struggles on with such extraordinary gallantry. Nine to dinner on Sunday – I don't know how he does it. I said to Henrietta I wondered what would happen to Hilton if William were to marry his girlfriend. She evidently hadn't considered for a moment that Bunny might not go on much longer wanting to live there alone and cook for his girls and their hosts of friends whenever they chose to descend on him. After a silence she said she supposed it was 'unimaginative of her'.

### September 30th

Returned from a weekend with the kind Penroses and Gwen Herbert[1] – a delightful person, not a streak of dross in her. She and Margaret played chess almost all the time. I thought about Henrietta and Sophie incessantly, chiefly in the middle of the night, talked about them a little and tried to assuage my restless anxiety with the unguents of sun, wet flowers after heavy showers, walks and rest.

Lionel talked to me about his Polish girl and I of course at once saw his side of the situation. No one has behaved badly, and the pain involved is built in to the pattern of events.

### October 4th

Lunch with Georgia yesterday. I got her to talk about herself, and about the world of the hippies. She had lots to say, and the fact that she sees their charm makes her testimony more valid. 'Their world is a world of hallucination and they are happy in subjecting themselves to its excitement. When they don't get their drugs a dreadful boredom comes over them, only to be stifled with more drugs. And of course their hallucinatory visions don't lead to *activity* – *God* no! They couldn't paint a picture or write about what they experience. They are totally passive.'

### October 12th: The Slade

Henrietta seems to be moving towards a possible solution. She is trying to arrange for Sophie to go to the same state school as little Frances Behrens[2]; what's more, Jane Garnett[3] has been angelic and

[1]  Widow of A. P. Herbert.
[2]  Child of Harriet and Tim. She and Sophie are great friends still.
[3]  Wife of Bunny's eldest son (by Ray) Richard.

very helpful, and may be able to put her up in term-time in their Islington house.

Dadie is here, and his company is always exhilarating. His mind moves much at the same speed as mine does and we often take the same point of view. Pouring all yesterday afternoon, with squelching grass and dripping rose-bushes, a howling wizard wind crashing against the windows. Raining softly all this morning. Only at lunchtime did that grey lid start sliding back showing a pale blue sky, and about four this afternoon Dadie, Eardley and I set out for a brisk walk. Incomparably lovely views in all directions, trees still fat with grey-green leaves, very rich blue shadows and the distance clear and remote.

### October 13th

To dine at John Fowler's[1] last night in his very pretty house near Odiham. He seems a nice, sad, kind man. The evening was awkward – the other guests were Michael and Rachel Redgrave.[2] Dadie made much of the honour it was to meet such distinguished people, but did not warn us that Michael Redgrave was as heavy on hand as could be imagined and generally drunk. He was in fact both and had just fallen into a muddy ditch on his way to dinner. I sat next him and at once realized what I was in for when I looked at his lost, impassive face, like a stuffed fish behind glass. I did my best; Eardley, on his other side, never addressed him once, and Dadie was laughing and shouting with Rachel Redgrave (very nice she seemed to be). My task was hopeless. I had to repeat everything to Michael Redgrave, who was totally uninterested in all of it, except when I admired his spectacles. After dinner there was a long walk in the dark to the 'studio', and I couldn't see a step and fell down and barked my shin, bleeding like a stuck pig – mainly after returning home and taking off my stocking. I was greatly touched by Mattei's extraordinary gentleness and consideration in bringing TCP and Elastoplast while I spattered the bathroom with my blood. Dadie cheered us on from the sidelines and Eardley vanished altogether. Hating the sight of blood, perhaps?

[1] Well-known interior decorator.
[2] The actors.

## October 16th

Jane and Richard have agreed to take Sophie in for this term at the Islington school to give Henrietta a break. I went and saw her there, a happy, busy little sprite who jumped for joy when she told me what she did at school, described the singing and dancing and showed me a picture she had painted. It would be dreadfully sad to uproot her from this flower-pot. I came home and wrote to Bunny, telling him that after all Amaryllis was not prepared to have Sophie to live with her (a perfectly mad idea) and 'hadn't realized what would be entailed in time and energy'.

## October 26th

I have come to Ireland for the Wexford Festival, and am now at the Busaras, or bus station, Dublin. Last week the leg I had damaged at John Fowler's nearly a fortnight ago swelled up, and I went to see the doctor. 'Keep it up as much as possible' was his verdict, and I am thoroughly bandaged and hamstrung. Sophie is with the Garnetts. I woke this morning to a vision of Sophie as I saw her yesterday, happy, gay, proudly showing me her little attic room at the top of the Garnetts' house, pleased with the dress kind Kitty West gave me for her, and talking happily about everything and everybody. I went to fetch her from the Canonbury Road school. First I saw her familiar blue coat hanging from a peg with every letter on its label in a different colour. Soon I saw her running downstairs, smiling happily at me. There was no shade of angst about her school. The little house in Alwyne Villas was abuzz with life, boys[1] and friends. The re-potted plant has been stimulated to put out green leaves in this fresh earth. I was full of gratitude to Richard and especially to Jane, whose sheer goodness has rung the bell.

And here I am in grey, soft old Ireland, drinking a glass of Paddy whisky and about to eat a snack before my bus goes.

## October 29th: Wexford

Desmond, his brother and sister-in-law and I are in a soothing, gentle, cotton-wool atmosphere here, friendly, warm, faintly damp and quiet, except for nightly jollifications which keep the three

[1] Oliver and Ned Garnett, Sophie's first cousins.

Shawe-Taylors awake more than me (I brought ear-plugs, having been warned). The musical part is tremendously enjoyable. *Fair Maid of Perth* on Saturday, dramatic and exciting music, well produced but not altogether well sung. Last night Rossini's *Equivoco Stravagante*, which was a riot, very pretty to look at, and greeted with thunderous applause. Before it we were invited to a grand dinner for critics and their friends in the hotel. I first saw Desmond as I emerged out of the bathroom on Saturday evening, already pretty frenzied because the water was not hot. 'I think we *must* start dinner at seven-fifteen,' he said, but turned up twenty minutes later himself. In the bar I found his brother Bryan and Jocelyn his wife; I like them very much. To hide my bandaged leg I bought myself a beautiful long black and gold silk Indian kaftan, and am delighted with it. At the critics' dinner party I sat next to the hotelier, a cherubic and far from stupid man. Irish jollity blazed up in no time, with plenty of drink and Irish coffee to end with – delicious but quite astonishingly stimulating and my mind was active hours later.

There are a few familiar faces – Andrew Porter[1] and Derek Hill[2] with Celia Goodman's friend, the Princess of Hesse.

### *November 4th: London*

Dined with Magouche. After dinner a troupe of young came in – Georgie, Antonia and Jean-Pierre's[3] sister, and a boy who had just been sent away from school for smoking cannabis.

Someone mentioned the words 'good', 'moral', 'ethical' – it might have been me, fresh from talking about G. E. Moore with Paul Levy (more of him soon). A visible shudder of horror went through them all. I asked the expelled boy why he disliked the words? F: 'There's nothing wrong with "good" or "moral," is there? What do *you* think "valuable" then?' 'Oh well, you know, it's rather diffiuclt. I'd have to think about that. I suppose nowadays it's mostly – you know – material things like television sets.'

But what of Paul Levy? He is a young Jewish American from Harvard who has come over with a grant to write about G. E. Moore, and I met him at Oxford and the Cecils at Cranborne,

[1] Critic and great friend of Desmond's.
[2] Painter.
[3] Georgie's boyfriend and later husband.

and talked to him a bit about Moore's theories. He declared he would like to find a Bloomsburyite who wasn't a Moorite – I put up a tentative hand. 'Why?' he asked. 'Because he didn't *really* refute Hedonism,' I said, 'and used "desirable" as if it meant "ought to be desired" instead of simply "is – or can be – desired", so introducing his own naturalist fallacy.' I scored a hit with this random shot. 'Oh, well, that's exactly what our modern American philosophers say.' I was loth to risk any further less successful plunges, and though I tried to draw him on his own views he wouldn't be drawn. He immediately won me by talking of Alix (with whom he spent two days) with enormous admiration. He's quick, intelligent, sympathetic, interested, amusing. He has given me Lytton's Apostles papers to read – they are well written, thoughtful, and mature compared to the yardsticks of some of today's young. But I must beware the danger of intolerance, and sticking up for the friends of my own youth, who were intolerant themselves and perhaps vain. As Alix said when I visited her yesterday, Paul Levy might be a very clever confidence trickster, but I'm prepared to bet he isn't. I took to him very much.

From Alix I went to the Carringtons where I was given to read a lot of correspondence from Carrington to Alix and (both ways) with Lytton, and also Lytton–James. An interesting letter of Carrington's to Alix described the Watendlath situation exactly as Ralph did, and twice referred to Gerald's 'Larrau plot' for Valentine to divert Ralph's attention. During the weekend Julian Vinogradoff[1] rang up to say that there was a paragraph in the *Daily Telegraph* announcing that someone called Ken Russell was going to make a film based on Holroyd's book. She is frantic – Noel too was very upset. I loathe the idea, but haven't yet sorted out my feelings about it.

### November 25th

The Ken Russell film has occupied my mind nearly as much as the question of Sophie's school did, and my thoughts about it came somewhat to a head this morning. I flew into action, partly because Rosamond suggested my ringing up the Society of Authors and consulting their legal expert. She says – and I have had various opinions on the subject, some disagreeing with this – that as Alix has

[1] Only child of Lady Ottoline Morrell.

the copyright for all Lytton's letters and I for all Carrington's and her diaries, she and I could make the film more awkward for the producers by refusing the copyright of any extracts to the film-makers. I am going however to see Holroyd this evening and find out what they do propose to do. According to the paper there will be some 'sensational casting'. Who in the world will play Lytton and Carrington – and is Ralph to be in? He must be, of course, and I mind this much more than the possibility (suggested by some of my friends) that I might be in it myself. I mind the idea of the false Ralph they will create very much indeed, whether rationally or no.

I rang Alix, who had received the news passively the day before, appearing to think it was nice of Holroyd to write to her about the project. She believed what he wrote: that he hoped the film would increase the sale of Lytton's books.

I have been supported in my bellicose attitude by Noel (who writes frequent agitated letters) and very much so by friends like Faith Henderson, Rosamond, the Penroses.

Many other things have happened: Henrietta came to see me looking very pretty, with her hair cut short and curly. She told me she had begun taking lessons at a drama school, which had given her an audition and may take her on.

### November 28th

Michael Holroyd was very friendly and I'm glad I asked him to come. He even said he was glad to know what we all felt about it. Perhaps nothing is gained; it may be out of his hands and in the tougher ones of the BBC and Ken Russell. But he has admitted to obtuseness in not realizing what pain would be caused, and said he is sorry, and will do his best to prevent it. This morning he rang again to say that he had made his protest.

Last night to Eliot's *Cocktail Party* with Wynne and Kitty. In its way it was riveting, though apart from Alec Guinness and the heroine the actors weren't good. There is also great sadism to my mind, in the play itself. Wynne was in a strangely keyed-up state perhaps because of his intense feelings about the myth of the Crucifixion, and he sees Eliot's Celia not as a 'saint' as I did, but as Christ himself. He frantically resisted any attempt to discuss the play in the intervals, but wanted to do so at length and in detail afterwards – and we did so over a bottle of wine in my flat. Wynne said he had been deeply moved by the play, which I had already guessed from his stifled sobs at one point. He was suspicious at first of me as an anti-Christian; he sometimes accuses me of teasing him for being a believer, but I'm most careful not to do this now I know he is such a serious one and the boot is really on the other leg. He attacks me — lightly, usually — for being a rationalist. Well, I hope I am one. It was an interesting evening, because of Wynne's first-rate intelligence. This afternoon he rang up to apologize for being irritable 'mostly to my wife'. I certainly didn't think he had been to me, except when Kitty and I were told we mustn't discuss the play in the interval, which I thought uncalled-for.

### December 1st

I give up. I shall become a recluse. I've had a letter from the BBC, speaking of the proposed Lytton film as a certainty — there's no sign of Michael having affected them in any way — and they hope for my 'approval and support'. What to do next? I beat against a stone wall, supported only by Noel. I still propose to battle on, though with very little hope. But I must not get megalomanic, and think that my futile flappings can make any difference.

### December 15th

Julia and I had a long telephone talk in which she implicitly claimed to be the only person who didn't find life worth living. It was after 5 p.m. and she at first said she had 'only just got up', then 'a young man has been here, washing up last night's dinner party. Really, I hate these social occasions and I don't find they relieve my loneliness at all. It takes me two good days preparing for it.' I said she was lucky to get someone to wash up on Sunday. 'Oh well, I had to bribe him. I paid him three pounds.' There followed an attack (the second within a week) on Margaret, for not having filled her hot-water bottle properly *last* Christmas!

I'm very anxious lest taking in Sophie should be too much for Richard and Jane. I have been to Alwyne Villas several times to see her, when she was away from school with a cold and earache, and I found her being devotedly looked after and quite gay, and she was sweetly affectionate to me. When I called her 'sweetheart' and asked 'if she minded', she pondered a long time and then said, 'You can call me anything you like – because I *love* you.' I think about her a great deal of the time, and at others brood over this somehow defiling and disgusting Ken Russell film.

In three days' time I am going for a whole fortnight to the Slade with Eardley.

## December 20th: The Slade

I have dived into still waters, like the little tarn above Ullswater where I bathed among water-lilies a few years ago. Peace – *yes*, unutterably soothing, and of course I keep asking: why do I stay in the clangour and frenzy of London, wound up like a clockwork mouse, inner mechanism whirring even when picked off the ground, palpitating senselessly, restless without purpose, flying to the telephone and then deliberately calming my voice? Why, why, why? I was not a little doubtful what it would be like here alone with Eardley in the total isolation of the Slade, without telephone or newspapers. But *at once* it applied a gently soothing poultice and I really do believe it is exactly what I needed.

Do I jabber away too much to Eardley? The first evening we went over our main preoccupations – mine, Sophie's future and the Ken Russell film, Eardley's, his Crichel studio. That was all right, just, because he said himself that he was sick of the whole subject and going to give it up, and the acute Mattei had realized the very strong underground emotions at work in him about it.

That snag having been by-passed, he's as usual, excellent company – thoughtful, honest and kind, and I have really enjoyed being here. This afternoon I took my first plunge into the muddy lanes in perfectly still winter weather, under a pale pink, blue and grey sky, and picked a large bunch of ivy, polypody ferns, holly and skeleton plants and grasses. Happiness.

## December 23rd

The settled peace and calm here has exceeded my expectations. Only the weather is wild, and for the last two nights flurries of rain and hail have hurled themselves against my bedroom windows with such a deafening noise that I've had to sandwich my head between two pillows. We listen on the wireless to the news of the three astronauts who are attempting to encircle the moon, I with fascinated horror as

159

if forced to witness a gladiatorial show, while to Eardley it is 'romantic and glamorous'. Yet he is a timid, rather than brave man, afraid of blood and pain, who, though by no means a pacifist, avoided risking his life in the war I'm not sure how and daren't ask.

I go walks by myself every day and prefer it that way. I keep up a tin-whistle piping of trifling and repetitive thoughts, and do a lot of looking. This afternoon up the hill opposite by a sunken lane with ivy everywhere – climbing up the trunks of all the trees, trailing down again and carpeting the ground, thus doubly binding the trees to the earth, tall dark evergreens are decorated with old man's beard like the spangled cotton wool on a Christmas tree.

Eardley and I talk with ease and absorption, a lot of course about the astronauts and whether our attitude to their performance is morbid, sadistic or gloating. I think it is all three. At times the wireless reports from outer space are so terrifying as to be almost unendurable.

### Christmas Day

Mattei got back last night. This morning thin flakes of snow are slanting down through the mist. Eardley looked out of his bedroom door to say that the astronauts had safely started on their return journey.

### December 28th

The astronauts 'splashed down' safely yesterday afternoon about five. The American wireless report was confused and undramatic, and (apart from the horrifying suggestion that the capsule might bounce off the Earth's atmosphere and continue revolving in space till they died) I personally felt – inaccurately – that the greatest danger was over when they turned from the moon's orbit towards home. At first I felt they would fail – thank heavens they haven't and we are spared the squelching deluges of ghoulish emotion in which everyone would have indulged. Reactions are touchy, and seldom quite right. Eardley says he 'misses the astronauts', and at lunch today Mattei announced, with quite a smug expression on his handsome face, that '*he* would instantly have volunteered to go to the moon if he had had the chance. What does one's own life signify for the good of humanity?' No one, I felt, no one should ever boast of being brave in some ordeal they have never had to be tested in.

## December 29th

My stay is nearing its end. I have very deliberately slowed my tempo, and taken things at a very steady pace. It has been a nursing-home cure, with very few moments when I have had to screw myself up to do anything. Last night we went for a drink with neighbours, meeting there two appalling figures straight out of the Ark. Brigadier Antrobus was voted 'all right', for he scarcely opened his mouth. Mrs Antrobus sitting next to me, was a ghastly female. The subject of Bedales came up as usual, and everyone looked at me as some sort of freak. I asked Mrs Antrobus if she would recommend a child to go there. 'Why no – you see they have no religious instruction. And then I'm a *square*,' proudly. We prattled of possible snow, nice walks, and cars. 'We have two. You see we have to fetch our daily, and we don't want to do *that* in the Daimler, so we keep a Mini.' Eardley was impressed because the Brigadier had been at College in Winchester, 'the highest possible intellectual standard'. Well, much good does it seem to have done him.

My thoughts are turning homewards and nestwards, and with that of course comes anxiety about the various people for whom I feel responsible. Snow covers much of England.

# 1969

## January 3rd: London

Now that I have – only this morning – handed in Carpentier to be typed, the chief thing I have on my agenda is my battle with the BBC. It is not yet over. Robert nobly came to my assistance and wrote a letter to a high-up person (David Attenborough, no less), sending me by telegram the news that this great man had 'promised they would not go ahead without my consent'. He warned me they might go on trying to obtain it, and so they have. I found a letter from Swallow of the BBC, asking me in very polite terms if I would meet and discuss the matter with him and Ken Russell himself. I hardly dared say no, but Robert advised me that I must. It would be fatal to make them put themselves out to persuade me. So – greatly daring – I wrote to say 'it would only waste their valuable time, as I had Attenborough's written undertaking not to go ahead.'

Standing up to this incomprehensible and now rather dreaded juggernaut makes me tremble. What am I protecting so tigerishly, obstinately from the BBC? Ralph, I believe.

With the Cecils last weekend. David talked so hard about Laura and Angelo[1], on a winter walk, that his own pace got slower and slower till we were standing quite still in the middle of the road, surrounded by trees and fields brilliantly lit by glorious (but not very warm) sunshine. And I almost laughed aloud, but also nearly lost my train, when he did the same thing while talking on the same theme on Monday morning's drive to the station. From crawling we almost ground to a halt, but just caught my train, and found Raymond, Pat and Munro Wheeler on it.

At Basingstoke we got into a carriage with a man taking his obviously dying wife up to hospital. Very distressing, and I felt

---

[1]  Hornak, now her husband.

deeply sad on his account. He was supporting her so kindly and yet there was that 'gloating' that I detest in his look and manner as he bent towards me and whispered 'leukaemia'.

I rang up Bunny last night and was sorry to hear that he was worn out by too much hospitality. He'll kill himself at this rate, and I do wish I could persuade him other things were more important, for instance Henrietta's health and welfare. Sophie is now back in London, but I've not seen Henrietta for a long time, and would like to.

### January 10th

The BBC situation ended with a loud bang. My polite letter to Swallow was met by an almost grovelling one from Julian's Central European boss. It came by return of post and when I saw the red letters 'BBC' lying on my hall floor, I trembled. I felt persecuted, harassed, badgered, 'why can't they leave me alone?' Hearst, as he's called, hadn't really read my letter and thought I was complaining of wasting 'my' time, not that of the great Russell and Swallow. He began all over again about Russell's eminence and outstanding skill. Would I come and see one of his films? Next morning I woke early, writing letters in my head. Robert and Cynthia, and Julian were coming to dinner, so I rang Robert to ask him to bring Attenborough's letter – my pass to freedom, without which I do see that the project would certainly go through. Robert at once urged me to write my mental letter *at once*, and post it *at once*. Why, I wonder? Was it because he feels engaged in this particular battle or likes battles in general. Anyway I did, and am sorry. I wrote in violent indignation, saying I had Attenborough's written assurance they would not go on without my consent and I would *never* consent. That I hoped Russell would find another subject and leave us in peace and that this correspondence might now end. In fact I said: *shut up*.

When Julian came, he was appalled; so much so that I really felt very ashamed of myself. I should have kept my original coolness throughout; it's never a good plan – or very seldom – to fly off the handle. Anyhow I have, and it's given me a certain relief. I was becoming obsessed by my battle with this huge Megatherium, the BBC. They are now 'the enemy' to me, but of course I'm deeply sorry to have upset Julian by my bad behaviour to his boss.

## January 12th: Crichel

At lunch Raymond suddenly said that the real point of Drake's expedition to Cadiz was that he burned a lot of wood stored there to build the Armada with – he pronounced it to rhyme with Maida Vale. Desmond in delight and wonder: '*That*'s something you would hear in no other house in England!' We discussed the rival merits of 'armaida' and 'armarda', without any good reason transpiring – but with *much* feeling! There were the usual indignant exclamations over grammatical incorrectnesses in the papers. When I showed Raymond a page Gerald had written and sent me about Ralph, what looked at first like being his only comment was 'I think he should say "disinclined *from*" not "to".' Afterwards he said delightful things about Ralph, that were music in my ears – about his extraordinarily acute intelligence, his taking an interest in everything, the remarkable warmth of his personality making people love him, and he was almost the best company he'd known, and what fun and jokes one had with him.

## January 22nd: London

Penroses, Georgia, Bunny and Pat Trevor-Roper came to dinner. Bursts of Roman candles from different quarters until nearly one. Everyone unselfconsciously but vigorously themselves (except perhaps poor Lionel, who is not at all well): Bunny saying, 'Sex begins at fifty,' Pat explosively appreciative and bubbling, Georgia quite splendid. Two nights ago there was a 'grand' party at the Dufferins for Duncan's birthday. Eardley and I got there at nearly eleven and hardly dared enter, the house looked so pompous and dead. But we at once saw countless familiar faces – Bunny, Amaryllis, Henrietta, Raymond, the Connollys, Quentin and Olivier, Holroyd, Mary Hutchinson, and some glamorous hippy young. Georgia (coming late) was caught by Bryan Guinness and I almost laughed, her face went so rapidly dead under the withering fire of his amiably booming conversation. Raymond 'thought Eardley seemed chilly' and wondered what's happened about the studio.

The Ken Russell film crisis is not yet over. Robert rang up to tell me he had had a letter of protest from Attenborough because I took his undertaking as a pass to peace and freedom, and wouldn't see Swallow and Russell. He still firmly says I mustn't, but that they are sure to try again. From Julian too I get the no doubt false impression that the whole telly world is a-buzz with this crisis, and I feel amazed at the extraordinary way I am venturing to try to stop their plans – also sick sometimes when I think of it; it's so very unlike the sort of thing I generally get involved in, so public and immolative.

### January 24th

Well, I've had a sight of the enemy – the great civilizing force of television at close range, and I must say it was not impressive. They occupied my flat from two to five yesterday afternoon in order to photograph Bunny in a 'congenial setting' speaking about George Moore. The net result of at least fifteen people's work, or what passed as such, will be (so a female friend of Julian's told me) about two minutes on the screen. In they poured, technicians with huge, black, helmet-shaped lamps on legs, camera men (at least five of these I should say), two near-gentlemen, one in public school clothes, another with long hair, Chinese moustache and a thick Irish sweater, neither of whom appeared to have anything at all to do; the director, with a massive head, who didn't know what a violin-stand was; the interviewer who retired into my bedroom 'to change his shirt and put on a wig'; a little girl detailed to assist in this operation; a big, blowsy make-up girl who did no making-up and sighed for a set of Scrabble; two other females, one – Julian's friend – whose only task during these three hours was to give me a cheque for five guineas for the use of my flat. Fascinated and inquisitive at first, I soon became dead bored, and sat in my bedroom reading *The Tenant of Wildfell Hall* (equally boring in another way). I took an occasional peep at Bunny sitting in the glare of the lights, with his beret pulled over his poor eyes to protect them, like a man under torture. But his soft and measured tones went on and on, unperturbed. Most of this host of people had nothing, or almost nothing to do, yet contrived to look as if they thought they had. None had brought a book, but total silence was called for when shooting was going on. I couldn't help commiserating with them; they looked surprised. They smoked a quarter of an inch of innumerable cigarettes and piled them up on any likely or unlikely object; they trooped into the lavatory and peed remorselessly and loudly, like horses. Julian's friend told me they were trying to make this documentary for three different sorts of people – the educated who had read George Moore, the literate who might want to, the illiterate, who wouldn't (I paraphrase her). '*But you can't do that*,' I said. And their activities seemed, though polite and well-meaning, futile, unimportant, sterile, anti-life. I felt that if they were not bored they ought to be.

## January 26th

Perhaps I was too hard on them, for in fact they 'meant well', as I was aware. And looking round the world this seems to be true of rather few — not true for instance of the disgustingly cretinous football fans, busily destroying the trains and buses that take them to their pleasure, or of the murderously vicious speeders, or those who are so avid for their material gain as to lose sight of everything else (a lot of strikers probably). I don't know quite where in the dismal picture to put people of near-criminal stupidity like the delegates at the Vietnam Conference who have wrangled on and on about the *shape* of their conference table while people go on dying and fighting; the perpetrators of violent films, feeding the sadism of the public, including children, so as to earn a little more money; psychologists who tell everyone they must be aggressive because aggression equals activity and creation; and everyone who contributes to the materialism of the present day, and in order to make money sinks all standards to the lowest common denominator. It's impossible to look at the *Radio Times*, it's so vulgarly hideous and aimed at those to whom past beauty is non-existent and present beauty is sex only.

What has psychoanalysis done for the world, when so much violence has still to be released both in fantasy and action? And can people have been even sexually liberated if they need so many strip-tease joints, which one would imagine could only gratify the bottled-up or immature? Why can dress designers not consider the shape of the female form, and why must they so painstakingly deglamourize it? Why must the young either drown reality in drugs or yell slogans of destruction like children in a nursery?

I have just (Sunday morning) passed a little group of black-haired men standing opposite the Spanish Embassy, shouting at intervals: '*Asesino! Asesino!*' They are to demonstrate this afternoon against Franco's declaring a state of emergency in Spain.

## January 27th

I face a new week with only a few dregs of courage and no opinion of myself whatever. A visit to the Kees yesterday was somehow frustrating; a delightful and intelligent Czech was there followed immediately by Cynthia's mother; in terms of human communication it was non-existent.

At the bottom of this feeling of pitch-waver and wobbling-bicycle is self-disgust at my relationship with Julia being no better. Our last meeting followed on our both being taken by the Kees to see *Così fan tutte* and, of course, we discussed it, and, of course, disastrously. She had endured hell during the first half, feels opera isn't a valid art form, hates the human voice, thought the two female singers 'wobbled' atrociously. I tried to defend the exceptionally steady Yvonne Minton as having merely that life in her voice vibrato gives a violin. Julia: 'Oh well, I hate the violin anyway.' I suggested she gave up trying to go to opera and that she 'didn't really like it'. That was the unforgiveable remark and should never have been said – oh *no* – though absolutely true. Why couldn't I let her be? I was indignant because I knew she had gone to the opera determined to hate it and find fault, because Cynthia had been well aware of this, Robert's own pleasure marred, and their kindness to her ruthlessly manhandled.

Leaving the Kees, I went on bungling and blundering, nearly ran out of petrol and quite ran out of money; went to a concert at the V and A, Yvonne Minton again singing well; the rest didn't move me, and I was stifled by the body odour of a man sitting next to me. I fear this creeping aboulia. Is it because I have no new translation ahead? Oh, help! help! But I really know there is none available, and that I need a crack of the whip to myself.

It was the Kees' nice Czech who introduced the theme of whip-cracking. He had heard the phrase being used among Oxford dons, by Rowse the historian, about student protests. But he soon applied it to the Russians and Czechs. 'People don't seem to understand', said Rowse, 'that the Russians had to do it.' Then he made the sort of patronizing apology to the nice Czech, who in his soft, deprecating and humorous voice, said that of course he was at Oxford as an individual and expected to be treated as one, but he couldn't help also being a member of the Czech nation.

## January 28th

Margaret rang up and asked to come and see me yesterday. Her troubles are really grim – Lionel with leukaemia and the torturous situation about Dunyusha. I know Margaret tends to fantasize a good deal so have to have my grain of salt in readiness when she tells me that Dunyusha's one object is to come to England, supplant her as Lionel's wife and have several children. The letter I was shown from her did not support this view, but actually thanked Margaret for being nice about her abortion and sending her flowers. I'm sure she wants to come to England but can she want to found a family and settle down with a seventy-year-old professor with leukaemia?

In a feeble attempt at organization, I've finished translating the surrealist story by Magouche's Spanish lodger, and rung up the typist to discover whether the Carpentier is finished. It seems likely that it is or nearly. So that this week should see the end of current work – and then what? I suggested to Margaret she might care to slip across to Holland if Lionel goes to Poland next month. I think the idea pleased her. Then in the evening Henrietta came to see me again, and we had nearly four hours of wholly relaxed *tête-à-tête*. There's no question of her wanting to remove Sophie from Jane's care – she says nothing but nice things about Jane.

## February 7th

Very nice evening with Eardley and the young Powells[1] last night, and one alone with Bunny the evening before; for nearly seventy-seven he is a model of energy, activity and enthusiasm. We talked a good deal about Carrington, whose letters he is editing. For once he seemed disgusted with all his family – 'I'm fed up with the whole brood,' he muttered. Angelica has again postponed her return, and he read out a letter saying 'she felt guilty about breaking her word to Jane and Frances, but couldn't leave Taiti (?) in the lurch.' This is a Moorish boy of eighteen, whom she is trying to get out of Morocco. As he left, he said kindly, 'it's been such a comfort talking to you.'

---

[1] Tristram and Virginia.

## February 15th

A lovely evening with Julian last night, a visit from Henrietta who said at one moment, 'Perhaps I ought to try and earn some money.' As she'd just spoken of her drifting state I suggested it really might make her happier to clamber inside some sort of iron maiden.

## February 16th: Hilton

Henrietta and I drove down here yesterday morning. The cold is deathly. Yesterday in the drawing-room, with electric fire, radiator and smouldering logs, I was so paralysed by it that my fingers refused to write. In bed I wore a vest, flannel night-gown, bed-jacket and winter dressing-gown, and over all that an eiderdown which I'd smuggled in in the boot of my Mini — yet I was no more than comfortably warm. But none of this mattered beside the ghostly melancholy that drips from these walls, apparently unnoticed by its inmates Bunny and William. Bunny in a handsome suit of blue check, steps about as briskly as a young man. William retreats into his room with huddled shoulders and tootles on his oboe. Henrietta and I sit in the dank, cold, lightless drawing-room.

It was nobody's fault that Sophie was babyish and endlessly demanding, and on the whole Henrietta was patient and sweet to her, until (unable to bear any more) she spoke to her in a rather remote voice, whereupon Sophie lay on the ground and sobbed as if her heart would break. I took her away almost by force, and read to her in my room, feeling heart-broken myself.

## February 18th

Henrietta, Sophie and I drove back, through falling snow at first. I'm only too aware of Henrietta's desperate unhappiness. She left Sophie with me in the afternoon; after one rush to hurl herself into her mother's arms as she was leaving, she became almost at once far more grown up and lively. She read brilliantly from two little books I'd bought her, sat picking out tunes with real pattern and rhythm on the piano for some time and sang several songs perfectly in tune. There was nothing but jollity too when we got back to Alwyne Villas, where Richard was awaiting us like a benign father figure. In fact she seemed a very 'all right' little girl, and undoubtedly bright in her wits.

## February 20th

This is the 'dead' of winter and no mistake. Last night it began to snow; tiny but dense flakes, whirled by the wind, magically converted London into some sort of Japanese pantomime. Paul Levy came to fetch me to a concert at the Festival Hall, appearing frosted over with the lightest, finest snow – one flake of snow had settled in each of his tight orange curls, making a charming effect. When we came out from the concert the snow was several inches deep, and the cars in the park had had a huge communal blanket thrown over them. I like Paul and enjoy his company.

## February 28th

'And he hadn't for a good while done anything more conscious and intentional than *not* quickly to take leave.' Janetta? No. Henry James (*The Golden Bowl*). It, *The Golden Bowl*, has been my solace and surprise during two days confined to my flat with a disgusting cold. Only in the isolation of my bedroom was it possible to attend completely to the amazing changing iridescences of this slowly inflated balloon. And even then, in rather small doses. Thus taken I bow down to it as never before. All its subtleties are significant, and their shifting glow made the quiet grey of my walls, when I looked up at them for a rest, almost reassuring.

Dear Craig[1] has died of a heart-attack on the way to work. Oh what sadness, and it made me think of other great friends gone and sadly missed.

## March 5th

Shaking with sobs, convulsed with doubt, neurotic pains and other symptoms, changing his mind five times daily, poor Lionel – a pitiable prey to love, at seventy – has at last posted off to visit his girl in Warsaw. Margaret has stood up to the stress of it all most heroically, her worst moment being when he implored her to ring up Dunyusha and say he wouldn't come – *he* couldn't, as her voice melted him. But Margaret couldn't, because she knew she'd be blamed by them both afterwards. She merely said Lionel wasn't well,

---

[1]  Macfarlane, my solicitor and a great friend.

and Dunyusha got him to the telephone and persuaded him to come. One of Margaret's treats during Lionel's absence was to be a weekend in Amsterdam with me, but this has been 'on' and 'off' so frequently that I stopped thinking about it. Now it seems we are going, and the day after tomorrow! My prayers are directed to Margaret's not getting involved in the hectic world of fantasy as she did last summer in Austria – but I'm afraid she has given Lionel her telephone number.

### March 6th

Julia for a long talk on the telephone this morning. She told me Bunny went to see her about her Carrington letters last night, worked his charm and has carried them off in triumph. We talked about Julian's forthcoming radio programme on Virginia, to which he has asked her to contribute. 'But I don't think, with her relations alive, I could say what I want to.' 'What would that be?' 'Well, Leonard used to say that he wondered why people stared after her in the street, but I could tell him it's because she wasn't *at home in her body*, wore such awful, cheap clothes and moved so ungainlily. But of course I can't say that. If it's just going to be another outpouring of adulation, what's the point of that? Then I don't happen to admire her writing very much – all this harping on beauty and describing life in terms of flowers and frills. It's girlish gush like Rosamond's. And I should want to say that too.' I wonder whence comes Julia's terror of people getting too much or too unqualified praise – that is except in the case of Chekhov and Saul Bellow.

Also there's a certain arrogance in her assumption that her criticisms might damage Virginia's reputation. But she ended on a sad wail: 'Nothing gets any better, and I start drinking whisky after breakfast now and can't eat.' She pays two cooks to cook one meal each a week at three guineas a go.

To the first night of *Fidelio* with Desmond last night; old Klemperer conducted remarkably slow tempi but got a terrific accolade from a mixed and excitable audience, just for being so old. The *Fidelio* was Anja Silja, a tall girl with golden-red, shining hair (which she shook out of its cap when revealing her identity), a stage presence that was electric, highly moving, and striking, restrained eloquence of movement. As for her singing, she opened her mouth

172

in a wholehearted black O and sang like a wild thing for all she was worth.

When we came out for the interval I asked Desmond what he thought of her. 'Well her clothes worry me rather. Of course she looks very elegant and beautiful, but too modern when compared with the others. More like something out of the King's Road. And the others, not very Spanish really. Like a fancy dress party.' So he went on for quite ten minutes – I could hardly believe my ears. Then I said: 'Yes, but what about her *singing*?' and he became extremely interesting. It also seems she has been having a great affair with Wieland Wagner while singing at Bayreuth, and creating a scandal. She certainly has 'star quality'.

## March 7th: Amsterdam

Never have I been less aware of leaving the ground and again returning to it. Our aeroplane sat on the Tarmac for a good half hour, waiting for 'space', before setting off into thin white mist. Here it is several degrees colder, and still, with brilliant, thin, metallic sunlight. Our hotel in the modern suburbs gave Margaret and me a late lunch of ham and eggs, after which we made off into the town, and walked and walked. It is dead of winter here still, no sign of life in the spidery, black twigs of the trees along the beautiful network of canals on the way to the flea market in the old Jewish quarter, and Rembrandt's house. We dined with a Dutch medical family, friends of the Penroses – an excitable geneticist and his tense wife. Their three attractive adolescent children were well-mannered but rebellious. I sat aching on a backless settee, interested by this glimpse of Dutch life but at the same time almost bored by the conversation; my role that of an 'extra'. The children excitedly brought in new records from *Hair*, on the sleeve of which one read about sodomy and masturbation. Talk about drugs – Dr van den Bosch is very much interested in them and apparently strongly against even marijuana, though the Penroses for some reason think he takes drugs himself. Back to cubicle bedroom with narrow monk's bed, but bath and hot water.

## March 8th

In the Rijksmuseum we saw among other things a temporary exhibition of frescoes from Italy. Here we met Mrs van den Bosch and her intellectual mother-in-law who lives at Haarlem. When I

173

admitted to not caring about Franz Hals she was greatly shocked, and I was horrified to hear later that she is an expert on him and a very scholarly old lady. After leaving our friends we set off to take a boat trip on the canals. In our glass-topped boat, trapping the warm sun, we glided deliciously about, while an extremely beautiful girl described things to us in four languages. Late lunch in a small tavern.

To a concert in the evening – we are very close to the Concertgebouw – Peter Pears, and a small orchestra playing Mozart *divertimenti* very beautifully.

## March 9th

Still we walk and walk, along the lovely streets and canal sides (this morning through the university). The weather is brilliant and cold as a knife. Another touristy trip – to Edam, Volendam and the Island of Marken. All the guides are excellent linguists, good-looking (this one was male), quick-witted and fond of making cracks about lavatories, prostitutes or drunks. Thoughts on the Dutch: they seem to have an appetite for life, and are clever, vital, efficient, reliable and funny (Amsterdammers particularly). But perhaps also somewhat coarse, unpoetical, unsubtle and lacking in nuances.

In the afternoon the excitable Dr van den Bosch drove us to Haarlem, where we spent an hour in the museum, and I realized that Franz Hals painted two superb pictures.

## March 19th: London

Low, depressed, not feeling very well. The hugeness and blackness and emptiness of the hole in my life stares me afresh in the face. I suppose it might be possible to get into some new gear, but I feel I've somehow lost heart.

Janetta, after all, arrives today for a fortnight.

Another small pin has perhaps fastened down a flapping portion of the foreground. Bunny asks me to drive out to Magouche's in Tuscany with him in five weeks' time. I've said yes. So the future takes a sort of shape, and I have a feeling this is an annually repeated pattern.

Janetta's low and gentle voice on the telephone has made sense out of confusion.

# March 23rd: At the Stones[1] (Litton Cheney)

I saw Janetta twice, and the ease and pleasure in our communication has changed my outlook. The pleasure of loving so unique a person whose affection I'm profoundly grateful for, can't be exhausted. When I say she's 'lost' and 'gone' I'm lying. What's more, in spite of arriving in this inclement, grey ice-box I think it has given her great pleasure, and perhaps some of the mental stimuli lacking on the 'coast', to see her friends and realize how very much they want to see her. Her life with Jaime sounds fine. There's no major source of worry in any of the three girls, only the flooding of poor Tramores (swollen windows and doors, bulgy, soaked books, wet-marks on walls) is a great grief – I admire the realistic almost self-mocking way she talks of it. This – since realism has always been the quality I most value – is brought home to me by finding myself in the presence of nervous collapse here at Litton Cheney, on which I'm afraid I've failed to make any impression. Reynolds is in a state of grief, self-laceration and mourning, and has been so for ten days, because he ordered two large trees that menaced the house to be cut down. It is as if they were murdered corpses lying there, and the gap in a hedge left by their fall is an agony to him. Janet found him yesterday looking at it with tears pouring down his cheeks and his hands over his face. On our first evening he referred to 'the knot of his utter misery and guilt'. Then and next morning I tried all I could think of by way of reassurance. I went to look at the trees; he had covered their stumps with ivy-fronds like flowers at a funeral, but I moved them aside and declared with conviction that the proportion between phloem and bast was wrong, that the rot had clearly set in, and they must have been dangerous. I told him that where the gap looked like a raw operational wound it would close up and nature take over, and very quickly too with spring at hand. I told him the extra light and sun (shining yesterday luckily) were an asset, and that there was something as a landscape gardener, artist and tree-lover he could treat as raw material and mould to his design. I went round and looked at all his other splendid trees, and said he was anyhow not suffering from tree-starvation. I said that man had always grown trees and then cut them down and burned them, and that logs and fallen trees were handsome, healthy objects. I tried sympathy pure and simple, saying how deeply I had suffered from a fallen tree at

[1] Reynolds and Janet.

175

Ham Spray, which was quite true. I tried a slightly tougher line, saying that what was done was done, and that however much one loved trees they were not people. I got a little tougher still and said that irrational emotion could only be dealt with ultimately by one's own courageous effort. If one *wants* to starve or grieve to death, no one can stop one.

I think he believed me when I said the trees had begun to decay, and for a moment pure sympathy had some effect. But by yesterday the black cloud of mourning was there as before. I hadn't had the least effect.

Both nights he has read aloud to us from *Middlemarch* in a low voice, with evident pleasure and well, but so very softly that he seemed to deny our presence as listeners. He is an intensely charming man but at the present moment one wrapped up in his own neurosis – and I admire Janet's patience and kindness to him.

## April 1: Stowell

I drove from the Stones to spend a night here and Auberon and Teresa Waugh came to dinner. Teresa is a character, with bright wits. He is full of odd hates. A nice evening though, and on Sunday we drove to Job's Mill and lunched with the Baths. Jonny was there. It is a ravishing place, and Henry was dashing and funny.

## April 9th: Crichel for Easter

The divine weather stayed with us all the while and turned on the heat as well. We sat out between the glass shelters; there was croquet; Moses panted in the shade. I did *not* however preserve the silence of an Indian Brave as I had meant, but am ashamed to say I discharged some of my melancholy (for it didn't quite clear up) on to Julian. Why the poor fellow should be treated so just because he's sympathetic I can't think. I look to see how the heroes and heroines of the memoirs and biographies I read deal with their last lap, and it is always (at best) a feat of endurance. I remember poor Edward Lear, and also Princess Matilde Bonaparte, a delightfully warm, good-humoured, enjoying character.

Raymond's face, just as yellowed and crinkled as mine, emerged distressingly from a harsh, cherry-red turtle-neck pullover patterned with peacocks' tails. Etymological problems filled the air between him and Desmond with fine dust, although Julian and I put up mild pleas for tolerance, variety and change. Then, over and again, Raymond gave proofs of his sweetness and affection, and returned from a ruler-wielding schoolmaster to a 'very cuddly man'.[1] Desmond ran about in his youthful and attentive way, worrying me in view of his recent eye operation and of the fact that he was clearly anxious about certain renewed sensations in the operated eye. Pat returned straight from Nigeria on Saturday and showed seemingly casual indifference to these very natural fears.

All in all there were lots of enjoyable, even hilarious times, walks of course every day (and every day the buds swelled and tiny tufts of green appeared on the larches), talk and laughter; not very much – but some – music, visits from the Cecils and Cressida Ridley, and a very nice evening at Kitty West's.

Raymond suddenly, *à propos de rien*: 'I know I've not got a first-class nor a second-class brain, but I'm cleverer than most people.'

## April 11th

Here I am back in London and this summer weather goes on. Last night Eardley and Julia came to dinner. I remembered how when this same trio met once before Julia complained that Eardley 'didn't once look at her' but addressed all his remarks to me, so I did my best to adjust matters differently. After Eardley left I perhaps rashly gave her another drink, and she suddenly (in the middle of talking of something quite else) launched on a tirade against me. It began (like a political speech often rehearsed): 'I think there was a time you and I didn't see each other, after we left school, so it was impossible for you to know that I had a piano and played on it endlessly, jazz only of course, but I understood how to make variations on a theme and so on.' This, coming out of a conversation about a totally different subject produced a rather mad effect and I thought it better to remain quite silent and let her flow on. She landed up of course on our musical conversation of January 27th. 'So you see you were wrong to say I'm not musical.' In vain I said that I'd not only never said this but never thought it. She collected her coat and finally went out of the front door saying something like 'this is a horrid way to part.' It is indeed.

[1] As he was called by Caroline West when about three.

Of the Campbells: F: 'How was it?' J: 'Oh well, *awful* really. I didn't enjoy it at all.' F: 'Didn't you have the glorious weather?' J: 'Yes, that didn't improve things, I must say. Susan's such a thoroughly unpleasant and selfish character.' etc. etc. Of Robin she said she liked him, but didn't find him 'an interesting person to discuss art with'. That 'he was quite obviously desperately unhappy with Susan, but the funny thing was that after Susan had been yelling at him she saw them hugging, quite lovingly.' The children made life impossible, and in spite of lying down all the afternoons with a bandage over her eyes she felt ghastly, ill and exhausted. There was much too much social life. I asked if she thought she would have been better staying in London and she said yes, and that she'd thought seriously of coming away.

As for the anatomy of my recent melancholy, Princess Matilde Bonaparte put it in a nutshell by saying, 'Griefs seem heavier as one gets older.'

## April 12th

Yesterday I went for some music with Margaret and Shirley[1] and the pianist Anne, and I stayed on to supper. I told Margaret about Julia and her response was typically kind: 'Oh poor Julia. It's really pathetic.' She thinks Julia feels love-hate for me, but I'm not so sure. I think it's pretty undiluted hate, coupled with a certain dependence because of the extremity she's in.

Lionel says that Beakus is contemplating suing Holroyd for what he wrote about him.

I liked a story of Julian's about Elizabeth Bowen. Asked by an interviewer what she felt about growing old, she thought and said: 'The gr-gr-GRR-great thing is to keep the car on the road.'

## April 13th

One result of my awareness of Julia's dislike is that I cling to those friends whose affection I feel sure of. Went last night with Georgia to a baddish film and afterwards she insisted on standing me an expensive dinner while she confided in me some of her problems. Does her stalwart Scottish boyfriend really have marriage in mind?

[1]  Margaret's daughter.

recently she has fallen to some extent for a Number 2 and is suffering from the usual stresses – conflict, guilt. She is deeply romantic about love and I doubt if either of these fellows is good enough for her. Is it perhaps ceasing to be valued – just as money and things become more and more so? I've been reading an article by Quinton on marriage in which love isn't once mentioned – in the Stendhalian sense, or the sense of rapturous companionship, of two minds emptying into each other, of support, of affection, or the touching emotions represented in Rembrandt's *The Jewish Bride*; nothing but sexual satisfaction and reproduction. I shall continue to believe that it is far the most valuable thing in the world.

## *April 15th: At the Campbells, Pitts Deep*

Robin, meeting me, says he called at Julia's to return the umbrella she had left in his car, and she sent a message to say she was 'very angry with me', which seems to argue that she is unaware that I too have reached the end of this particular tether. Robin went on, chuckling, to tell me she had said, 'Everyone thinks Frances so bloody marvellous, or wise – Minerva and her owl – but she's *not*!' Any of our mutual friends who have been so foolish as not only to think it but tell Julia so have done me a great disservice.

Cold armies of clouds battling in the sky, daffodils swept suddenly flat against the ground by gusts. A little friend of William's is staying, with the result that I sleep in the cottage and there's a good deal of rushing in to say, '*Mummy*! He threw *earth* at me!', constantly calling on their parents to show omnipotent benevolence.

Waking this morning (Sunday) I looked out of my bedroom straight over the sea channel to the Isle of Wight. The tide nearly high; a quiet sheet of softly rippling, pale blue water sheened with gold and on it two swans drawn up near the beach, gilded also by the early sun, with their necks, beaks and heads plunging about under the water – an ecstatic sight. One or two other sea birds were swimming about or crying faintly in the distance. This animal and vegetable peace and tranquillity, suggesting the beginning of the world, made me think with horror of human beastliness, noise and rush, motor-bicycles, bombs, smells and advertisements. Such a serene morning sight is cosmopolitan too and links up with other mornings remembered, in Spain, Scotland and Turkey. The common element in them all is serenity.

Julian asked Raymond what he would like to have possessed that he hadn't got. His own would be 'long legs'. Mine – serenity.

Walking in the Beatrix Potter wood I found a rarity – lungwort growing perfectly wild, also primroses, slowly clumping, miniature leaves on hazel twigs, and stagnant ponds full of young iris spears.

I was rung up last week by a literary frog who wanted to come and see me because he was 'writing a book on Lytton Strachey'. Professor of English Literature at the University of Paris, he was a plump, middle-aged man with a stuffed appearance and moon face. He fitted himself into my wing armchair and became almost speechless. I didn't know what to tell him. In the end he asked me a few questions, mainly about Carrington, because he said he had read her letters to Lytton, and not been greatly impressed. 'Even by the drawings?' I asked. He shrugged: *'Je ne suis pas Carringtonien'*

## April 19th: London

I have had what I most enjoy – three quiet evenings running with one companion: first Isobel [Strachey], then Joan [Cochemé] and last night Julian. Julian of course was the most stimulating, and we talked away till going on for one, covering much ground and spilling plenty of beans – he about his relation with parents (full of guilt that was quite uncalled for, as I tried to persuade him), and how he would like to have children. What a waste it is that he shouldn't and a wife to. Then about Virginia's books, and Janetta's character, and many other things.

Now here I am stuck like a fly in my last weekend before departure for Italy, and London weekends have a curious stickiness. I went to visit Sebastian[1] in his hospital ward; he was sitting up in a chair looking perfectly all right, with his sister Velda and two other visitors. The huge, long ward with light flowing in through tall windows, strange machines here and there, a murmur of talk, and on every bed figures stretched in varying stages of misery, decline or recovery. One in the next bed looked in a very bad way, his poor, thin face (spectacles on nose) and domed forehead reminded me of Eddy (Sackville) and wore the same look of distaste. Here so many dramas are proceeding, with mutes on but one is well aware of them, and

[1]    Sprott, an old Cambridge friend, and fellow student of philosophy.

hardly dare let one's eyes drift into corners. The feeling is that this isn't real life – but in fact it most certainly is.

## April 20th

Preparing to leave today for Hilton, tomorrow for Europe.

Yesterday I went out to Kew to lunch with the Kees. Cynthia had been having a bad go of her internal complaint with quite a high temperature and lay pale and limp and sad in her bed. Robert and the children looked almost indecently robust, but Robert was more relaxed than usual, and talking very freely about love and marriage as we walked among the magnolia trees (some scorched by frost) in Kew Gardens. He tried to make out that he had 'no real feelings for other people or desire to help them in distress', why I can't imagine for no one does so much.

## April 21st

To Hilton through rain and a horrible combination of new, young, green leaves and dark, lowering, plum-coloured sky. Found Bunny tired and with a cold, and I feel a qualm of dawning responsibilities. Amaryllis disturbed William and his girlfriend Linda aloft at their love-making. They came downstairs and she is just what I expected, with dark eyes and hair and firm little round features; quick like a robin, full of friendliness. She and William are very lover-like. We played trios, which I loved. At dinner we talked about drama, old and new. Amaryllis said that the trend of modern drama was to make speech unnecessary and concentrate on gestures and attitudes. But I wonder why they are all so keen to pare down everything until only skeletons are left. Why in heaven's name make things 'unnecessary'? I said so long as things were good the more of them the better. Linda asked why I thought so, and I told her it seemed to me a matter of simple arithmetic. Amaryllis sometimes looks beautiful in her cloud of hair, but how nervous she is! Plates rattle as she hands them, she smokes endlessly and talks of going out to Tramores 'for about ten days' though she has just been to Italy. Where will she get the sixty odd pounds? In argument Bunny fruitlessly opposes everything modern. I try – equally fruitlessly – to sit on the fence.

## April 22nd: Arras

Arras is the end of our first day's journey. Almost as soon as we reached Southend airport 'Mr Garnett' was called for on the loud speaker. He at once thought Angelica (who is ill) must be dying, but it was merely that our hour of departure was earlier than he had reckoned with. We were carried over the sea at a stately pace. Looking down I could see its sandy floor through shallow water, and very soon, we were across and near Calais. Threading tiny 'white' roads we passed on to Arras and arrived with no map of the town, at rush hour, and in drenching rain. Bunny had a vague recollection of a big place where he had once stayed with Angelica. We asked in cafés and circled the suburbs and at last found a rather grand one. Dinner in a cheap restaurant while young men sat singly with newspapers, or in pairs talking their clever, delicate language.

## April 23rd: Aisey-sur-Seine

In a charming little village inn, cheap, clean, with window-boxes of egg-yellow pansies and the lovely combination of cream-coloured stone and grey paint. A few yards away, the 'infant Seine', as Bunny calls it, glides and then tumbles under an ancient bridge, and cows like Alderneys, a soft mouse-grey, are driven along the village street. Weather still wretchedly cold and wet but neither of us is wretched. Bunny's stamina is amazing. We drove from nine till seven yesterday with a fairly long break at Meaux – a detour made simply in order to buy its special mustard, but I enjoyed seeing the noble cathedral after lunch in a restaurant humming with noise. 'What famous man was its bishop?' I asked Bunny, who couldn't remember any more than I could, and then inside we saw it was Bossuet. Beautiful country from Meaux to the Seine, trees only just coming out but grass brilliantly green, cowslips, fat white cows looking as if they gave excellent milk and butter. Bun is very good-humoured, but I feel I must be the only female he has travelled with in separate rooms, and only hope he doesn't feel humiliated before the hotelier. His deafness is greater than I realized and in the car almost total. I lean towards him and project my remarks loudly towards his ear, but am nearly always greeted by a cheerful 'what?' A very good dinner: leek soup, trout, and goat cheese, before a wood fire, with an excellent bottle of wine. Bunny thaws out in the evening; at lunch, either from deafness or fatigue he appeared to me curiously shy. He talks affectionately of Magouche. Of Henrietta he says he asks and knows nothing.

## April 24th: Bonneville

South of Geneva and surrounded by ominously towering, snow-capped mountains, quite spoiled by *usines*, chalets and pines. Had difficulty in resigning ourselves to stay anywhere. Here we are in a straightforward commercial, which may be terribly noisy. My room looks out on a pink-blossomed tree and snow mountain, and I have the window wide open to fill it with fresh alpine air before sealing it hermetically. Meanwhile I'm sipping whisky and feeling happy.

## April 25th: Piacenza

Well, what a place! 'Pleasance' says the map ironically, in brackets. There's a holiday in the town, with flags and pleasure-seeking crowds. Unable to find the most modest of hotels, I stopped a promising-looking passer-by, who turned out to have a disastrously cleft palate and made ghastly noises, though obviously wanting to be helpful. Fired by his astonishing energy, Bunny insisted on leaving behind Pavia, which looked much nicer, and it's my rule for happy travelling to give in on such points. Anyway, we are in for the night in a modern hotel on the outskirts, whose staff are hissing with exhaustion after serving holiday meals all day. There's no question in Bunny's mind of slackening our pace, and what he said about dawdling along for five to seven days is rubbish. No time to buy a postcard, look at a single sight, take a stroll, yet in my foolish credulity I thought this was what we should see eye to eye about. Each morning he's eager to be off, and off we go. I feel like Alice and the Red Queen. This morning we headed towards the Mont Blanc tunnel, slightly dreaded beforehand but quite unalarming. Bunny expected forty kilometres of it, I twenty, and there turned out to be only twelve.

Out into soggy snow and sun; we coasted down the Val d'Aosta and had our first picnic by a stream. Last night at Bonneville I lay awake for three hours wondering if I could suggest a little less haste, but of course I didn't and again we drove all day, often at about seventy miles an hour, at which speed the little car is bumpy and erratic. I can't but admire this stupendous feat of endurance in a man of seventy-seven, but by evening his hand shakes and his face is red, so my pity is often aroused. And I regret the places whizzed by unseen, and wonder what I would do if he had a stroke driving at seventy miles per hour.

Interesting conversation, *en route* about homosexuals. They are 'frightened of sex', says Bunny, and their life is 'lacking in richness'. Stopped for a drink in the Piazza Cavour of a nice town called Vercelli and had an argument about Garibaldi. I asked the boy who brought our drinks what holiday it was. '*Di fascismo*', he said sheepishly and incorrectly.

## April 26th: San Sano

We have arrived and I have come to my senses and see the past four and a half days in a new light. Magouche was not expecting us before Monday at earliest, and our thundering advance now plainly shows as a valiant and obstinate attempt on Bunny's part to beat the band, and prove that he's not a dead dog yet, but a *man*. I can't help retrospectively resenting not having spent at least one more night on the way, looking at Italian towns, searching for flowers or lying in the grass after picnics. I may be hypersensitive about outstaying, and in this case anticipating, my welcome. In any case Magouche was, of course, much too polite not to greet us warmly, though she has a couple of Italian visitors and their little boy already staying in the house, and hasty bed-making had to be done. And I could so well imagine her muttering 'Good God, it's not them already!' as she ran downstairs to meet us.

Her house stands bold, solid and dominant on the rounded summit of a hill, looking out over other softly rolling hills and valleys thick with oaks and olives, towards Siena. Its central tower has two rather low openings onto a loggia, which give it a somewhat grumpy expression. Matthew and Maro[1] are nest-making vigorously, planting trees, gardening, planning swimming-pools and garages. The furniture is solid to match the house, simple, a little austere, and there's nothing for prettiness alone and no pictures on the walls, windows rather small according to Tuscan farmhouse tradition, central heating. Almost the best room in the house is an enormous

[1] Magouche's eldest daughter and her husband, son of Stephen and Natasha Spender.

bathroom, with a vast bath that can never be completely emptied. Moved by the same sort of impulse as Janetta with Tramores, Magouche, Maro and Matthew have created something very different. I don't know who is responsible for what.

## April 27th

Breakfast-time announces itself without a watch by the sound and delicious smell of coffee being ground and toasting bread. We sat outside under a mulberry tree which is only just starting to unwrap its buds. Hot sun. On this southern side of the house there are preparations for a lawn to be made. Sat in the sun reading and writing till it was time to start on a picnic which was to speed the Italian family to Rome. We ate beside an artificial lake. After lunch Magouche and Maro flung themselves shrieking into the water; Bunny took Matthew off to fish; I went looking for flowers, fell down and returned with bleeding legs as usual, and the dear little boy, Albertino, made love to frogs. Suddenly Matthew burst into applause as Bunny was seen at the far end of the lake capped with his white hair, preparing to dive off a long board, which he actually did twice, with great heroism, for the water was icy. The Italians left for Rome.

## April 28th

Getting into the San Sano way of life. My bedroom is severely simple, with a hard monk's bed which I find very sympathetic. I'm impressed by Matthew and Maro's unfashionably energetic lives. Matthew digs and waters and chops wood all day long, comes in with red cheeks and eats huge meals. Maro, smooth but pallid, looks as if consciously trying to produce a child, but doesn't. Two women from the village come in and help. Bunny strides off to the porch of an old barn and sits at a stone table writing. We drink a lot of the local Chianti and eat minestrones, pasta and home-made brawn. Everyone becomes jolly over dinner; Bunny tending to hold forth.

This afternoon I walked downhill through a wood of oaks whose leaves are still downy, crumpled and pinkish-grey with youth. Everything is behindhand and there are not many flowers, but a good many spider and *purpurea* orchids.

## April 29th

The veils covering yesterday's sky have grown denser and streaked, grey and threatening, an unbecoming roof to this most eloquently beautiful landscape. But it is warm still. Lorries have been arriving and depositing huge mounds of earth on the flat space destined for the lawn, bringing ugliness and confusion and breaking our calm.

I walked with Magouche to a farm on the next ridge. The ground switchbacks gently, what is seen changes at every step and in the long, bright green grass or on the limestone rocks some flowers are at last appearing. Magouche has been unfailingly warm and kind to us all, and looks so handsome and strong that I can't help minding her lack of a mate, at present.

Next to my room is a pleasant landing with some books and a table and the window, where I sit identifying my flowers.

## April 30th

Fine blue morning. 'Let's take a picnic and go to Volterra,' said Magouche at breakfast, and no one expected the skies to open and deluge us with rain. It's tantalizing to be in such lovely country with extraordinary things to see all round, and find such disappointing weather. I think of Orta and Sicily, scenes of two other dubious Italian springs. Matthew and Maro stayed at home controlling their mounds of earth and lorries. Bunny, Magouche and I picnicked by a sweet little Romanesque church on the way to Volterra, and Bunny put away a quite alarming quantity of red wine and a good deal of food too, which, however, had no effect on him until we were nearly home, when he looked as though he might collapse. 'Are you all right, Bunny? Have you got a migraine?' 'No, not a *migraine*.' He is ashamed of every sort of weakness, so that it's difficult to know how seriously to take it. As he grows older and tends to feel tired, he turns to wine to help him out, rather than give in, and presents a tragic spectacle, reminding me for some reason of the dramatic news that de Gaulle was rejected by his compatriots two days ago, with a last dreadful '*non.*'

I'm slightly preoccupied by several adjustments or the lack of them. I wonder if I've become more critical of Bunny through seeing him here. Magouche is quite angelic to him, and they would appear to be on better terms than they were on their travels last year. But human beings are so walled in behind castellations that after months of feeling 'this is easy, all you must do is be interested and appreciative', the sense of contact suddenly disappears behind a curtain of non-communication.

As we approached Volterra we saw it across the valley preparing to wrap itself in a dense sheet of rain, and then down it came in floods streaming over the huge, many-coloured paving-stones of the noble streets till they looked as brilliant and variegated as pebbles under water, olive green, purple and burnt sienna. We ran into the Duomo, Baptistery, the small but interesting Pinacoteca and the extraordinary Etruscan museum. Arrived home, we put the exhausted Bunny to bed and our soaked clothes to dry, and Magouche, Maro and I sat over a wood fire drinking whisky and talking female pacifist talk, and saying how we disliked those intellectuals who pride themselves on our having 'kept the peace' by means of the bomb race. And at a very jolly dinner in the village restaurant, I said what I thought of people who 'dismiss' all Germans – namely that they were racists as much to be condemned as anti-Semites and anti-blacks, and that we must remember what a huge contribution to civilization the Germans had made.

### May 1st

Tears – an unexpected development. At lunch-time it was still cool and cloudy and we lunched indoors. Bunny was talking, as he loves to, about figures of the past – Rupert Brooke in this case. How James [Strachey] had been in love with him and then carried off Rupert's girl, Noel Olivier. Maro said: 'You mean he couldn't get one, so he thought he'd have the other.' Bunny did a full, glaring half-turn and burst out in a pressurized voice: '*No*, it wasn't like that *at all*. Don't always assume the worst of people; just *for once* try thinking well of them.' She carried it off well, though daunted, and said she supposed it came from belonging to the persecuted Armenian race. It seemed to have blown over, but later when I was at my table looking up my flowers Magouche whirled through like a ship under full sail saying, 'Now everyone's in tears – Maro *and* Bunny!' I could indeed hear Maro's sobs and hysterical voice, then Bunny walked quickly through with a red, folded, gloom-stricken expression.

I'm on Maro's side. Bunny was quite unnecessarily fierce; he can't both insist on talking about his old friends and also jealously guard them from the comments of those who didn't know them. But this is just what he does want to do, and last year there was an explosion over Tommy.[1] The first premises of Maro's character have to be accepted, and she sometimes talks without thinking, but I like her energy and directness, and her devotion to Matthew all these long years is very touching.

Peace was confirmed by a long walk for all of us except Matthew, who keeps to his dedicated life of physical activity. The favourite of the two cats came too – a tabby tom with apricot underfur, who trotted down the woods with his tail in the air, displaying his furry balls, and then got lost. Flower-hunting; Maro dug up everything. Bunny tried to leap into the air to get down a strange form of mistletoe from an oak. We crossed the river, traversed the other side and waded back through icy water and so home. I'm slightly alarmed lest Bunny's exhibitionism gets him into serious trouble.

### May 2nd

Better weather at last and steadily improving. Magouche and I drove to Siena together. The beauty of that truly glorious town knocked me backwards just as it had on my two previous visits, though possibly the Duccios in their dark, velvet-hung gallery crowded with Italian schoolboys and girls, seemed to ask for admiration so insistently that they got less. With lunch in the piazza, pictures, duomo, cafés and postcards, we passed six hours very happily.

Dinner of globe artichokes and chicken; anecdotes from Bunny, intercepted by long pauses. Laughter, drink and bed.

### May 3rd

Perhaps too much drink, as everyone admitted to sleeping badly, and acid home-brewed Chianti may have been to blame. Sunny morning. Yesterday's post brought a batch of letters; one from Janetta asking me to join her and Jaime in Minorca – so very soon that I quailed at first. Much as I love being with friends and staying in their houses, there's an effort in trying to fit in, understand, not grate on other people's nerves, which gives me a desire for the only form of true relaxation that now remains – being alone. And this, when it

[1] Stephen Tomlin.

happens, is often a bitter disappointment. But after this first shrinking response I thought how much I loved being with Janetta and Jaime and wrote to say, 'Yes – next month I would love to.'

Writing letters at the long, solid table on the breakfast porch, which faces north and is in shadow till tea-time.

Desultory afternoon, watering, reading, flower identification, while Magouche and Maro sat removing stones from the projected lawn, chattering and thumping like native women with their machetes. At dinner Bunny became curiously militaristic and blimpish (Matthew pretends to be taken with this attitude and is reading Kipling); Magouche said, 'We must avoid politics in future,' sipping camomile tea in the kitchen.

## May 4th

Magouche, Bunny and I spent the day in Florence. I don't like it nearly as much as Siena – its character has dwindled under the invasion of commerce and tourism, till it's just a large, noisy, bustling town in which are beautiful things. I sat alone in a café on the Piazza della Signoria, while the hideous voices of three Americans quacked on beside me about things and money, should they have ices or not, and whether there should be a discount on the bill. I only tried to see a few things, but enjoyed them. Magouche put me down outside the barrack-like church of the Carmine – walking alone inside I saw in one corner a band of upward-gazing worshippers and knew this was where the Masolinos and Masaccios were. They talked in hushed whispers only, in the awful presence of art. In the Bargello I ran into Bunny, his colour scheme of bright pink and snow-white startlingly at odds with the Donatellos and Verocchios. Somehow I don't feel his reaction to art is so much visual as literary, but it's strong, and he likes to look at what he looked at before. For lunch we drove out into the country to a smart restaurant in the stables of a Medici hunting-box. Depressed, unwelcoming waiters, but the best meal we'd had in Italy.

## May 5th

Magouche's great outgoing warmth is much in evidence here, and to Bunny she is extraordinarily sweet, but perhaps there is an element of destruction in the way she eggs him on to prove his strength and youth, takes him on immense walks through rivers, or – above all – asks him to roll the new lawn. He came in so redfaced and done for after this that I exclaimed in horror and said he shouldn't do it. Magouche: 'I know it. But one must ask him to do things sometimes or it's so depressing for him.' Reminding me of Janetta long ago, pressing Ralph to eat and drink more than he should, 'to cheer him up'.

### May 6th

Magouche likes a generous way of life and to go shopping with her is an eye-opener in lavish spending. Late in the afternoon she and I walked to the village dressmaker and ascended for a fitting to her dark shuttered room, entirely filled by a bed for three. Below three Norn-like females sat stitching, giving me the sort of glimpse into other lives I love. Afterwards we walked on through lovely woods and the cold inclement afternoon. I tried to turn the conversation from Magouche's girls to her own life, but she gently and politely resisted and said at present she had none. Yet later on, when we had lost our way and let ourselves in for a long, long walk she began talking of Gorky,[1] and I feel that he is now more real than Jack Phillips[2] or even Robin Fedden. She compared Gorky with Othello for jealousy. He was beside himself, if she talked to anyone else. She had 'given him everything' and believed everything he told her, much of which turned out to be lies. Her honesty and recklessness and destructiveness all appeared in the last act, 'when he became paranoic' and violent and threatened suicide. Did she think he would kill himself? Yes, on the whole. She could see no other end. She took the children and went to her mother; he telephoned to one of his friends saying he was going to hang himself and then he did. Did none of his friends hurry to his side? I asked. Yes, but he was too late. She was young and the demands made on her by the violence and urgency of the catastrophe carried her through. It had become more painful later, and still obviously does obsess her. Yet she hasn't a morbid sense of guilt and looks at it honestly. He had been violent as well as jealous and his doctor thought she should take the children away. I suggested that she couldn't still have loved him. 'Oh yes, I

1 Her first husband, Arshile Gorky, the famous Armenian painter.
2 Her second husband.

190

loved him *tenderly*, but I couldn't stay with him. And, of course, the poor fellow had a series of ghastly calamities – serious cancer and a colostomy, his neck broken in a car accident, a fire consuming many of his pictures.' Magouche gave me oddly little sense of his personality, probably because I've known no one in the least like him; but she sets very real value on his 'marvellous work', and there was something deeply moving in this tragic, honest and terrible story. On our walk we reached a deserted farmhouse, solid and towered like Avane, with a steep green field running down to the river bed, a vine trained across the space between house and stables, a marvellous view. We picked stems of quince in flower and very pale mauve irises. Our devious return down endless valleys and steep hills nearly finished me off and I felt I was in the hands of the death-instinct. Does she remember I'm nearly seventy? On my return I lay prostrate on the sofa and drank rather too much whisky. Spenders in Siena today. Bunny in bed curing his cold.

### May 7th

Wet and cold. Writing, reading and flower-books all morning. Warmed up with a little weeding. Last night at dinner Matthew was critical of Maro's nagging, and cast fierce looks across the table at her, she responding with propitiatory ones and apparent alarm. Today they are honey-sweet together and she came carolling like a lark to breakfast dressed in shirt and trousers of palest pink. When Bunny had left the lunch table she had an outburst about the repulsive signs of age in him ('bags of flesh'). 'Will Matthew look like that one day?' she asked incredulously. Yes, and you too. It's rather a struggle trying to keep warm, and the solid house with its small windows seems dank and dark.

This evening a blazing fire was lit in the dark sitting-room and we all read except Maro who sewed. I read Freddy Ayer on William James, meaty and stimulating. Very jolly dinner. Very cold night.

A week tomorrow I shall be in England. I've suggested to Bunny driving with him as far as Pisa.

### May 8th

Got up early hoping to warm myself in a hot bath, but for once the water was merely tepid. I've got into more than a full quota of English clothes. Magouche decided that we must defeat the cosmos by driving off somewhere regardless, and we had a most delightful excursion. At San Gargano we saw a ruined abbey and (far more exciting) a round church decorated with zebra stripes, unrestored and lined with perfect Lorenzetti frescoes. On the way to Massa Maritima we picked orchids and other flowers, and the sky became royal blue in patches. Arriving home we saw a car outside the house. 'Who *is* it?' cried Magouche in alarm. It was Miranda Rothschild,[1] her present husband Ian Watson and a solid little girl called Da'ad, child of her first husband – an Arab – who ill-treated her and died a violent death.

## May 9th

In bed this evening, rather drunk and in a flux of contradictory emotions. My first reaction to Ian Watson was physical repulsion from his too red lips sunk in a black beard. Then came a certain sympathy because of shared views on various subjects. Also awareness of the kindness and intelligence behind his high, well-shaped forehead (Julia is quite right – I do value foreheads and hate their absence). Miranda has a neatly pretty face and very short hair and drops her ceaseless chit-chat like water on a stone in a flat 'silly little me' voice. She is at once irritating and rather charming.

Here in my bed I've also been thinking perhaps ironically about Italy, its really pretty dreadful climate, vast stores of beauty (natural and otherwise), its handsome friendly inhabitants all with rotten brown stumps of teeth and intestinal worms, eating their plates of pasta and drinking the sour Chianti that tears at the entrails.

This morning in spite of the continuing horror of the weather we set off in the Watsons' car, leaving behind Da'ad and the Spenders. Miranda had pattered away at breakfast: 'I had a dream about Bunny. We'd been talking about marriage, and at the end of it he said: "And as for *love* – I think it was merely an invention of your grandmother, Mary Hutchinson."' Bunny responded with a rosy delighted beam. It was something he almost might have said. Lunch in a small town restaurant, Sienese pictures at Asciano and then to Pienza where the serious rain began. Huddling from the weather we saw the sights of this lovely little town better than when I visited it a

[1]  Daughter of Lord Rothschild (Victor) and his first wife Barbara.

few years ago with Raymond and the Cochemés. Miranda – sitting at the back of the car with Magouche and me – never stopped her prattle for a moment and I began to be maddened by it. She doesn't understand stillness and quiet, or how to soak in impressions, she is self-absorbed to an alarming degree – everything comes back to herself. They are supposed to be looking for a house to buy here, but whenever we see one she sets up her dismissive monkey-chatter: 'Oh no, no. There isn't enough bareness, not the right sort of trees. I don't like it, do you Ian? It's too *bushy* – too *pubic* if you know what I mean. No, I really want a sort of *castle*.' She's obviously a spoilt, little rich girl, but scratch her and you find a bohemian eccentric, and perhaps a 'bitch'. 'Bitchily' is one of her favourite words and it was applicable to what she said to Magouche about Matthew – she was 'worried about him. There seems to be no *joy* in his painting.' She's quite a good mimic – favourite targets Paddy and Joan.[1] She spars openly with Maro, who gives as good as she gets. Maro is fond of talking disparagingly about 'awful old hags of nearly fifty' or 'horribly ugly girls', with an arrogance that would be un-charming even if she were younger and more beautiful than she is. 'Just as a matter of interest, do you never want to have anything to do with ugly girls?' I asked her. 'No. I'm a fan of beautiful girls.' At dinner I had quite an interesting conversation with Ian from which I gather he's deadly serious, works at research into Byzantine art, can't really laugh at himself, had a stormy childhood rejected by his parents ('I was *extremely* violent'), and now loathes violence, has undergone periods of depression and insomnia, is very neurotic in fact. At Oxford he was often intensely unhappy, was befriended by Maurice Bowra, and 'five out of ten of his friends committed suicide.' He found his best friend dead, a brilliantly successful young man. How true it all is I don't know, but it tumbles out with adolescent excitement, many 'you know's' and 'sort of's'.

## May 10th

I've seen another facet of Miranda's character. Da'ad spent most of the morning with me and was so good and sweet and the day so fine that I hadn't the heart to shoo her off. Then, when we were all in the kitchen, she did something that annoyed her mother who had

[1] Leigh Fermor.

responded inadequately to bunches of flowers, and kept rigorously aloof. (Yesterday she left her all day with the Spenders.) Miranda hissed suddenly, 'Do what I tell you! *Obey* me!' and added something in venomous-sounding Greek. Da'ad backed into the dining-room and stood glaring out of green eyes and muttering 'horrid pig' under her breath. I don't think Miranda saw I was there – she shot after Da'ad and slapped her violently. 'That hurts,' said Da'ad in a low voice. 'It'll hurt you more next time. You're a *naughty* little girl. You're *never* nice to me! Never!' (Mounting hysteria.) The odd form of this complaint is significant I think.

Yet, later when I became distracted by the loss of my bag with all my traveller's cheques, passport, etc. it was she who really put determination and kindness into her search and found it in the long grass.

But the beauty of the day! That's been the great thing. All that we've longed for and expected since that first picnic. This gentle landscape engendered an idyllic *Month in the Country* atmosphere, and nearly everyone worked hard on the lawn, rolling and raking and removing wheelbarrows full of stones. I walked alone down into the riverbed and back, picking flowers. Some pretty awful visitors to dinner. An Irish poet, thin-lipped and egotistic, his stupid, attractive, sexy wife. A little boy of four who romped and talked unflaggingly and without quarrelling with Da'ad till 2 a.m. Ian had rather typically brought a spit and started too late roasting a side of lamb on a much too weak fire. It seemed as if it would never cook and the visitors were longing for more drinks and sitting with empty glasses. They brought also a bearded au pair boy on his way to Balliol, a lower-class Communist, quite clever probably, but with his back to some invisible wall or other, and almost speechless. At last we decided to tear the half-done meat with our teeth and say how marvellous it tasted. The guests now showed an immense capacity for putting away the drink and stayed and stayed disastrously. The benches we were sitting on grew very hard, yet it would be fatal – we felt – to move upstairs. A conversation flared up (and led a brief crazy life) as to whether you would save a Cézanne or a spastic child in a fire. Maro threw herself rather hectically into defence of art, the poet and au pair boy were passionately pro-human-being (the child somehow became a 'plastic child'). I threw in Shakespeare and Mozart's works with the Cézanne in an endeavour to make a *reductio ad absurdum*. Then the poet began a very long, boastful story with carefully studied gestures, about how he got out of the RAF in spite of being, as he repeated several times 'an athlete, their champion runner'. Maro and Matthew said afterwards they had heard this story several times before and his wife always laughed at the right place. Magouche, Maro and I held a council of despair in the kitchen: how to get them to leave? We tried yawning and letting the conversation drop – no go. I went upstairs to bed, and the poet's wife (who was Frieda Lawrence's granddaughter) seems to have said to Magouche, 'Do go to bed. I'm afraid I can't possibly get them to come away.' What a desperate state of things! Miranda had gone to bed before they came, suffering from 'cramp in the stomach'. Ian said almost proudly that they both had terrible migraines and when I started to discuss cures as a fellow sufferer, he said, 'Oh I'm just absolutely *out* and delirious for five days. Nothing's any good.' Lawks.

### May 11th

The weather is now quite perfect and we've had I think the best day of our stay. The Watsons went off house-hunting in the Volterra area. The rest of us and Da'ad took a picnic to the valley below the deserted farmhouse Magouche and I discovered last week. Wading through long grass, past a spring of purest water surrounded by a little wall and tufts of mint and fern, we came to the shallow river, took off our clothes and rolled in the cold water. After our picnic some lay and read, I looked for flowers and then we walked up the hill to the farm. The view it looks out on is now clad in much denser but still fresh greenery: oaks, chestnuts and cypress, and behind is a sort of tableland with vines, quince in bloom, white iris and apples. A poetical, Virgilian day, ending in a serene afternoon.

Then the Watsons returned, Miranda chirping on like a wire fence, about what a horrible day they'd had with football crowds and motor rallies, waste paper, road accidents and a bad lunch. Yet there's something likeable in her and she is so hungry for love that she plays it for all it's worth. But her child doesn't love her and she knows it. I've rather fallen for this solid, reasonable, good-tempered little Da'ad.

Our breach with England has been complete because of an Italian postal strike. I speculate about them all from time to time – Sophie, the Kees.

195

This evening at dinner Miranda talked so wildly that I think she must have been taking drugs. Afterwards she came and thanked me for 'being so nice to Da'ad'. F: 'Well, she was nice to me.' M: 'I'm the only person she isn't nice to' (again). 'She adores you, you know.' I said what I could think of about Da'ad's alrightness, and since Miranda seemed to be making an appeal of some sort I gave her two kisses.

Odds and ends:

Maro calls Matthew 'my little love', 'my little darling' in spite of his being six foot five. It is not irritating, rather touching in fact.

The view from the lavatory seat is the finest I ever saw. I wonder why they've made the lightest, largest room into the bathroom-lavatory.

Ever since Magouche and I played *Otello* right through on the gramophone I have had it on the brain, without a moment's freedom from it. And always, always I keep coming round to Desdemona's despairing cry 'Ah Em*i*lia!' What does it mean? Do I, like her, want to be saved from death?

## May 12th

Another brilliant morning. The Watsons who at first were going to stay 'one night', obviously intend to dig well in, and leave Da'ad here while they go house-hunting. Slight electricity in the plan-making this morning. Miranda starts an interminable rigmarole about the horror of female bodies and pubic hair. Bunny gets up and hurries from the breakfast table in ostentatious disgust. Ian reproves her. I am anxious to leave the day after tomorrow, Wednesday (my flight from Pisa is the day after), so as to look at Pisa and not feel rushed. I suggest to Bunny driving with him as far as Pisa, but he is obstinately disposed to put it off till Thursday. He is trying to persuade Magouche to come with him to the frontier and he rather obtusely fails to realize that this would not be much treat for her, that she's always doing that journey and would have to return in a hot train. I think she only wavered out of kindness, affection and worry at his going off on his own.

Finally Miranda and Ian set off house-hunting, leaving Da'ad with the Spenders, who got exasperated and locked her in a bedroom. Bunny, Magouche and I to Siena which was frustratingly shut, and afterwards picnicked on a grassy flowery bank in the shade of huge oaks, looking out over startlingly green fields at a village heaped on a hill. A leisurely and delightful day, seeing several small and charming 'sights', a beautiful miniature romanesque cloister, and a curiously self-contained village through which we strolled, keeping in the deep shadow and ignored by the inhabitants, peering into cellars where beautiful large-eyed cream-coloured cows or oxen lay in straw, and into blackened bread-ovens. Suddenly a van arrived and unloaded a lot of boxes of day-old chicks, and all the villagers at once came to life and buzzed with excitement.

Magouche told us more about Miranda's short, selfish and disastrous life. Ian is considered to be doing a hard job amazingly well and that he deserves whatever financial gain he gets from it. His own family is Catholic and have disinherited him.

We were sitting happily over our finished dinner at ten-thirty when they arrived, Miranda whining for food.

Matthew and Magouche draw Bunny on to talk about the great figures of the past he has known and he seems to revel in this, to me embarrassingly, and unaware of the vein of mockery in their affectionate appreciation.

## May 13th

Really hot. Matthew is curiously hearty at times. 'Well! *How*'s everyone?' or '*How*'s life in the big city?' I dare say we'll go early on Thursday morning as he plans. So be it. I can't struggle, but I think it would make it easier for Magouche if we went, since the Watsons show no signs of doing so.

Now, 11 a.m., the house is silent and surrounded in incredible beauty and peace. Matthew is hard at work in the garden in his Harrovian-style straw hat. Maro has gone off with the Watsons to look at an empty house which Miranda will of course find 'too pubic, if you know what I mean'. Bunny was flushed with pride at breakfast, having woken in the night and done some work, but he has gone off in dudgeon to his 'rabbit-hutch' outside the barn, because Magouche has told him she won't come with him. According to her he slammed the door in a rage. On principle, I'm quite sure he wants to be kind, gentle and considerate, yet he has a snubbing 'you don't know anything about anything' line with Maro. 'Please be *quiet*,' he actually said to her once, 'and listen to me.' I don't feel he realizes the sceptical tolerance the young feel for the old. Magouche has with masterly generalship contrived to keep everyone happy, and now seems even to have reconciled Bunny to taking me to Pisa tomorrow. Miranda has given me a message for her mother saying she'll 'be back in about ten days' and is 'house-hunting'. Scuffling in the pubic hair! Little Da'ad was exceptionally good and willing last night, did quite a lot of ironing and some cooking and endlessly combed everyone's hair, always ending (even to me): 'You look quite sweet now.' I can't help being touched by her; 'No need,' says Bunny, 'She's made of indiarubber'.

We spent our last and blazing hot day gently, but in the afternoon descended to the river bed and had a really delicious bathe – all but Miranda who lay in her bed in a darkened room.

### May 14th

Bunny and I got off at last, at about noon. Both Magouche and I have been worrying about his journey to the frontier along the hateful and perplexing autostrada or the dangerous and terrifying coastal road. We picnicked in a sea of poppies and long grass, stopped at San Gimigniano when all was shut, and reached Pisa at four-thirty. I heaved a sigh of relief at being still alive after the last lap of my journey with Bunny, though I don't usually consider him a dangerous driver. I liked the look of the Hotel Nettuno on the Lungarno, old-fashioned and its long past days of grandeur commemorated by a photo in the hall of the unmistakeable bulk of Queen Mary getting into a limousine in 1925. That was shortly after my first visit to Pisa, when the Campo Santo and its frescoes in all their brilliant perfection gave me a major aesthetic experience, like seeing the Parthenon for the first time – it may have been partly its quality of 'firstness', but so it was. I wanted now to see what the effect of American bombing had been – but oh my God, I nearly burst into tears when I did. It was like looking at the face of a great beauty mashed up in an accident, or Avane's hills covered with skyscrapers, but much much worse; for instead of that dazzling and complete freshness I so well remember, only a shattered wreck remains, a ghostly spider's web in parts, with huge white patches and much gone altogether. It's enough to make one a pacifist simply to know that it was destroyed by our allies' bombs. Bunny now decided to stay the night in Pisa instead of pressing on, and took a room in my hotel. So after a rest, we walked out into the town dominated by the university students at this hour, and little cars tearing about with squealing brakes. We sat in the tiny animated Piazza Garibaldi watching the students drinking what looked like water, but may have been vodka. A jet-black Othello was pouring his passion into the ears of a blonde, long-haired Desdemona.

## May 15th

I've seen Bunny off, and hope he'll be all right. A hot day is opening its jaws to gobble us all, and I sit at breakfast listening to the members of an American bus tour jawing away about money and possessions. Now I'm on my own until take-off this afternoon. The hotel told me the museum was shut (it's a holiday) but I went there and found it open. There were some lovely things and no one looking at them – so a beady-eyed custodian fastened himself to my side, physically as well as mentally and boringly. Luckily his superior appeared and he made off like a shot rabbit. It must be a habit of his.

## May 20th

London again. Dinner with the Penroses; they were anxious to look at the television programme in which the American astronauts were being presented to us 'live' inside their module. I found them faintly disgusting, I don't quite know why: aimlessly moving, with their mouths steadily working at chewing-gum, they suggested foetuses in the womb.

Television is beginning to dominate conversation to a disturbing extent. I still have no desire to possess one, but look at other people's quite eagerly, sometimes in amazement at what they enjoy or even put up with.

A few days after the astronauts, Eardley and I were looking at Kenneth Clark in the last of his series on civilization wherein he delivered the salvo of his credo: 'I believe in creation rather than destruction, kindness rather than cruelty, gentleness, courtesy, etc. etc.' It was unexceptionable, but he lost some of my respect by prefacing his talk with 'I must reveal myself in my true colours as a stick-in-the-mud,' said in a tone of relish. He *doesn't* think he is one, so why not have the courage to stand up for his beliefs?

## May 31st: Mottisfont[1]

This is my first visit here alone, and I have been dreading it and wondering how I should manage without Ralph to walk, talk and laugh with in private. Why put myself to these hurdles for no purpose? Who cares if I manage or not? I knew four other guests were coming but not who they were. They all assembled on Waterloo platform – or all but one – the Lennox Berkeleys, Burnet Pavitt[2] and a Spanish decorator called Esteban. Not till I had been in the house some hours did Boris appear and then of course everything became much more congenial at once. His face has sharpened and saddened, his upper lip whitened. Late on Friday night the last member of the party arrived, a female beetle-expert from the Natural History Museum, grey-haired but with a charmingly girlish slim figure and something boyish in her striding walk. Self-contained, efficient, intelligent, she struck a note of freshness in this settled cushioned world. And Maud battles on bravely against increasing age, and pleases by her sudden outbursts of individual sense of humour and low infectious laugh. Over one of the lovely streams that swiftly flow to intersect the garden there is a slippery bridge and we were told how on a previous visit Frieda fell off it and went right under the water in all her clothes, got out dripping and rat's-tailed and had to be revived by hot baths and whisky. At the end of her description Maud said softly, 'It was extraordinarily enjoyable.'

The beauty of this water-divided garden moved me as I wandered to the river's edge on Saturday morning, joined by Maud who kept up a steady, dispassionate monologue.

Now comes the afternoon rest and I've gone off to my quiet room whose bed was too smooth and soft for sleep last night. I lay in my bath this morning and thought how insipid was its nursing-home green with the peach-coloured walls. There was such a curious absence of stimulus in last night's conversation that after I'd turned the light out tunes rushed to fill the vacuum in my head, and I was haunted by the thought of the huge trees standing round in the dark garden as if listening.

---

[1]  Home of Mrs Maud Russell.
[2]  Musical bachelor, a director of Covent Garden.

### June 1st

Getting the hang of it a bit: the smooth, swift water, the green garden, Boris, Lennox. To be waited on by silent, obsequious servants always embarrasses me, so does the assumption that for the likes of us this is all right and life is *not* real *nor* earnest, and diseases and disasters don't exist; we favoured few are here in the world just in order to glide from day to day supported by these many invisible hands. But to me it was worth coming here solely to hear Boris say to me twice 'I love you' last night across the dinner table, and then to urge me to write about the past. I would almost have liked to say, 'Yes I will.' He told me a story that may be true but I remember nothing of it. 'Do you remember a party in Gordon Square? You sat beside me and told me that Partridge was making advances to you and you didn't know whether to yield to him or not. And you said, "What shall I do, Boris!" So I said, "Of course – yes – go ahead."'

### June 2nd

Back in my flat, quite exhausted by the effort to seem to glide. Yet I don't feel 'it wasn't worth it' because every sight of Boris is valuable. I remember the beauty of the garden, absorption in my Conrad novel, the personalities of Lennox Berkeley and the beetle-woman, piano duets played by Pavitt and Lennox; croquet. On Sunday when the rest of us were strolling in the grounds Boris (who has a bad knee that suddenly gives under him) fell on the paving stones outside the house. He gave a characteristic imitation of how he deliberately put out his hand to 'save my spectacles', and then – finding he couldn't get up – took a book about the Marie Celeste out of his pocket and lay there reading until the butler found him half an hour later and helped him up. What a pleasant shock to find butlers are human. Wandering one morning in the lower corridors I asked the younger of the two how to get into the garden, and said I had no sense of direction. I was surprised and pleased when he said, 'Nor have I.'

### June 10th: Kitty's cottage

Came here in my Mini last week to get some peace from the tribes of painters in Halkin Street and from Mrs Murphy's holiday. From Thursday till Monday Kitty and I quietly pursued our companionable ways, I working at my translation, she going to her shop. In the evenings gardening, whisky, wireless and early bed. It was very kind of her to let me come, and even stay on till I go to Crichel on Friday. Yesterday morning she went to London for two nights, so here I am on my own; as I plodded the lanes and fields bathed in sudden heat that made me want to get into the shade I realized that I was perhaps experimenting to find out whether I could ever live alone in the country. Not entirely impossible, I feel, after only twenty-four hours' solitude in glorious weather. I most certainly find strangeness and tranquillity in this gentle, countrified world, walking through the boggy woods carpeted with creeping Jenny, and the completely gone-to-seed fields are a real pleasure, but would I not quickly exhaust a neighbourhood?

Before bed I listened to a programme about Wilfred Owen on the wireless which nearly reduced me to tears. I put him in a small class of rare talents.

## June 14th: Crichel (Sunday of a gloriously fine weekend)

Boris is dead. Desmond told me on Friday night and it shook me horribly. Could he have had a feeling that he was near his end that last weekend at Mottisfont? I got the impression that he had moved as it were into a different key, and now it is as though his declarations of affection were a sort of valediction. Oh the sadness of losing one old friend after another! And the hole he leaves in the universe seems very large and black. He must have died only five days after I left Mottisfont, and of course I wonder if his fall had something to do with it.

Tomorrow back to stern reality and life on my own, after being pillowed as I've been for quite a while on other people. Desmond and I have got on very well as solitary inhabitants here. We had the whole of *Idomeneo* from Aldeburgh on Friday night – glorious. Last night part of a Bellini opera – *La Straniera*, poor stuff. Kitty's party came to drinks and croquet: Caroline West brought over her Ghanaian lover, bearded, *shiny* with blackness, white teeth flashing and a high giggle. I thought him an intelligent and kind, friendly man, and admired the way he didn't turn a hair when Kitty said her plumber had 'worked like a black'.

Today was far from solitary – Richard Brain and an interesting young man called Jonathan Price who is about to take the veil came before lunch and for the night. His austere face lights up at times with a radiant smile. Desmond lay back in his chair on Saturday night groaning at how much he had to do. 'I shall set you a good example by going to bed early,' said I. He declared he would too, but went on filling the house with a noisy, thumping Berlioz *Te Deum* until between twelve and one. Last night we had a high-powered and intellectually tough conversation until bed-time, well shared among us all, about Wittgenstein and what his effect had been, and ethics, Blake's poetry (illustrated by records of music by Elizabeth Lutyens and Britten). Richard Brain is a great talker and a confident one; Jonathan Price is unlike anyone I've ever met; the quality of his mind was like the feel of a new stuff in my fingers.

## June 18th: London

Trying not to whirl like a twist of paper in this maelstrom and lose my country-found strength. It's harder to breathe deep and slow in this town where everyone is hurrying, and I find I am looking forward to two days and one evening on my own.

## July 1st

Janetta and I spent a lovely, warm, English summery weekend, all 'blooming, buzzing confusion' with Anne and Heywood, going on Sunday to the *Fairy Queen* in Blythborough Church. But she came down at least one morning with her face small and pinched from a sleepless, worried night, remembering how her children so often said to her after they had made some awful mistake, such as refusing to take their exams, 'Why did you *let* me do it?' Yesterday she obviously still doubted whether she and Robert should have given the necessary consent.[1] But of course any other behaviour was impossible. Even the ghostly adumbration of heavy parent behaviour would be more suitable to a quite different civilization.

Heywood and Anne rolled out to meet us, smiling and rotund, like Mr and Mrs Bung the Brewer. It must be happiness.

In the warm summery haze, and gentle vegetable beauty, I picked my way happily around fields of clean, strong corn where grew

[1] Georgie (who is under age) wanted to marry Jean-Pierre Martel.

'weeds' (or flowers) in very clean, strong colours (red of poppies, blue of bugloss, yellow of charlock, chalk-white of campions). I had a feeling of having 'stepped sideways out of life', due partly to pain-killer drowning slight toothache which has left a dreamy impression of the weekend in my mind. And all those East Anglian figures floated in and out too – Jonny, John and Sheelah Hill, Lucy. I loved being with Janetta, noticed her anxiety over Georgie with sympathy, and was amused by her longing to travel first class. I said (about this last) of course I would if it was crowded and she wanted to, but that I had an egalitarian feeling that there should be no such thing. 'Oh I don't,' said Janetta (gratuitously for well I knew it), 'I think it's so nice that someone who is old or not feeling well can pay extra.' I pointed out that these weren't necessarily the people who could afford it.

## July 5th: London

I think it may have been no accident that, finding myself sharing a taxi from Liverpool Street with Nancy Raphael[1] we suddenly plunged into questions of practical philosophy such as 'what one was at', and 'how perhaps one wasn't at anything' and about values, and collecting a string bag of pleasures, and whether there was rhyme or reason in the universe, and friendship, and love and death. In fact, I suppose, all the things I had been wanting to talk to Janetta about, but somehow didn't have a chance.

## July 7th

Dinner with Patrick Kinross, Janetta, Paddy, Julian and Coote Lygon. After dinner Magouche, Miranda and Ian Watson. Very enjoyable. Relations between children and 'Mum and Dad' being on my mind, I brought them up to Julian at dinner. Violent resistance. *Yes*, of course they were responsible for everything that befell their families. Much later, drink taken, he returned to the subject and the true reason for this forcefulness was revealed – a recent crisis in his own Mum and Dad's life: their decision to leave Kingsland, his desire to keep it for himself. He said a great deal, much that was very interesting, touching on his deepest feelings. But my position is not shaken in that I do think it futile to go on blaming them, and blaming

[1] London neighbour, and new friend.

their Mum and Dad, and so on, back and back in an infinite series. One should, except in a few grizzly cases, be able to enjoy being one's own man at seventeen or eighteen, shouldn't one? Two struts awkwardly supported my argument at the moment, that's to say the feeling that the old should remember their youth and not behave like old colonels, and that the young should shoulder their own lives and not sit back and blame their parents all the time.

Janetta looked tired and ravishing in a pale yellow Moorish trouser suit. How little is distilled from hours of talk.

## July 12th

The tempo got faster and faster, culminating in a *prestissimo* that whirled through Georgie's wedding day, a French-style wedding day beginning with lunch at the Ritz for twelve or thirteen encircling a big, round table. *Luxe, calme et volupté.* Walking the long and spacious corridor, to see with pleasure Jaime advancing towards me, and soon afterwards, Rose, looking very much herself; Nicky, brown, strong and *décolleté*; the amusing, provocative face of Serge. Robert arrived last, and blew Cynthia up for 'doing the placements all wrong'. I sat between Julian and Jean-Pierre (very fine in white linen suit and black shirt). Georgie wore a black trouser suit; in the evening, in a white one she looked really lovely. Moving in three cars through one of London's 'worst traffic congestions', we at last reached the Register Office at East Sheen, watched the ceremony performed in a Nissen hut surrounded by hideous bunches of flowers, and returned to our bases to gasp for a while before setting out for the evening party at Kew. That was exceedingly pretty and well arranged.

I'm now awaiting Janetta for a last supper before she returns to Spain.

## July 15th

A flawless, pale blue sky spreads overhead. Heat tremendous, tropical. I spent last evening by myself, reading and listening to the wireless, in a cotton dressing-gown, mopping myself with a damp sponge. Yesterday Joan [Cochemé] and I lunched in the square garden, lying in the shade on an eiderdown, drinking iced orangeade. The heat somehow intensifies impressions, such as of the delicate strong beauty of Ben Nicholson's paintings seen afterwards. He is a great painter I believe; just as at this moment (still in bed) I am questioning whether Conrad is, after all, a great writer. Yet I approached *Victory*, which I'm now reading, full of expectation and backed by several enthusiastic commendations, one from Frances Phipps. At once I was struck by a strong, male smell reminding me of Kipling; he is horribly at ease and relaxed in his own masculinity (like Kipling), rolling about in it as in a club armchair. And I don't like this boy's book-adventure-*Huckleberry Finn* flavour, nor its glorification of violence. Not at all. I rather think a novelist *must* have some femininity in him even if he's a man, like Henry James and Proust.

## July 19th: Thorington Hall

I've spent two nights alone here with Margaret. Warmly and admiringly as I feel towards her, it disconcerts me and makes me feel lonely when she drops instantly asleep after dinner in an armchair each evening, only to come alive again when the television news is due about ten-fifteen.

We spent nearly all yesterday driving to see poor dying Frances Penrose – a good seventy miles and back again. I'm not used to visiting the dying, indeed I don't think I have ever done it before, and on the way there I wondered if it would be difficult to avoid speaking about future plans or refrain from bursting into tears. Margaret was more panicky than I was, but also more stoical. In fact our visit was less harrowing than I had expected, because we found Frances extremely well looked after, peaceful and resigned, half out of this world already, and obviously not in great pain or discomfort. A little confused at times, but with her hostess instincts still touchingly alive. She seemed pleased by our presents (mine was some half bottles of champagne). Over lunch I persuaded Margaret that an hour of our conversation before lunch and half after would be all she wanted or indeed could stand. After two drinks her poor mind got in a muddle. 'Where is my sister-in-law?' M: 'Do you mean me – Margaret?' F: 'No, I know Frances and Margaret were coming, but so was my sister-in-law. Where is she?' Soon afterwards she settled down for her afternoon rest with an almost happy smile, and we stole away, knowing we would never see her again. I for one didn't find that strange, yet it had seemed important to give her this symbolical evidence of our affection.

This morning Margaret suddenly said that Frances had always hated her, and she longed to know why. 'It couldn't be because I was better at work when we were at school?'

Now I'm packing in my pitch-dark, oak-panelled bedroom, in preparation for my drive to Hilton for William's[1] wedding.

## July 22nd

In the last twenty-four hours men have landed on the moon, and for once I wish I had a machine with which to view this extraordinary event. Yet I confess I have very ambivalent feelings about it. At dinner with Tristram and Virginia Powell last night it was the chief topic of our talk, and Jonny said he had sat up virtually all night: he was a keen moon advocate. How the young talk about the television, the wireless! I am positively alarmed by the obsessional nature of their interest, much as I am when I see a too large child in a pushchair, with its mouth stoppered with a 'comforter' or 'dummy'. It's not so much the passivity as the lack of choice, the uniformity of this sucking-in process that I see as baleful. By discharging an identical dose of soporific liquid – and it does often send people to sleep – into the mouth of every child and adult in the country, it must surely standardize them, even if the diet were good – and of course most of it is bad.

But I've left out William and Linda's wedding, which was a very jolly affair, though it now seems like a faded dream. The evening was fine enough for plates and glasses to be taken out into the garden where the midges devoured us. The first person I recognized was Sophie looking very charming in a pretty, white muslin frock, excitedly running about with her cousin Edward Garnett and other smaller and larger children. Late in the evening came Tim Behrens, grinning endearingly out of his ruined face, Serge and Nicky (very handsome in a long, white dress, with Bekalelis[2] firmly plastered on one hip), and the narcissistic Mark Palmer in golden velvet trousers. Some moved off to the pool, and I saw the naked shapes of Tim and Fanny Garnett fling themselves in. Serge was telling everyone the egocentric news that now that his film was going to be produced he had lost all desire to do it. A groaning board of food, cold dishes,

[1] Garnett, my nephew.
[2] Their son, now an artist.

Stilton cheeses; the drink supply began to run short later and had to be supplemented from Bunny's cellar. William and Linda seemed very happy; Linda had invited a large, vital cohort of her friends and relations; a difference in lifestyle between them and the rest of us had been invisible until they'd had a good deal to drink when they suddenly exploded into noise and laughter, kicked up their legs, filled the drawing-room, thumped out 'For Me and My Gal' on Angelica's piano, danced wildly about and fell down. Angelica did I think join in – but I shamefully couldn't imagine how to amalgamate with their boisterousness and soon after left, to return to the hotel at St Ives where Angelica, Duncan and I were staying. Lunch next day in the garden off remains.

### August 4th

I'm suddenly committed to go to Portugal with the Kees a week tomorrow. I don't know whether I'm looking forward to it or not, and hope it isn't just the fruit of some dreadful restlessness. Meanwhile I have been 'managing' fairly well. *Linguistics* (translated from Spanish) is just on finished – thank God. It really has been a corker.

### August 9th

Appallingly hot. This afternoon I met Georgia and we went by mistake to a tedious French lesbian film, in which two naked girls rolled about together ecstatically. Coming out I walked for a while, saw London with fresh eyes and was astounded. Or was it just the weekend look? Such motley, hideous crowds straggle along, sowing a trail of cigarette and chocolate papers. Mostly young, all nationalities, but I looked for beauty – began to panic, and searched without success. It was more like what I imagine Yokohama to be than London. Then climbing on an empty bus I swirled through Piccadilly Circus, and there was the space round Eros, stuffed, packed and jammed with a dense crowd of drop-outs, lay-abouts and hippies, in large, floppy felt hats or fur coats in this heat. What was particularly striking was their stagnancy; they lay, sat or stood washed together like the odd bits of orange peel and wrapping-paper in the run-away of a sink, totally passive and seeming in a prison or a zoo because of the surrounding railing.

I got home, undressed and sat naked in my dressing-gown listening to Haydn and Mozart on the wireless and mugging up Portuguese. But the roaring sound of cars dashing through West Halkin Street disturbed me. What is happening to the world? Whatever it is has speeded up, and I don't think there'll be time to put a brake on it.

## August 10th

Awake to another heavy, hot thundery day, and a pang of dread – yes, real dread of Julia's visit because it is so rattling to know the irritation I am sure to produce, the current of hate that I may so easily loose in her. That I should be in a state of fear before a face-to-face meeting with another human being (and she my oldest friend) gradually seemed absurd and I awaited her arrival in the end with calm. Well, perfectly well, the evening went. Julia made, I think, an immense effort not to complain too much of her own life or of anyone else. She looked extraordinarily young and pretty, and spoke rationally. No signs of pill- or drink-given confusion; her voice was gentle. What a pleasure! I have the impression that she's in some way taken steps to tackle her life and problems. There was a farcical touch of course. She said, 'I can't open more than a tiny slit of a window in my flat in this hot weather because of this mad cat that comes in at the window and claws at everything.' She took pains to say that Robin and Susan had been really kind, 'in spite of the awful things I say to Susan', but told me how appallingly Robert had behaved to Cynthia over the cardboard plates for Georgie's wedding. 'I'm frightened of him,' she said. There was high praise of Jean-Pierre, and Georgie had been very charming to her (Julia) when she'd met her at Kew, but she noticed she had her 'sullen expression on' at her wedding party. She had received Julia's present without a gleam of pleasure, but had written 'a really affectionate letter afterwards'. Not a word about Janetta. By common consent we kept off that and other controversial subjects, and snatched at any chances of agreement, and not a few arose.

## August 14th: Portugal

I enjoyed the journey in a muted sort of way. Cynthia's mother[1] came and sat beside me in the aeroplane; we looked down at the mouths of Garonne, Douro and Tagus spread glisteningly below in turn. Robert met us at Faro airport and as he drove ran down

[1] Sylvia Judah.

everything, unconvincingly, and as a sort of insurance against disappointment. I can see he likes it really, and so do I, what with the limpid sky, carts with dogs running under them, women wearing scarves over men's felt hats, the pure and scented air, decently built houses, some brilliantly coloured, or white, or outlined in royal blue. Ours seems to be solidly built with plenty of wood, tiles and whitewash and a very nice shady eating-terrace. The children are brown, naked seals already.

I'm greatly struck by Robert's practical geniality. He wants to be – and so far has been – supporting to everyone, including Cynthia, and quite exceptionally so to her Mum – 'Sylvia' now to me – who obviously dotes on him; he wants things to be all right.

Down to the beach this morning by innumerable steps and a rocky path. The sea is cold on first impact, then rustles round one like silk. The very hot sun is tempered by a cool breeze.

### August 16th

Our ship is still afloat, no signs of a leak, except that Cynthia is clearly driven mad by her mother. Robert appears to be a model father, husband, son-in-law, friend. Drugged with sun and sea, mental life is in abeyance; I read at different times of day a detective story, Beckford's Portuguese journal and a novel in Portuguese, an earthy story of sex, violence and class war, which I can barely understand.

### August 18th

I'm now thoroughly embedded in the life of the others and trying to get on with them all. I mustn't forget Sylvia is there, nor show when delicious little Sarah is too much of a good thing. I'm particularly anxious to be 'all right' with Cynthia, and not let my delight in Robert's company and mental processes lead to ganging up with him. And I do admire her tackling spirit and have never found her more attractive looking. But Robert's endless benignity and *patience* (yes!) give her no cause for complaint.

Full-scale Sunday excursion yesterday, very successful. In hot, still weather we drove to the cathedral and Moorish castle at Silves (densely planted with cannas, hibiscus and bougainvillaea) and on up to the Caldas de Monchique. Found it all just the same as in 1934, only there was this time a Sunday concourse of peasant picnickers happily spreading their bottles and food on stone tables in the shade of huge trees. If only they wouldn't spit so. Hearing the dreadful preparations as they come down the path one longs to shout: 'Oh *do* just wait till I've gone past!' But of course they don't. They needs must void themselves of their beastly gobbets anywhere and everywhere. We had our picnic on a hill-top under some fine cork oaks: these and many other things – for instance that the Portuguese radio should play Schumann – fill Sylvia with innocent amazement. Everything smelled delicious under the speckled shade and we ate tender little roast chickens, bread, fruit, cheese and wine. In sweltering heat we piled into the car and drove on to Marmalete and Monchique, and then – craving a bathe – made for the nearest sea at Praia da Rocha. It was a sorry sight, rapidly turning into Torre-molinos, with monster blocks of flats, night clubs and battalions of cars. The tiny tartanas still ply to and fro, looking rickety and absurd. Drove to the furthest beach and bathed in a beautifully calm evening sea. Sylvia showed childish disappointment at having no bathing-suit, and Cynthia gallantly lent her her own white one, in which her mother stalked into the sea looking like a Raemakers cartoon of famine. Sarah hurled herself into the movements of swimming with enormous spirit and vitality, her little wet head sinking again and again. Cynthia has a very nice figure in her swimming rig.

### August 20th

I drove Sylvia for a shopping excursion in Tarvoeira village and afterwards to the beach for a short rough bathe. Robert has begun to work at the dining-room table. Irish news is bad, and disturbing, as it impinges on what he has been trying to say in his book.

About four we all drove off along the coast eastwards and I was overjoyed to find the little chapel of Nossa Senhora da Rocha where I went with Ralph. My memory of his pleasure in it, so exactly in tune with my own, was strong enough to produce a haunting strangeness in the fact that he wasn't still there beside me, but I loved its white simplicity, blue tiles and little many-sided spire; but though everyone seemed to like it, nobody did so quite enough to please me. Below were two beaches linked by a tunnel, on one of which we stationed ourselves, slowly withdrawing from the large rollers till we were

211

right up among the brilliantly painted, obviously functioning fishing-boats. Sylvia gallantly sat in a hole dug by the children above the water-line until the sea rushed in and made her look like the sages in the *Just So Stories*. Then the Kees vanished leaving her surrounded by interested Portuguese children. She has a sort of dignified humour in such situations which warms me to her. Robert's black head vanished out to sea among enormous waves. Sarah's courageous little figure looked fascinating in minute shorts and a wide-brimmed Portuguese hat.

11.15 p.m. I always thought kindness was Cynthia's quality, yet she is sometimes quite fierce to her poor old Mum. The first time was when she arrived very late from the beach and we had been unable to persuade Barbara the maid even to start preparations for lunch until two-fifteen. Sylvia said harmlessly enough, 'We're all starving.' Whereupon Cynthia exploded in a burst of indignation.

But tonight has been *much* worse and I'm at my wits end what to do. Poor 'Grandma' knocked one of her already swollen legs (insensitive too from diabetes) on a rock on her way up from the beach. She made light of it, but when Robert and I returned from Portimão we found her sitting on the sofa with her leg up and a horrible great purplish-black swelling as big as a tennis-ball on it. I had never seen anything like it, and was appalled. She was supposed to be going with Robert and Cynthia to have a drink with the landlord, but Robert and I suggested she stayed with her leg up. When Sylvia went out to say so to Cynthia, who was making a mayonnaise on the terrace, she answered her mother's 'Robert doesn't think I ought to go out', with 'Oh Mum, I'm *sure* he couldn't have said that! Why ever *not*?' implying that she was making a fuss over a mere trifle which should be ignored. So Sylvia went, but returned early and put her leg up again. I was reading to Alexander, but whenever I looked up and my eye caught this terrible blackberry-coloured object, I was so horrified that I lost my place in the book. I brought her her supper and tried to spoil her a little. She said: 'You'll make me burst into tears if you're so sympathetic.' Alexander was worried too, and kind and helpful, escorting her to the lavatory. I was in two minds whether to go over and beg Cynthia and Robert to telephone for a doctor (there is a telephone at the landlord's), and I really thought they'd have had the sense to do it. Not a bit of it. When she had gone to bed with painkillers and sleeping-pills I asked if they didn't think they should now do so. 'But what could it *be*?' said

Cynthia, and Robert: 'If it's not better in the morning, we will,' but I felt they both thought I was fussing.

12.15 a.m. We're in for a bad night – and what *else* I wonder. Cynthia went to see her mother and administer belated sympathy after settling another of Sarah's outbursts. Poor Sylvia has begun to groan 'Oh *God!*', and if I were her I should indeed be frightened. I hardly feel it's worth trying to go to sleep, what with the agonized sounds coming from next door, the incessant barking of a dog and the probability of more yells from Sarah. So I'm trying to read Beckford, but my lamp gives a dim light and his personality depresses me.

### August 22nd

My prognosis was alarmingly correct. Sylvia's moans and groans were so distressing that I went into her room some time after 1 o'clock. She tried heroically to be polite, but was obviously in agony. So I went down and knocked Robert and Cynthia up, saying that something must really be done. Cynthia was still sceptical. Robert, following on her heels, came in to say that the swelling on the leg had got very much worse and he was going to telephone for the doctor. All his enormous reliability in an emergency now came to the fore, and (unable to get into the landlord's house) he drove off to the village nightclub and somehow got the address of a Lagoa doctor. All this took some time, while Cynthia stayed with her mother, and I went down for a slug of whisky which I felt sorely in need of. What a relief, when Robert returned with a stalwart, black-clad figure behind him – an English-speaking Portuguese doctor. I listened to the proceedings from my room, heard him say Sylvia had ruptured a vein, and that she must either have an operation next morning or keep the leg quite still, until the blood was re-absorbed. Robert said afterwards he made Johnsonian jokes, smoked the whole time and fished out his implements from his pockets or a grubby old bag, remarking that the danger was infection. While he applied an ointment to 'disperse the thrombosis', I could hear from exclamations that the whole great swelling had burst and blood gushed out. Cynthia hurried for a basin, and apparently the pain was instantly relieved. The doctor bound the leg up tightly and soon after went away, while I was swallowed up in oblivion. But my God, supposing this had happened without the doctor being present!

When I came down this morning Cynthia was obviously feeling remorse and shame, and mollified me with an apology and a kiss. Robert described his taking the doctor home and how he turned out to be a 'radio-amateur' and had forced him to listen while he contacted Canada.

## August 26th

A perfect day to visit that best of all Land's Ends, Cape St Vincent; then on to Sagres, and down a rough cart track, until the car had to be abandoned and we walked on down a magically wild valley to a vast deserted bay, with tilted stratified cliffs and the rollers breaking in a mist of shining spray on miles and miles of hard sand. The sides of the valley were covered with tufts of sea-lavender and horned poppy and peopled with little birds. I hung back to botanize and saw the four silhouettes of the others walking into the glimmer of this incredible beach, like the figures at the end of a film about the shape of things to come. Cynthia walked off along the beach and vanished in the mist, in a desire to be alone, perhaps, which is something I can always sympathize with.

But there were unaccountable delays on the way home – a drink at Lagoa was very pleasant, but by the time we got home it was very late, the doctor had been, Sylvia had had to hobble round lighting the lamps (or sit in the dark), both children were exhausted and had screaming fits, and Cynthia herself was dead beat and went early to bed.

One evening in the course of conversation I said I thought it was important for children to accept the fact that adults too had their rights. Dead silence from both Robert and Cynthia. Then the young wife of Dr Wolfson, who is studying for a PhD, told me on the beach how difficult it was to work with the children in the room. I asked if she had no small room where they weren't allowed, and she seemed amazed at the idea. 'But children can and do accept rules,' I said, 'and they can also have a place where adults sometimes aren't admitted.' 'Children first always' is now the almost universal practice and I think it's disastrous.

This morning all is serene. Incredibly hot; England tomorrow.

## August 27th

Packing begins. Sylvia seems no worse; Cynthia complains of a very sore throat. Barbara the maid arrived with a look of self-pity gleaming through her spectacles and said that *'tudo roda'* – everything was spinning. We all worry about Sylvia's journey.

I've just told Sarah to stop squirting her grandmother's bandaged leg with her water-pistol or 'I would spank her.' She rushed off bawling to her mother.

## August 28th: London

Grey, old, noisy, friendly place. We got to the miniature maelstrom of Faro airport and at the last minute I managed to get a seat in Sylvia's aeroplane, instead of one an hour later. She was taken in a wheelchair to a privileged seat and another chair met her on arrival. I went along to see she was all right and found the ambulance men looking dismayed. 'You mustn't put your foot to the ground!' cried one. 'We must get an ambulance.' But I heard later that there was a strike of ambulance men and she had to wait two hours. She's now in St George's Hospital.

## September 2nd

Whirling days. Immediately after Portugal, off I went to Crichel for Bank Holiday – Dadie was there, a great life-enhancer and stimulator, laying the dust of etymology and raising that of general conversation. He has an excellent effect on Raymond of whom he takes devoted care. One sometimes hears him accused of heartlessness, but in practice one can't fault him.

And now I must begin ordinary working life and a new translation. Julian came yesterday, and told me among other things that he has been 'cohabiting' for the last fortnight with a girl called Tammy. 'No love-making though.' Amazement, gratification, speculation. I have always hoped for something like this and thought it possible – but if it doesn't develop into a proper love affair I suppose it may not last. He very naturally 'doesn't want to analyse it' and is 'suffering from shock'.

## September 5th

My day with Sophie delighted me. I think she really is fond of me, and before she came she rang up on the telephone for a long talk, ending with a swelling organ note: 'And I *love* you! You're my very *bestest* Granny!' Of course I spoil her, and her times with me are nearly always treats, not the routine of life, because her wide smile with a large gap in the middle, her strong limbs and energetic run, her quick responsiveness are all a joy to me. There wasn't a wail, pout or sulky moment all day long – she was happy and busy all the time. We lunched with Isobel and Amy[1] (a very pretty little creature now) and when they weren't busy playing we followed their pounding figures into Battersea Park and up the Tree Walk. Among the nursery rhyme records I gave Sophie for her birthday was one of Vivaldi's 'Spring' from the *Seasons*. I put on my own record of it while she was here and was amused by her immediate grown-up reaction in a surprised voice: 'Oh, it's the Vivaldi!' This of course is the age of happy promise and hope, but why not enjoy it? She told me quite a lot about her visit to Iceland with Henrietta. There were 'no trees', 'a lot of rabbits but they were grey', and 'it was very cold and I was nearly blown flat.'

Bunny, who has been to see me since I got back, told me more: Clancy[2] somehow failed to get his ticket, and Henrietta and Sophie went on ahead. The hotels were frightfully expensive, so Henrietta talked to a group of Icelandic students who invited them to join them. They went with them to an island, where an appalling storm blew up, and the lifeboat was sent to fetch them back. On it (practically its captain, as Bunny told the story) was a huge, handsome, splendid old man, whom Henrietta fell for. 'What good English you talk,' she said. 'Yes. I was married to an English wife – a poetess. Her name was Iris Tree. I have a son by her.' He later invited Henrietta back to meet the son, and she fell for the son and is now in Sweden with him. Clancy did eventually get to Iceland, but I imagine he was odd man out.

## September 8th

Frances Phipps came last night, arriving at a quarter to seven and making the business of cooking our dinner almost impossible by her ceaseless talk. But what did it matter? What did, however, was that

---

[1] Her grandchild.
[2] Henrietta's boyfriend at the time.

she seemed to be for the first time feeling the pathos of her own decline. She sat gazing at me with extraordinarily penetrating fixity from her beautiful pale eyes, now beginning to be clouded with cataract, and I felt it to be the gaze of a drowning person saying 'Help me! Help me!' Tortured by sciatica, seeming to read less well every day, hampered by her immobility (how can she ever see Eardley or Julian, who live up so many flights of stairs, when even getting into a taxi is an undertaking?), she still keeps her courage and spirit, but they are cornered and at bay. I was even aware that her wig was a wig. And when the usual topics – of our horror at and rejection of violence and war – came up, neither of us could think of anything faintly hopeful to say. I have remained saddened and a little sunk myself today. When I went out into the Knightsbridge hullabaloo, the modern world had become incomprehensibly chaotic to me, like the 'noise' of the worst Broadmoor[1] patients, swamping and confusing. I have no part in any of it, and it is an effort which I force myself to undertake to venture into the flood in my new shiny plum-coloured Mini.

### September 12th

Dinner with Julia last night. In order to meet on common ground it seems we can only talk critically of people, plays and books. She spent the first hours talking about Carrington, mainly in order to prove that she was a unique person and a genius, yet she couldn't resist an occasional backhander at her. The Kees had been to dinner the night before, quarrelling on the way and arriving separately. But Cynthia told Julia that there 'had been no trouble at all in Portugal'. Her 'tough line' with Robert, noticed by me, is deliberate according to Julia, who also declares that Cynthia is 'utterly fed up with Robert' and only stays with him for the sake of the children.

Latest Julia story – when staying at Thorington, she sat down on the lavatory and 'did what she had come to do', but when she tried to get up found she couldn't! 'I was caught in a vice, my dear, an agonizing pain! And when I did get away I was bleeding. I looked and saw the seat was badly cracked. So as I'm always so rude these days, I went straight in to Margaret and Lionel and complained about it. Margaret said she knew about it; someone else had complained three

---

[1] Visited by Ralph and me, when he wrote a book about it.

weeks ago. I said, 'Well I do think you ought to have put up a warning notice.' Margaret said a new one was on order. Lionel looked very cross indeed and went off to look for a file, muttering, 'The princess and the pea!' Or pee?

Yesterday to a party given by Jane Garnett for Sophie's sixth birthday – about nine little girls and one shy little boy. She has never in her life had such a party, with such a spread of jellies and cakes, balloons and crackers, such games and prizes, combining to produce radiantly appreciative faces and rewarding the hard work Jane must have devoted to it. Sophie was a delicious little figure at the head of the table, intoxicated with excitement and showing a good deal of social talent.

### September 17th

A call yesterday from Henrietta, just back from Stockholm and 'wanting to see me'. She comes tomorrow, and it may be my imagination, but I felt she was pregnant with news, decisions, I don't know what. Bunny came to see me in the evening, and talked a great deal about Carrington in whose original, ambivalent personality he is deeply submerged.[1] As a result I dreamed that Carrington had gone mad and wanted to murder an innocent but foolish upper-class young woman and her children. Or rather she wanted *me* to turn the knob that would let poison gas into the room where they were sleeping. Nearly mesmerized by her persuasiveness, I suddenly realized what I was doing and refused. *Who* can that 'innocent but foolish' etc. have been?

### September 22nd

Henrietta arrived looking smashing in such a romantic yet tasteful style that I was quite bowled over. Her hair had been cut in a longish Renaissance bob, she was very slim, and wore a diaphanous, striped tunic over black trousers. Talk of Iceland and Sweden; she was off to dine with David Galloway.[2] I'm in the dark about her love life. I think Clancy is out of favour, she groaned at his name.

Soon after she had gone, came Julian and his dear little Papagena, with whom I played violin sonatas.

---

1   He was working on an edition of her letters.
2   Burgo's friend and executor.

## September 24th

Besides the languages of clothes, voices and so forth, there's one of movement. Pathetic old people trail in an almost useless limbo, or poke their heads, or shuffle, manifesting their dislike of advancing to the tomb. My own elderly disease is humming. There's practically always a tune in my head, so out it tends to come and (as I sometimes realize by head-turning in the street) quite loudly. I keep frantically trying to stop, but fear the habit will return, like Julia's sniff. An old lady buzzing like a very loud bee in the grocer's gave me pause. It's a way of talking to myself, I suppose, yet I did it before I was alone. Burgo told me of it. Oh my aloneness – I see it now as a horrible, long streak, like the trajectory of a bullet or rocket, leaving behind everything most valuable. I hate the increasing distance between me and them, and its length only seems to increase the pain of recollection and deprivation.

I've had Julia here again, and with much the same result; I have to make an immense effort to avoid provoking her. She described meeting Tim Behrens and Amaryllis – lovers so it seems – along with Bunny. Her praise of Tim, particularly of his ravaged appearance, was extravagant and (I feel) doomed to subsequent collapse. No one she had met for the last thirty years had struck her so. Great praise too for Amaryllis's beauty, but a curiously conventional response to the situation: 'It seemed to me odd somehow. In my day we didn't *do* that sort of thing – go about publicly with the mistress, leaving the wife at home, and I don't think it's the way to preserve the marriage.' Everything is seen in the light of its application to her own position. For surely she must remember that Bloomsbury went about openly with their mistresses – Clive with Mary, Duncan with Vanessa? And how does she view now her position as Wogan's mistress, when he was still married to Rosamond? I wonder if she ever thinks of that. It has occurred to me before, and this supports it, that her hostility to me is partly because I 'went off with a married man'. She sometimes talks genuinely about Carrington, sometimes she sees her as herself I believe. One daren't ask her if she really believes so forcibly in the marriage tie and is against divorce, extra-marital affairs, etc. It is too near the bone. But I think I may have spotted a source of her hostility to me.

Last time Bunny dined with her, there was again extravagant praise: 'the wittiest man she knew, quite brilliant' etc. etc. And there

219

is always the implication that the person in question has turned over a new leaf. 'I never remember he was like that in the old days.' However, poor Bun, on second hearing (with Tim and Amaryllis) he was 'quite slow and dull, with nothing at all to say for himself. Why *is* he like that? Such a pity!' – echoing her own famous portrait of Lady Tomlin (her first mother-in-law), but, more than that, I was distinctly aware of a challenge, a wave of indignation aimed at me, although I'd been amazed by hearing what a wit Bunny was, and had contented myself by saying he 'could be amusing and delightful company at his best'. 'Well, it's rather odd that he's never been like that in all the long years I've known him. Is he a man of moods, or what?' Yes indeed; who isn't?

### September 30th

A weekend with the Campbells at Pitt's Deep, savouring very happily that beautiful and peaceful scene. Sympathetic talk – with Robin, who awaits news of his promotion in the Arts Council with some anxiety. Susan, keyed up and packing too much in, screams at her boys – or rather through them at the universe. My journey down there by train was infinitely long, owing to a derailment and consequently missing my connection; the journey home appallingly crowded. I was overtaken by one of those attacks of anti-plebs feelings which I so strongly disapprove of in principle – dismay at seeing how they just sit for hour after hour, gazing in front of them, and do not read even a paper. Sole exceptions in our cattle-truck: two young people seriously poring over a magazine article entitled 'Is your cat a nut-case?', and a sweet-faced nun reading in a little book about how to get nearer and nearer to her Saviour. And everywhere hideousness, lack of taste, people treated as cattle, shuffling through the cattle-truck. Husband angrily to wife: 'Why do you act so *stupid*?'

Getting home, I found some beastly advertising agency had bundled a mass of hideous, coloured hand-outs in at our hall door. Angrily, and resentful of this visual outrage, I bundled them out again onto the pavement.

## October 11th

An unusually social spell – so I have promised myself several quiet evenings of blessed privacy, which I am ready to protect with lies. Yet I enjoyed much of it, operas, a dash to Cambridge (Munia Postan's[1] seventieth birthday party and back to Robert's fiftieth); *The Doll's House*; buying new clothes rather recklessly and uncharacteristically; hurtling on. Frances Penrose died last week; no more hurtling for her, I thought with a quiet sort of envy. I realize now how elderly people become preoccupied by their wills and tidying up. I have not seen a great deal of Janetta, but I expect her any minute now. We went together to Ealing Studios to see a preview of Julian's film on Virginia[2] – I found it very moving, and very good too. Indeed it quite carried me away. Julian put in a brief appearance at a rather ramshackle evening at Magouche's but disappeared (preoccupied) to see his Tammy, who is ill.

## October 14th: London

Janetta and I passed the afternoon looking at pictures – moving from French impressionists (in a dazed, smelly mob) to the splendid Turner rooms, and thence, on the way out by accident, into a room of modern horrors: 'targets', huge orange canvases vaguely splodged, and in the centre of the room a giant object of iron painted bright red, which would have had more point if it had actually been a fire-engine or threshing-machine. Janetta and I looked at each other aghast. The nerve! The witlessness! And what are the guardians of the Tate thinking about? Julia defends this (or more probably Lawrence) by saying that one 'must have examples of the work being done'. I can't see why it has to be classified as 'work'. Years may pass when nothing worth doing *is* being done, and then – what point in recording the fact?

## October 22nd

Quiet, beautiful, still, misty days. Janetta again to boiled egg lunch, and a walk for a quarter of an hour in Belgrave Square gardens, picking up the parti-coloured, flattened, plane leaves, just as I did

---

[1] Cambridge history don, friend of my brother Tom.
[2] *A Night's Darkness, a Day's Sail.*

with Nicky a year or two ago. She talked, more freely than usual, about frustrations in her life. How much does she peer into the future, I wonder? And what does she see there? Julian last night told me I *'ought* to go out to Spain this winter and see her'. But 'ought' seems irrelevant with someone one loves so much.

Irritation – I have thought about it a lot lately. I suppose it may be the grinding of a mechanism that is driven too fast. Which is more upsetting: to realize that you are irritating someone you are fond of or to be caused irritation by them?

Tam came to dinner last night with Julian, Janetta and Raymond, and I again found her intelligent, interesting and charming. Knowing Raymond and Julian would talk together at dinner, I put Tam next to me. Janetta complained of her being 'over-confident' and noticed that though she had given up drinking she smoked all the time, so was 'obviously an addict'. How can the latest arrivals be fitted into the pattern that is already there in the complicated marquetry of inter-relationships? I feel sure that Tam isn't second-hand in her ideas, and I don't find her aggressive. And I cleaned my slate afresh before this last visit.

## October 28th

More and more do I find my satisfaction in relation with friends, and a possible drawback is that I am temporarily elated and inspired by a session with some of them (Georgia, Eardley or Julian), soothed perhaps by a quiet visit to the Carringtons; and then, arriving in my flat again in the emptiness of Saturday, a cold foggy hush envelops me. The eternal question: could I get along, as I may have to, without my translations and without depending on other people?

I dislike, and try to avoid any feeling of bungling or even flat pointlessness in a human contact. Last night, quite a jolly dinner party: Tristram and Virginia, the Harrods, Julia. Billa was friendly, lively and funny; I warmed to her. Roy bent and looking older, sometimes a trifle off the point, but not ranting about Vietnam. They stayed to the last, and Billa exclaimed in astonishment at Julia: 'She's rather alarming; she doesn't exactly *come to meet one* does she?' and then: 'How extraordinary she looks! Is it a wig she wears? And all that on her eyes!' It wasn't said as cattily as this sounds but in a tone of mild surprise, and I expect I'll get something of the same sort back from Julia, the ironical fact being that Julia herself rates a friendly *accueil* so high that the lack of it puts you straight in her doghouse, and I don't think she has the smallest notion how many people feel her to be formal and forbidding.

## November 6th

Rattling on through some experiences that go too fast to leave any imprint whatsoever. One of these was a dinner in honour of Sebastian [Sprott] at Bedford College. About twenty sociologists and other academics who all called him 'Jack', not a single figure from his Bloomsbury past, except me. As I expected, Baroness Wootton, with her long, pouchy, bulldog's face (intelligent, very) and, down near the bottom of it, a small crimsoned mouth, parting into a smile of much sweetness and humour. On my left at dinner, a sociologist I had met at Sebastian's bedside in hospital, an easy friendly fellow, on my right a 'Doctor of Politics', young, fresh-faced, non-U accent, bright all right but oh, how *borné*. He couldn't go to Russia or to Spain because he 'disapproved of the regimes. You see when I'm abroad I like to be friendly with people and I couldn't there.' I suggested that people could be thought of as such, individuals, people, all different, not as identical with their regime, or indeed not political animals all of them at any rate, that good (not harm) came from exchanging musicians etc. with every other country. I thought I'd been lucid, even eloquent. But he only repeated: 'You see when I'm abroad I like to be friendly with people and I couldn't there.' It's the same thing as not being able to listen to Cortot playing the piano because he played to the Germans, or thinking *all* Germans are beastly and always have been in spite of Mozart, Bach, Heine, etc. It's the same as the fuss now going on because the Springbok football team from South Africa are over here. As A. P. Herbert pointed out, people who are booing and yelling at them are practising apartheid themselves.

## November 11th

The thundering past of time is now and again unbearably sad – a stream of coloured and emotionally tinged images whirling back into the mists of forgetfulness. One of the things that makes me specially aware of it is winding up my dear old clock each week. The noise it makes and the movement of my arm as I do it carries me back to a mental picture of MAM[1] winding it – in which house I'm not quite sure. And I feel a sort of identity with her.

Last weekend at Stowell, with Magouche and Patrick Kinross.[2] Although I have charted my course there now and am therefore comparatively at my ease, Magouche was patently *not*, and this affected me. Nor was Patrick enjoying himself, and as for Mary? None of us really saw her. She goes up for a 'kip' all afternoon from lunch till five and to bed again at ten-thirty. On Sunday Philip drove us three guests, sadistically I almost feel, to the top of an exposed hill in ghastly weather and left us there, to climb down it in wind, sudden deluges of rain and hail, slipping and sliding on the smooth, wet grass, with sodden shoes and soaked legs. 'Hell! This is the last country walk I ever take,' said Patrick, whose huge frame crashed to the ground more than once. And I was thinking, 'Why should we be forced to do anything so disagreeable as this in the false guise of entertainment?'

Mary vanished again for the whole afternoon, and we three visitors left (with relief) after high tea. Philip is reasonable and agreeable part of the time, then with blazing eyes will make some outrageous remark. I was talking about the insane and now abandoned plan of having forty London telephone books. 'Yes, well, I was all for it. If you wanted the others you could pay for them. Why should some *little baker* in Wandsworth have as many books as I do?' 'Why shouldn't he?' I said.

### November 21st

I'm surprised by finding so many things still intensely enjoyable. At a Handel concert, I remember especially my pleasure in watching the movements of the string players coiled round their instruments.

Then I enjoyed giving a dinner party last night and four of the guests have rung up to say how much they too enjoyed it – it was to Christopher and Joanna Mason,[3] Eardley, Bunny, Magouche. Afterwards Duncan arrived and was made much of.

Looking forward unreservedly to a relaxed weekend with Heywood and Anne, and now sitting in a cold cattle-truck of a train

---

[1] My mother.
[2] Writer and authority on Turkey.
[3] Painters; Joanna is Carrington's niece.

waiting to start. A visit at lunch from Julian, whom I've not seen for some time. Poor Tam has been very ill with pleurisy – he suggested it was of neurotic origin and confessed having 'behaved badly to her'. A taxing situation, in which he must have longed for bachelor freedom, irritated by her incessant cough and incessant smoking.

Desmond, back from Africa, invited me to the BBC to see this second moon landing on a colour set there. 'Or are you anti-moon?' I was moving toward the decision that I was, but this was a chance to find out, so I accepted rather to his surprise, and after a buzz of frantic planning over the telephone off we went and were ushered into a tiny special viewing studio. 'You must lock the door,' they said, 'or you'll get a crowd in.' We both felt that would be uncivilized, so we left it open, and it was soon a black hole of Calcutta, with large men trampling on our coats and hats. Beside some exaggeratedly lifelike portraits of announcers and the technical experts of Houston, we saw in a dim blur – we would not have known had we not been told – Conrad descending the ladder on the moon. It was a humdrum, ordinary sight, he might have been putting his feet down on Paddington platform; nothing could have seemed less magical, and they kept up a dreary murmur of figures and letters; peppered with 'Attaboys' and 'OK's, or at most 'it's fantastic'. I regretted the once inviolate, white-faced moon of yesteryear. But our experience was short-lived, as the telly-camera went wrong, and we soon after went away.

My foreground is richly invested with the figures and faces of charming, loveable friends – but the background is dark and louring. There have been horrifying revelations of a deliberate massacre by the Americans in Vietnam of literally hundreds of civilian natives. And after a shocked response from most quarters, George Brown burst out shouting: 'Why don't the Americans stop weeping and *get on and finish the job.*'

## November 22nd: Snape

It is every bit as delightful being here as I had hoped, beginning with Heywood's ineffably sweet smile gleaming through the station darkness and opening the way to cascades of talk.

This morning, like some benevolent military commander, he conducted me on a long and beautiful walk past the bird sanctuary of Minsmere along a grassy track between Russian pine and birch woods, the still air heavily scented with wet pine-needles and the dead but tall and heraldic bracken, bright yellow as were the tops of the trees, making gleams of false sunlight in the soft, grey day.

## November 23rd

New arrivals – Harriet first, with her children Frances and Algy. She is a sweet charming girl, prettier than before, notably *good*, and intelligent. Lucy arrived later in a cotton blouse with bare midriff, long, crumpled, black plush skirt, and a face that was thin and unhappy. She has a bad effect on Harriet, whose amiability leads her to adopt the style of whoever she is with, and their long pointless exchange drifted like this. 'H: What was the party like? L: Oh well, it was sort of *mar*vellous *ac*tually, I mean *rea*lly (mumble-mumble). H: What happened exactly? L: Oh well, everyone got absolutely *ter*ribly drunk, and (lowering her voice) ter*rif*ically stoned, and it was sort of am*az*ing. H: Tim and I think it would be *so* nice to give a *really* grand party before we leave London, I mean a sort of *proper* party, a re*cep*tion, yes, that's it, a re*cep*tion. L: Oh, yes, *do*, how sort of *mar*vellous! H: I mean not in our house, but somewhere like the *Ritz*. You *know*? L: Oh yes, how wonderful. H: Well not *ac*tually the Ritz, but (I don't know) I think a sort of reception would be rather marvellous.' And so on. This is no criticism of the Hill girls; it is the 'in-talk' of the day.

## November 25th

Homeward bound, snug in a carriage with a man who where Lucy would be 'sort of' or 'you know' puts 'bloody' and very fast too: 'My bloody missus goes to bloody sleep every time we have to go by bloody train to bloody Leeds. She can bloody sleep everywhere.' He was well-dressed and prosperous-looking. I found myself staring amazedly, secretly wondering if he was mad and his friend really his keeper.

Lucy opened up a little before she left with Harriet yesterday evening and of course I therefore take to her. She has got herself a secretarial job for one week with the journalist Quentin Crewe. She told me she couldn't bear the idea of working at the same thing for more than a week or two; she supposed she was 'terribly restless'. L: 'If only I could find something that interested me.' I asked: 'If you had plenty of money would you be quite happy, and not bored doing nothing – no work?' L: 'Oh yes.' I said I thought this was clever, that it was difficult. How would she spend her time? 'Well, perhaps take some sort of course a few afternoons in the week.' I marvelled, but didn't say so, that in their hippy aversion to 'work' they don't realize that the only difference between it and a course is that you get paid instead of having to pay, and that it's entirely for *yourself*, and not for anyone else at all.

Harriet and Lucy gone (Harriet on her way to Italy). Heywood, Anne and I had a peaceful evening with the children, to whom I have lost my heart. I think I got on quite well with Frances who gratifyingly said at breakfast 'I don't want you to go.'

It was a pleasure to get up early and see out of my window an intensely blue, (though not yet fully light) sky over the bright yellow trees – a foreign look.

## November 27th

The Julia situation has gone very very far beyond a joke. She came to dinner here alone, her eyes half-closed with 'sedation', her poor legs tottering under her, her hatred of life hanging in my sitting-room like the mushroom cloud from an atom bomb. She began at once on her weekend with the Hills (she went the weekend before I did). I swear I didn't encourage her. And there was nothing but criticism: 'Really these country weekends! One hopes for a breath of fresh air, but not a bit of it. Nothing but driving round in a closed car to heavy lunches in hotels.' Heywood had already amusingly but not unaffectionately described her visit to Snape. She lay in bed, receiving the breakfast tray brought up by Anne but not touching it till nearly lunchtime, and after lunch retired again. One day he'd driven her to the sea in hopes of decoying her for a walk, but she wouldn't get out of the car. To me she said perfunctorily, 'I always like seeing Heywood – and Anne too, of course' – whereas Anne had been enthusiastic about the fascination of Julia's conversation, and said 'it ought to be recorded on tape.' Then came the horrors of her present life, poured out with all the symptoms of persecution mania. 'I really do feel there's a jinx against me. Things happen to me that no one else suffers from. I told you about how I couldn't open the windows because a cat came dashing in, and about all the knobs coming off the doors? Well, then these shrimps started coming out of the taps with the water, and believe it or not they got bigger and bigger. Then – just to show you what it's like – you may have heard a thunderclap the other night. Well, it evidently struck my house and all the electricity went. Of course the landlord pays no attention to anything. And I get so many wrong numbers, and people can't get me when they want, yet if I ring the engineers they don't answer. And of course there are these mice still.' All this is viewed, not as the stuff of life, but as something keeping her away from her true life – her mythical writing. She even described how she was 'just going to get down to this one afternoon at last, when the doorbell rang and it was Amaryllis with a friend called Clancy.' She still gets her secretary to come to 'write all these millions and millions of business letters I have to deal with every day.' And in every shade and intonation one is made aware that she knows she is singled out by fate for these horrible frustrations. Perhaps even that she in a sort of way enjoys her persecution by fate. But the most dismal symptom of all is that she says she hasn't brushed her teeth for months, it's too much trouble. 'Don't you find they feel rather horrid?' 'Oh yes, but washing them would be worse.' Indeed, letting go with me as she did, and I hope it did her some good, she suddenly looked her age and ill into the bargain. I'm desperately worried about her. It's pitiful. I can't forget the tone in which she said, 'I hate my life. I hate every *moment* of it. Sometimes I throw things about and break them.' Is she going mad? I almost fear it. Her purple heart intake has gone up to six a day and her doctor now says she must reduce them. But what can she hope for? And when she has run through her Arts Council grant, what will become of her? Unable to sleep for brooding over her plight, I wrote her a letter to tell her how much her unhappiness upset me, and to suggest a change of scene, with which I would gladly help her financially.

### December 2nd

Julia rang up again today. I think my letter really pleased her, and it opened a possible door (which of course she will quickly slam like all others) that in itself may be a minute alleviation. She wanted to tell me of fresh disasters: all her cleaners and cooks had given up. (I dare say they find her too difficult.) The electric fire in her bedroom had gone wrong, and she had backache. Looking at her back in the glass – a thing she hadn't done for years – she 'thought it had become a very queer shape'! She's going to consult her doctor. Meanwhile she won't go away at present because she 'can't leave her doctor or her hairdresser'.

Margaret is anxious to get her to go to a wonderful analyst she has been consulting herself.

The pages of my life are filled with the graphs of other people's dramas. Whether to record them or not, I hardly know; but my own life is otherwise a blank.

The Penrose drama has speeded up and got so complex that I have left it far behind. Lionel has been in hospital for observation and treatment of his heart condition, and this, with the imminent threat of Dunyusha's arrival, set Margaret dashing about like a whirling dervish, consulting his cardiologist, and a solicitor and psychoanalyst on her own account. How much of what she says can one give credence to? They all, including the psychoanalyst, Doctor Schoenberg, sympathized with her and – according to her accounts – said something must and should be done to stave off Dunyusha's arrival. The head of the Medical Council, the Home Office, the Immigration Authorities, all were to be invoked. In fact, absolutely nothing was done by any of them, and Dunyusha is now here. Yesterday Margaret was 'very glad she hadn't stopped Dunyusha coming', and said that 'she had done Lionel a world of good.' When she comes this afternoon I may hear a different story.

A cold but beautiful weekend at Cranborne, with David, Rachel, Laura, Julian, electrically full of cross-currents of thought, responses, jokes. Two iced walks, one with Julian, one with Rachel, under a perfectly clear sky, but talking so hard as barely to observe the light powdering of frost on creamy fields, and long winter shadows from trees that still had a residue of withered foliage on top, and almost black yews.

Rachel talked mostly about her children, Laura especially. Julian now describes Tam as the 'girl who is staying with me at present', and I'm sure this indicates a change. It is sad, but if it won't work, it's probably best that they should realize it before any bones are broken.


### December 4th

I saw Julian and Tam at Magouche's and talked to Tam as best I could through the veil of her blue-tinged glasses. The Kees and Raymond were also there. I had gone in after a gruelling four hours' concert dress-rehearsal at Guys' Hospital. These last rehearsals are of course the high point of my orchestra; they are dramatic but not too serious. Rows of underpaid nurses and medical students (after working for hours in the wards) stood singing away at Purcell and Bach. Another nurse, with her head topped by a tiny bonnet, scraped away on a violin. Some medical horns blared in the background. Our plump Cupid of a conductor was fairly tough with us, but made it enjoyable; and going in and out of the noble arcades of the hospital contributed something to the feel of the evening. Margaret drove me there, and there was of course more talk of her anxieties.

### December 6th

Last week was dedicated to the orchestra as never before – two marathon four-hour rehearsals and two concerts, one in Southwark Cathedral, one in Westminster Central Hall. In Southwark the setting once more provided a potent ingredient, though the sound was carried aloft to the roof in a blur. I walked about looking at the tombs, and talked for a while to Mr Johnston, a male nurse from Ilford, who told me dirty stories originating from Sir Thomas Beecham. I would be happy to be rid of my little Austrian partner; when concerts come on she develops a competitively aggressive schoolgirl side, ludicrous in someone over seventy, which makes her come in too soon and jockey for a more forward seat than younger and better players. It reminds me of the competitive aggression of the ski-slopes, and left me with a bad taste about the whole orchestra, joy though it is to me.

Last night out of the darkness Georgia appeared looking splendid in something like a suit of chain mail with a velvet tammy fastened by a brooch. I persuaded her to stay and have scrambled egg supper; there is almost no one I enjoy talking with so much. She soars and stimulates thought and response in kind. I try to remember what we talked about: how money and possessions were the Gods of today; the dread of 'work' among some of the young; activity and passivity; values, metaphysics – and the point of them, which is their power to make one leap off the ground even if Wittgenstein has for ever invalidated them; the intoxication of this leap; why does no one ever now talk about the Will; what is it?; the special point of poetry, and then of music; the importance of associative threads in all arts except music; the framework the mind imposes on reality in its attempts to grasp it – how much of what seems to be experience is reality and how much framework?; the random element and is it really random? A handful of pebbles from the beach – what you hold in your hand is a random selection, but each pebble is causally connected with some part of the sea-bed (says Georgia, who tends to think there is 'no real chance').

## December 14th: Hilton

7 a.m. Lying swathed in coats, vests, my thickest nightgown. Yet I have been awake for an hour, *penetrated* by cold. The wind sweeping across the soused cabbage-fields rattles my windows. Bunny has spent a lot on painting his beautiful house up, and it looks much cleaner, but who will be able to endure the icy bleakness of the winters here?

Last night, a repetitive conversation with Amaryllis about the impossibility of acting Shakespeare and the 'unnecessary' embroidery of his verse; she thinks Pinter writes better acting plays, and wants plays to 'get on with the action – speech is a distraction.' Bunny and I tried in vain to make her see that speech, even thought, were forms of action. Her desire to get rid of speech, reject it, seems to me puritanical and austere. Amaryllis fixes me with her enormous eyes as she talks in her low, soft voice; with her face surrounded by its cloud of tangled dusky hair she is like some sea-creature gazing from the depths of the ocean, while her long tapering hands make weird, weaving, octopus-like gestures. At times on our drive up here I thought she was waving me to the right or left, instead of merely trying to define her nebulous thoughts.

## December 16th

A visit from a psychoanalytic negress on Sunday – a very intelligent woman, with an expressive face whose mood varied from gaiety to deep sadness. She believes lives are made or lost by the parting of parents at two years old, and that psychoanalysis is the only cure. How they do cling to their mast! After she left, Amaryllis, Bunny and I agreed that 'they' ignored the part of their patient's life (twenty-three hours at least out of twenty-four) when they didn't see them; and also the therapeutic power of work. Amaryllis has a smile of great sweetness. I wish she didn't strike me as so unhappy.

231

Now I have had such a day of acting as psychoanalyst myself that I feel as if I were bursting at the seams. Julia rang up this morning, in real solid physical trouble, having cracked her spine by a fall, when under the influence of drugs and whisky. She asked me to buy her some cardboard plates to avoid washing up over Christmas, 'as everyone's ill and no one will be coming for four days. Then I suppose I'd better lay in some of that chicken jelly – Brands is it? – in case I get this Hong Kong 'flu with temperatures of 103 we hear about.' I asked her to make out a shopping list and dictate it on the telephone and said I would bring things tomorrow when I come to see her. Her voice had its harsh metallic ring and I couldn't help feeling that her deprivations and troubles seemed my fault to her eyes. (She told me she held Lawrence responsible for her cracked spine.) So I feel I'm *in for it* tomorrow evening.

## December 20th

At Rodborough Road I at last saw the mythical Dunyusha – and she's no fiend in human shape, no schemer or even vulgar flirt I would say, but a slight, pale, attractive and gentle-looking girl, with a high, well-modelled forehead. The only disadvantage: a compulsive giggle. What was I to say to Margaret who took me into another room after dinner to hear what I thought of her? In fact I said almost nothing. It is pain for Margaret, pain undiluted not to be told you hate Dunyusha on sight. Lionel had a touchingly apologetic air.

A very, very good evening with Julia, the best for years. She said of Lawrence, 'I want to ask you if you think he treated me cruelly?' 'Well, of course I think he caused you the worst possible unhappiness; more than you've ever had in your life.' 'Yes, that's not what I'm asking. Was he *cruel*? I'm not objecting to his wanting his sex life with Jenny but his throwing me off as a friend.' I negotiated this awkward corner by saying I thought him an extremely self-centred, egotistical man, though not deliberately unkind, and that in pursuit of his own ends he had perhaps been rather ruthless. She talked then of her writing, which is now entirely autobiographical but in novel form – the shape given by her own life: loneliness and desertion as a child, misery with Aunty Loo, and in her marriage to the heartless neurotic Tommy, and then peace and happiness (tremendously idealized of course by loss) with Lawrence, ending in the dark night of loneliness and desertion closing in again. 'A very good theme,' I told her. 'Yes but the trouble is it can't be published in my life time.' 'Nor in Lawrence's?' 'Oh, I don't mind *what* happens after I'm dead.' I urged her to go on with it none the less and enjoy her dedication to the writing itself, to the struggle rather than the final fruition, for the struggle was life. It had occurred to me that there could be a Henry Jamesian plot in which the novelist finished her book and then killed herself so that it could be published – a sort of *Revenger's Tragedy*.

Next morning she rang up to say 'the very moment you left me I found I had 'flu.' But in her new mood even this doesn't make her bitterly complain – 'flu *and* a cracked spine! 'I so enjoyed last night,' she said (and goodness so had I, and goodness there's no one like her at her best) 'and especially what you said about life being a struggle.'

The last note struck during the week before Christmas concerns the American philosopher Chomsky. Paul Levy came for a drink and we talked a lot about him. How grateful I am for being seduced into taking a hard bite now and again on such a philosophical crust. Also Paul was interesting, illuminating for me what had not been apparent in the pamphlet *Syntactical Structures* which I read before. I think I see where Chomsky is tending – back to Kant and *a priori* ideas. He is searching for the basic structure of the mind by means of patient excavation of the dry deposit of linguistics. Just as the eye can only see as it is built to see, the mind can only apprehend according to its structure. Well, I've long believed that in a way – I'm not quite sure what way. And I definitely sense a whiff of mysticism if not religion emanating from Chomsky's way. Paul made great play, as Chomsky does, with the creative element in language, and the way children and simple people soon learn to use language grammatically, and sentences they've never heard before. But they *don't*, I kept thinking; half the world repeats others parrotwise, and at the lowest level it's not much more communicative than the barking of dogs. Chomsky (and Paul) believe in some basic deep structure common to all languages – and don't we get back to God that way? I see language as only one among many means of expression – voice, dress, gesture, facial expression being others – learned with varying skill. So that from the child Mozart to an unmusical dustman is a very long leap.

## December 21st: Crichel

Off from London two days ago, laden with books and work and tins of Coca-Cola for Tam, for peace and escape in the country for over a week.

I drove to Crichel through a dank white landscape; at times white bees were flying at the windscreen. Got there before Raymond, Desmond, Julian and Tam. Raymond, seeing the Coca-Cola tins, looked and sounded disapproving. 'Oh, doesn't she *drink*? Well, I hope she's not a veget*a*rian.' Later, hearing the reason, and having taken to her, as everyone does, he respected her for it; and is in an amusing, lively mood, and at his sweetest to me. I was surprised by the thought, 'Does he *want* to frighten the young?' Tam and Julian seem happy together and in an altogether natural and un-embarrassed way for which I give them (specially Julian) high marks. I like Tam more and more, and her being seemingly quite un-shy is a comfort.

She gets on very well with Desmond, who obviously likes her, but all is not perfect between him and Julian.

## December 22nd

This reached a climax last night when Desmond – having deferred writing an article all afternoon in order to listen to records with Tam – retired after dinner to finish it, like a naughty schoolboy with his homework. The rest of us started playing paper games amid fountains of giggles and shrieks of laughter. Desmond came in, jealous, pathetic – 'What fun you're all having!' – and stood there in his bright pink corduroy suit, his face equally pink and his mouth turned down with disappointment. But alas! at this moment he caught sight of the libretto of a record lying on a table, forgotten where Julian had left it. There was a quick, short, verbal scuffle, and Julian's face was left with an X sign of irritation stamped across it. They ruffle each other, in spite of real affection and appreciation on both sides.

Now, Thursday, I'm alone with Des, all the others having gone off. I drove Julian to the Cecils at Cranborne and talked for a while with Rachel who was unwell in bed.

## December 26th

Desmond has great power to touch – he makes one feel that he craves affection and yet it never quite comes up to his hopes. He is aware of how his fussing upsets people and is sorry. He talked again of longing to retire and live entirely at Crichel. I was surprised, for his urge to hear music and be in the swim of it seems so strong.

# Index

239

Krips, Josef, 125

Lambourn (house), 7–8, 43–4
Lampedusa, Giuseppe, Prince of, 26
Lawrence, D. H., 4
Lawrence, Frieda, 195
Lear, Edward, 176
Leavis, F. R., 85
Lees-Milne, Alvilde, 1–3, 39, 116
Lees-Milne, James (Jim), 2–3,
    116–17
Lehmann, Rosamond: goes to opera
    with author, 9; Sicily holiday with
    author, 16, 21–31; mystical
    beliefs, 25, 27–9, 35, 50, 83;
    personal history, 30–1, 219; and
    Hester Chapman, 32; Sonia
    Orwell reads, 67; and proposed
    film on Lytton Strachey, 156–7;
    Julia criticizes, 172; *Dusty
    Answer*, 30
Leigh Fermor, Patrick and Joan *see*
    Fermor
Lena (Swedish au pair), 15
Levin, Bernard, 5
Levy, Paul, 155–6, 171, 273
Lewis, Cecil Day *see* Day-Lewis,
    Cecil
Lewis, Wyndham, 4
Lindsay, Lady Annabel (*née* Yorke),
    78, 79
Lisbon, 100; *see also* Portugal
*Listener, The* (Magazine), 65
Litton Cheney, 175
London Library, The, 4, 85
Long Crichel House, Dorset, 7,
    46–8, 107, 146, 165, 176, 202,
    215, 234
Lords Wood, 35, 131
Lorenz, Konrad, 38
Luisa (Spanish servant), 98, 100,
    102
Lutyens, Elizabeth, 203

Lygon, Lady ('Coote'), 204

McCabe, Charles, 12
McCabe, Mary, Lady, 10, 12–13
Macfarlane, Craig, 171
Maclean, Donald, 57
Maclean, Melinda, 57
Malet, John, 66
Margaret, Princess, 112
Mari (child, Spain), 93
Marshall, Margaret (author's
    mother), 224
Marshall, Nadine, 87
Marshall, Tom, 87, 130, 220n
Martel, Georgie (*née* Kee): character
    and appearance, 3–4, 6, 85, 104;
    and Hills, 3; author's affection
    for, 4, 6, 67; Janetta and, 41–2,
    99, 102, 108; in Spain, 43, 58;
    and Jaime, 97; author dines with,
    155; marriage, 203n, 204–5, 209;
    and Julia, 209
Martel, Jean-Pierre, 85, 155, 203n,
    205, 209
Martín, Rosario, 93
Mary, Queen, 2
Mason, Christopher & Joanne, 224
Meaux (France), 182
Methuen, Paul Ayshford Methuen,
    4th Baron, 3
Mijas (Spain), 55–6
Milford, Wogan Philipps, 2nd
    Baron, 10, 22, 30–1, 219
Minton, Yvonne, 168
Moore, G. E., 155–6
Moore, George, 166
Morel, E. D., 109
Morley College, London, 8
Mortimer, Raymond: at Crichel, 7,
    46, 64, 151, 176–7, 234; and
    Bunny, 11; entertains author in
    Islington, 59, 92; lends life of
    Voltaire to author, 98; and

243

proposed Lytton Strachey film, 157, 163; Mortimer praises, 165; Janetta encourages, 190; in Portugal, 211; writes on Broadmoor, 217n

Partridge, Sophie (Henrietta's daughter): at Hilton, 37–8, 170; qualities, 62–3, 89–90, 151, 170; visit to Bernardine, 73–4; at Kees', 89–90; and Janetta, 108; visits author, 130, 136, 151, 170, 216; in Spain, 147, 151; schooling and stay with Richard and Jane Garnett, 152, 154, 158, 164, 169; and mother, 170, 216; at William and Linda's wedding, 207; affectionate nature, 216; 6th birthday party, 218

Pavitt, Burnet, 200–1

Pears, (Sir) Peter, 174

Penrose, Beakus, 110n, 131

Penrose, Frances, 108–9, 206–7; death, 221

Penrose, Lionel: dines with author, 4, 75, 85, 92; on drug-taking, 51; essay on consciousness, 82–3; visit to Vienna, 108, 118, 122–3, 125–9; affair with Dunyusha, 119–24, 127–9, 152, 169, 171–2, 229, 232; lectures on chromosomes, 126, 128; on Beakus, 131; and Julia, 133–4; friendship and meetings with author, 135, 152, 165, 199; and proposed film on Lytton Strachey, 157; leukemia, 169; and Julia's lavatorial mishap, 217–18; heart trouble, 229

Penrose, Margaret: dines with author, 4, 85, 92; on abortions, 5; music-making, 50–2; opposes drug-taking, 50; timidity, 51; qualities, 68; Julia visits for Christmas, 75–6, 158; and

Lionel's essay on consciousness, 82–3; visit to Austria, 108, 118–29; and Lionel's infidelity with Dunyusha, 119–29, 169, 171, 229, 232; on Beakus, 131; and Julia, 133–4; friendship and meetings with author, 135, 152, 165, 199; and proposed film on Lytton Strachey, 157; visit to Amsterdam, 172–3; visits dying Frances Penrose, 206–7; and Julia's misfortunes, 217–18, 229; domestic anxieties, 229–30

Penrose, Sir Roland, 108

Penrose, Shirley, 76

Peto, Rosemary, 35

Philby, Kim, 57

Philipps, Anna, 56

Philipps, Wogan see Milford, 2nd Baron

Phillips, Antonia, 155

Phillips, Jack, 190

Phillips, Magouche (later Fielding): unhappiness, 84; Bunny and, 87, 91, 104, 189–90, 197–8; and Janetta, 99; author lunches with, 155; Bunny and author visit in Italy, 174, 183–93, 195–8; marriages, 190–1; in England, 204, 221, 224; at Stowell, 224

Phipps, Frances, Lady, 40, 77, 92, 206, 216–17

Phipps, Williams & Henrietta (née Lamb), 77

Piacenza (Italy), 183

Pinter, Harold, 231

Piper, John and Myfanwy, 13

Pirandello, Luigi, 25

Pisa (Italy), 198–9

Pope-Hennessy, James, 1–2; Queen Mary, 3

Porter, Andrew, 155

Portman, Suna, 53

247

# Frances Partridge

# Hanging On

## Diaries 1960–1963

'The oldest living Bloomsbury – and the nicest.'
Anthony Powell, *Sunday Times*

Frances Partridge is the oldest suriving member of the legendary
Bloomsbury group. Most of its leading members she knew well –
Lytton Strachey, Dora Carrington, Virginia Woolf – and *Hanging
On* contains many of her memories of them, as well as reflections on
her own life. 'You are infinitely refreshing,' David Garnett says of
her, ' – like the advertisement of some detergent or soap that takes
the film of dust and dirt away.' It is this ability to live life to the full
even in the face of adversity which makes Frances Partridge's
diaries so addictive.

'Frances Partridge's diaries are a breath from the other world of
Bloomsbury . . . it makes compulsive and enlightening reading.'
Julian Broad, *Vogue*

'Her diary, as always, is truthful and funny. She is sad, but never
boring. More please.' Mary Warnock, *Observer*

'As ever, beautifully written and observed. Neither sparing nor
pitying herself, her account of coping with tragic bereavement is
heartening as well as heart-rending. There is also a great deal of
humour.' Jonathan Cecil, *Spectator*

'Deeply interesting and moving . . . skilfully composed and
affectionately reminiscent . . . neither morbid nor unduly
sentimental.' Peter Quennell, *Country Life*

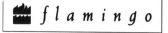

# Frances Partridge

# Other People

### Diaries 1963–1966

'The best of Frances Partridge's journals to date.' Barbara Everett, *Independent*

The publication in her nineties of Frances Partridge's diaries has been greeted as an unexpected literary discovery. *Other People* chronicles her life in the mid-1960s, when she is struggling to come to terms with existence after the deaths of both her husband Ralph and her son Burgo. 'I must forget myself utterly,' she writes, 'and sink into the concerns of other people.' This she does, an expert called in to deal with friends' divorces and sadnesses, 'as they would call in a plumber'.

An indefatigable traveller and relisher of conversation, Partridge is endlessly observant of people and nature, and passionate for ideas and for her friends. This passion for life in the face of adversity is one of the most attractive qualities of the remarkable women the reader comes to know through this book.

'Partridge's diaries, coming as they do so many decades after Bloomsbury was originally formed, are an outstanding testimony to those values which neither excessive praise nor vituperative criticism can obliterate.'                Frances Spalding, *Sunday Times*

'This book seems itself an example of that dying art of talk: serious, amusing gossipy, about life – and death. Frances Partridge's extraordinary achievement is to make this book, which is essentially about bereavement, high-spirited and entertaining.'
                Stephen Spender, *Evening Standard*

'This is a moving and affectionate book whose conclusion is that time does not heal the knowledge of loss but does alter it.'
                Elspeth Barker, *Independent on Sunday*

# Tolstoy's Diaries

## Edited and Translated by R. F. Christian

'A model of scholarship, one of the most important books to be published in recent years.'
A. N. Wilson, *Spectator*

'The diaries *are* me,' said the author of *War and Peace* and *Anna Karenina*, towards the end of his life, of the daily record he had kept, off and on, for sixty-three years. They open in 1847 with Tolstoy recovering from a bout of gonorrhoea and proceed to paint a full, unmitigated self-portrait of this giant of literature, whose political, moral and literary beliefs are laid out for us here in all their vivid, cussed splendour and singularity. The diaries contain the raw material from which Tolstoy carved his fiction and political writings; they teem with ideas; and they are marked by their frankness of expression, their raw candour and their ruthless self-examination. Anarchist, vegetarian, libertine, excommunicant, educationalist, soldier, self-taught cobbler, petitioner, difficult spouse, benign patriarch, and Grand Old Man of Russian letters: Tolstoy is a magnificently complex, even contradictory, figure. These enthralling, self-lacerating diaries confirm outright that he is not only a matchless writer but also a *man* of heroic proportions.

'Meticulously rendered and admirably annotated, as a picture of the turbulent Russian world Tolstoy inhabited these diaries are incomparable.'
Anthony Burgess, *Observer*

'Finely edited, both scholarly and easy to read . . . exceptionally rewarding.'
Raymond Williams, *Guardian*

'A monumental work of careful scholarship by the leading expert in the field . . . invaluable.'
Erik de Mauny, *Financial Times*

ISBN 0 00 654513 0

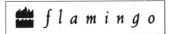

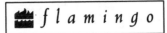
**flamingo**

Flamingo is a quality imprint publishing both fiction and
non-fiction. Below are some recent non-fiction titles.

- ☐ Wild Swans *Jung Chang* 0 00 637492 1 £7.99
- ☐ Evelyn Waugh: The Early Years *Martin Stannard*
  0 586 08678 1 £7.99
- ☐ Evelyn Waugh: No Abiding City *Martin Stannard*
  0 586 08680 3 £7.99
- ☐ An Angel at My Table *Janet Frame* 0 586 08586 6 £4.99
- ☐ Dr Johnson & Mr Savage *Richard Holmes* 0 00 654824 5 £6.99
- ☐ The Naked Civil Servant *Quentin Crisp* 0 00 654044 9 £5.99
- ☐ Handel and His World *H. C. Robbins Landon* 0 00 654460 6 £6.99
- ☐ Jesus *A. N. Wilson* 0 00 637738 6 £5.99
- ☐ Pursued by Furies: A Life of Malcolm Lowry *Gordon Bowker*
  0 00 654678 1 £7.99
- ☐ Tolstoy's Diaries *R. F. Christian* 0 00 654513 0 £7.99
- ☐ The Life and Lies of Bertolt Brecht *John Fuegi*
  0 00 686317 5 £9.99

You can buy Flamingo paperbacks at your local bookshop or newsagent. Or
you can order them from HarperCollins Mail Order, Dept. 8, HarperCollins
*Publishers*, Westerhill Road, Bishopbriggs, Glasgow G64 2QT. Please enclose
a cheque or postal order, to the order of the cover price plus add £1.00 for
the first and 25p for additional books ordered within the UK.

NAME (Block letters) _____

ADDRESS _____

_____

_____

While every effort is made to keep prices low, it is sometimes necessary to increase them at short notice.
HarperCollins Paperbacks reserve the right to show new retail prices on covers which may differ from those
previously advertised in the text or elsewhere.